# INDIGENEITY IN REAL TIME

LATINIDAD

Transnational Cultures in the United States

This series publishes books that deepen and expand our understanding of Latina/o populations, especially in the context of their transnational relationships within the Americas. Focusing on borders and boundary-crossings, broadly conceived, the series is committed to publishing scholarship in history, film and media, literary and cultural studies, public policy, economics, sociology, and anthropology. Inspired by interdisciplinary approaches, methods, and theories developed out of the study of transborder lives, cultures, and experiences, titles enrich our understanding of transnational dynamics.

Matt Garcia, Series Editor, Professor of Latin American, Latino and Caribbean Studies, and History, Dartmouth College

For a list of titles in the series, see the last page of the book.

# INDIGENEITY IN REAL TIME

## The Digital Making of Oaxacalifornia

INGRID KUMMELS

RUTGERS UNIVERSITY PRESS

New Brunswick, Camden, and Newark, New Jersey

London and Oxford, UK

Rutgers University Press is a department of Rutgers, The State University of New Jersey, one of the leading public research universities in the nation. By publishing worldwide, it furthers the University's mission of dedication to excellence in teaching, scholarship, research, and clinical care.

Library of Congress Cataloging-in-Publication Data
Names: Kummels, Ingrid, author.
Title: Indigeneity in real time : the digital making of Oaxacalifornia / Ingrid Kummels.
Description: New Brunswick : Rutgers University Press, [2023] | Series: Latinidad: transnational cultures in the United States | Includes bibliographical references and index.
Identifiers: LCCN 2022025216 | ISBN 9781978834798 (hardcover) | ISBN 9781978834781 (paperback) | ISBN 9781978834804 (epub) | ISBN 9781978834828 (pdf)
Subjects: LCSH: Zapotec Indians—California—Los Angeles—Social conditions. | Zapotec Indians—Mexico—Sierra Norte (Oaxaca)—Social conditions. | Mixe Indians—Los Angeles—Social conditions. | Mixe Indians—Mexico—Sierra Norte (Oaxaca)—Social conditions. | Internet and indigenous peoples—California—Los Angeles. | Internet and indigenous peoples—Mexico—Sierra Norte (Oaxaca) | Communication and culture—California—Los Angeles. | Communication and culture—Mexico—Sierra Norte (Oaxaca) | Transnationalism. | Zapotec Indians—Urban residence—California—Los Angeles. | Mixe Indians—Urban residence—California—Los Angeles. | Sierra Norte (Oaxaca, Mexico)—Social life and customs. | BISAC: SOCIAL SCIENCE / Ethnic Studies / American / Hispanic American Studies | SOCIAL SCIENCE / Media Studies
Classification: LCC F1221.Z3 K86 2023 | DDC 398.208997/68—dc23/eng/20221102
LC record available at https://lccn.loc.gov/2022025216

A British Cataloging-in-Publication record for this book is available from the British Library.

All photographs by the author unless otherwise indicated.

References to internet websites (URLs) were accurate at the time of writing. Neither the author nor Rutgers University Press is responsible for URLs that may have expired or changed since the manuscript was prepared.

♾ The paper used in this publication meets the requirements of the American National Standard for Information Sciences—Permanence of Paper for Printed Library Materials, ANSI Z39.48-1992.

rutgersuniversitypress.org

Manufactured in the United States of America

To the memory of Millo Castro Zaldarriaga and
Karl Kummels, my parents, who once migrated to
Los Angeles and invested their creativity into making
the city one of their homes

# CONTENTS

# INDIGENEITY IN REAL TIME

# 1 · INTRODUCTION

## Community Life and Media in Times of Crisis

How do we organize our lives when our familiar routine collapses under shutdowns and forced physical distance? Since early 2020, people all over the world have had to struggle with this turn of events. In response to the measures implemented to battle the COVID-19 pandemic, they have relied to a great extent on digital practices and new social arrangements that allow them to get on with their lives despite hampered mobility. From work (home office) and education (home schooling) to gatherings for private parties, conferences, and political campaigns (Zooming, FaceTiming), various aspects of everyday life were realigned to accommodate "social distancing"—although this would be a misnomer, since the real challenge is to cope with physical distance. Even countries that are leaders in high technology found it difficult to adapt. They had failed to ensure the widespread accessibility of digital equipment, know-how, and rapid, creative solutions that reorganizing community life calls for in terms of maintaining sociability, work, and leisure from a distance in the long run.

From the current global health crisis perspective, the protagonists in this book are pioneers of cutting-edge media initiatives, which they had devised when physical distance was imposed in quite a different crisis: the tightening of the border regime between Mexico and the United States from 2016 to 2021 intensified geographical separation, complicated temporal adjustments, and fragmented routines between the inhabitants of Oaxaca, a key migrant-sending state, and their undocumented relatives. When I began my ethnographic research on this topic in 2016, my intention was to explore processes of transnational community building in Los Angeles in the United States from two villages in the Sierra Norte of Oaxaca, namely, the Zapotec Villa Hidalgo Yalálag and the Ayuujk village of Tamazulapam del Espíritu Santo. I was particularly interested in the mass media that the villagers used for cross-border communication, such as internet radio broadcasts, communal multimedia platforms, and social media influencing. But I soon discovered a more comprehensive sociocultural dimension to their media enterprises. At stake was nothing less than the reorganization of family life in all its facets, including illness, death and mourning, large community celebrations, sports, and political meetings, across vast distances. Despite their illegalization and the growing danger of deportation, migrants who had worked and paid taxes in the United States for decades put this into practice. Storytelling, village costumes, communal labor, sports, live brass band music, and dance group performances, as well as the latest social media and digital platforms: these communication formats were combined in a fresh way for the purpose of sharing Zapotec and Ayuujk cultures and languages with a broad audience on both sides of the U.S.-Mexican border.

Radio Cantautor, Tamix Multimedios, Bene Xhon Videos, Video Aries, Radio Gobixha, and Multimedios Jën më'ëny are some of the emerging media facilities I encountered in the Sierra Norte villages and in Los Angeles. Following the transition from analog to digital, Zapotecs and Ayuujk ja'ay launched novel hybrid outlets, such as internet radio stations operating from their own Facebook page, team-managed multimedia platforms, and pages run by individual influencers.[1] These outlets popularized media formats that are cocreated interactively by the users. The names of these outlets refer to diversified identity horizons beyond narrow national and ethnoracial categories commonly used in Mexico and the United States, such as "Mexicans," "Americans," "Hispanics," "Mexican Americans," and "Native Americans": Tamix Multimedios derives its label from the abbreviation of the village name Tamazulapam Mixe, whose inhabitants identify for the most part as Ëyuujk ja'ay. Bene Xhon Videos takes its name from "fellow people," used as an ethnonym by the Sierra Zapotecs. Gobixha, an internet radio that broadcasts from Los Angeles, borrowed its designation from the Isthmus Zapotec word for "sun." Jën më'ëny means "shooting star" in the Ayuujk language. All these names express Indigenous knowledge systems and multilayered senses of belonging, from identifying locally with the Mexican home village and affiliation with the ethnolinguistic group to sharing ageless cosmological ideas about the sun and shooting stars as sacred forces. These media outlets enable present-day Indigenous lifeworlds to be seen and heard in public. Such dimensions are rarely granted space in the mainstream media of the cities and nation-states where Indigenous peoples reside. During the intensified crackdowns on immigrants, self-determined media outlets broadcast regularly about Indigenous cultures, wisdom, and languages, thus enabling their users to live together as a community in Los Angeles—where their conviviality was particularly threatened—and to extend this community in a transnational scope. Media practices in Los Angeles that I jotted down in my field notes in March 2018 provide insight into how creatives opened these spaces:

> While we are having breakfast together at her home in Koreatown, Los Angeles, Pam occasionally checks her Facebook page on her cell phone.[2] As she does every morning, she greets her numerous followers, notably in Yalálag, Mexico, with a blessing or a bit of fun. Pam, a house cleaner in her mid-forties, is also checking the news for information about raids, since undocumented immigrants here in this sanctuary city are threatened with so-called interior arrests.[3] Immigration and Customs Enforcement (ICE) officers are now authorized to detain immigrants

with no criminal record in the United States and deport them. It is March and more than a year into the administration of Donald Trump, who had issued this executive order in an all-out assault on immigrants. Since the 1980s, Indigenous peoples from the Oaxacan Sierra Norte have shaped Los Angeles as a city. But although they have long felt at home in the Californian metropolis, they are currently no longer safe walking on its streets. This also applies to Pam, who emigrated from Zapotec Yalálag to Los Angeles when she was sixteen, fell in love with a Yalaltec migrant, and has a grown-up son who is a U.S. citizen by birth. Her thoughts now revolve around what will become of her mixed-status family if she or her husband were to be deported.

Nevertheless, Pam also keeps checking her cell phone for announcements about local community events: A food fair, evening dance or *kermés* (community fair) in honor of one of the patron saints of Yalálag, or similar events hosted by other migrant associations from the Sierra Norte region of Oaxaca. Since the day I arrived, she has taken me to the many meetings and celebrations she attends on weekends, which are now more frequent than they were a year ago. Pam is well-connected on social media and is herself an actor in a self-determined media scene with countless followers. She uses her long bus rides to work to update her Facebook page. Media outlets run by Indigenous people and the information circulated by their interlinked Facebook pages give her a sense of direction and a platform to intervene politically despite being disenfranchised.

On Good Friday, Pam is summoned via Messenger to a Yalálag migrant association meeting at the house of a *paisana* (fellow countrywoman) in the neighboring Pico Union district. More than twenty members of the Comitiva del Panteón have assembled in the backyard. At a number of picnic tables they are preparing food to sell for the big dance that will take place the evening of Easter Sunday. Their goal is to raise several thousand dollars for the renovation of the cemetery in their Mexican home village by selling admission tickets and meals. While the women and men are busy working on the heaps of ingredients bought the day before—pulling apart *quesillo* strings, roasting chilies, and trimming cilantro—their actions are being transmitted live with a cell phone. Two women from Radio Cantautor, a new type of Internet radio, help chop ingredients in between reporting duties. They have set up a makeshift studio on one of the picnic tables and organized a livestream to La Voz de Yalálag (The Voice of Yalálag), the Internet radio station in the Mexican hometown. The producer, who comes from the village of Zoogocho, keeps the group entertained with some of his Zapotec songs, which he simultaneously broadcasts. He then asks the board members of the Comitiva for an interview. A few days previously, the hometown political authorities had withdrawn permission for the Graveyarders (*Panteoneros*, as they are jokingly called) to collect funds in Los Angeles on behalf of Yalálag.

Radio Cantautor and its audience, which lives in places like Los Angeles, Mexico City, Oaxaca City, and Yalálag, are curious about the conflict. Listeners in the home village are captivated by the pointed questions the radio producer asks alternatively

Reporter Nolhe Yadao (Woman from the Hill) from Radio Cantautor livestreaming the *pozontle* preparation in El Mercadito, Los Angeles, April 2019.

in Zapotec and Spanish. Some immediately post a comment on the station's Facebook page. "And what about the appointment of the wannabe officials?" one user complains, since the political authorities in the Oaxacan hometown have not officially recognized the members of the Comitiva in Los Angeles. The Comitiva treasurer defends their position to the radio audience, first in Zapotec and then Spanish: "We are doing all this for our dead and particularly for those who are dying now. They deserve a place of dignity to rest in peace.... We have just one goal: to help our village of Yalálag, because we were born there. Now we live abroad, in a foreign country where we often experience racism and discrimination. Our *compañeros* have different working hours but they asked for permission and switched their shifts. They do all of that so we can come together here and host our dance event." Once on the air, a Comitiva woman goes on to promote the dance: live *bandas* (brass bands) are its main attraction, formed by second-generation youth born in Los Angeles who, as musicians, uphold Zapotec traditions. (field notes, March 31, 2018)

These backyard media practices not only speak to people living in the urban context of the Californian megacity but also mobilize their compatriots in rural Oaxaca. A political project of transnational reach is being debated here, which members of the hometown association, who have lived in Los Angeles for decades, wish to and must coordinate with their fellow villagers in Yalálag, given that a novel cross-border Zapotec culture concerning death is at stake. The treasurer clarifies that the working rhythms of two countries have to be synchronized. The

Radio Cantautor reporter broadcasting from the dances performed at the Virgen del Rosario fiesta in Yalalág, Mexico, November 2017.

people keeping in touch range from peasants who work farmland to employees in the low-income sector and entrepreneurs with their own chain of shops. They not only communicate in a total of four languages—Zapotec, Spanish, English, and Ayuujk—but also ensure that their words, ideas, and actions are able to travel across this rugged transnational terrain and take root. To counteract disenfranchisement in the United States, Indigenous migrants carry out activities that have been described as citizenship practices (Strunk 2015) and politics of dignity (Castellanos 2015). Self-determined media have been harnessed to export communal practices and politics from Indigenous Yalálag and adapt them to life in Los Angeles. Media use is decisive for transnationalizing village governance, that is, for serving a hometown or satellite community office, a duty that villagers— without regard to their place of residence—may assume on a regular basis throughout their lifetime (a system popularly known in Mexico as *usos y costumbres* and called "cargo system" in the body of anthropological literature).[4]

This transborder community life unfolds via self-determined coverage with appropriated mass media: scenes of joint activity are broadcast live via cell phone to viewers in both countries. The radio stations report on topics that touch people scattered across numerous locations, either because they come from Yalálag or because their experience of transnational life is similar. Their interventions on the program refer to matters of everyday existence: How do you provide for death when leading a life far from your home village? Who is entitled to a say in a modernizing project, such as expanding the hometown cemetery? Do people who live in the United States have a right to represent the Mexican village politically? What role should self-determined media play in producing sociality, culture, and politics across immense distances? In a kind of twofold movement, issues of wider social significance in both nation-states are discussed via community concerns: How can the communitarian Zapotec or Ayuujk way of life be not only extended transnationally but also firmly anchored in cities like Los Angeles that have long denied Indigenous peoples a voice and visibility in cultural, social, and political life? What future do we envision for Indigenous life led at "homes" in several places and countries?

## REALIGNING SPACE AND TIME BETWEEN SEVERAL HOMES

From multiple locations in both countries, those who took part in the radio program actively opened a media space that not only bridged geographical distance but also navigated temporal discrepancies. I conceptualize media spaces as socially constructed both by communicative practices—what people do with and say about media (Couldry 2004)—and by everyday imagination and aspiration (Kummels 2017a, 13–17; Kummels 2020). The political empowerment that actors develop in these spaces illustrates that time is an integral component of their construction. Doreen Massey (1994, 251, 265) explained that due to its "lived practices" (Lefebvre [1974] 2009), a processual dimension laced with various temporalities and the possibility of politics is always inherent in space. In her view, social relations that occasionally interlock or dissipate in space call for simultaneous coexistence. By recording and commenting on live broadcasts, mediamakers produce simultaneity in real time when establishing a media space. Through simultaneous experience—sensing what distant others do at the same moment—people can incorporate the action of others into their own experience in a meaningful way (cf. Boyarin after Cwerner 2001, 23). According to Benedict Anderson (1991), experiencing simultaneity as a result of reading topical print media enabled people to sense, imagine, and thus create community. Based on these considerations, Arjun Appadurai (1996, 35) coined the term "mediascapes" to refer to the deterritorialized landscapes centered on pre-electronic or electronic media images enabling viewers in the late twentieth century to imagine themselves as a community. In the present case, mediamakers and users designed strategies to reconcile diverging temporalities such as those in the everyday lives and working schedules of people who reside in the rural and urban milieus of the two bordering nation-states. They purposefully involved audiences and places equipped with highly unequal technologies into a media space. Streaming facial expressions, gestures, words, and locations meant that media events could be shared with others, who would then empathize from a distance and show political solidarity.

During my fieldwork, I accompanied the creatives who launched these initiatives at a time of heightened exclusion as a result of the illegalization, immobility, uncertainty, and discrimination suffered in the context of international migration. The overall political constellation meant that Indigenous ways of life were contested on both sides of the border, on-site and in their transnational extension. Once Republican Donald Trump assumed the presidency (2017–2021), U.S. policy, already restrictive toward migration from Latin America, became even more rigid. It was implemented within the framework of openly racist political discourse that sought to benefit a "White America" through isolationism and protectionism. A series of executive orders led to raids by ICE that targeted unauthorized Mexican migrants. Indigenous people from the Oaxacan Sierra Norte, in particular, have for decades contributed significantly to the economy and the "Southern California lifestyle" by toiling as essential workers in the agricultural industry, in the urban restaurant sector, and as housekeepers and babysitters in the service sector.[5] Meanwhile, Indigenous groups living in Mexico were affected by other, equally consuming uncertainties that prompted continued migration north. Enrique Peña Nieto's PRI (Institutional Revolutionary Party) administration (2012–2018) introduced constitutional changes and structural reforms in a neoliberal vein that failed utterly to counteract the centuries of systemic inequality that Mexico's Indigenous population still experiences today. Blatant disparities in public education, access to telecommunication, and control of natural resources were addressed in a half-hearted manner, leading to massive resistance to government policies by the population concerned.[6]

The approximately 100,000 Bene xhon (exonym: Sierra Zapotecs) and 130,000 Ayuujk ja'ay (exonym: Mixe) who live in the Mexican Sierra Norte, along with roughly 100,000 members of these two ethnolinguistic groups who migrated to the United States,[7] all used self-managed media as a tool to circulate information in their own languages about their cultures, social grievances, and political claims across immense distances. Between 2016 and 2021, I explored how mediamakers met the challenges of the time by following the everyday lives of crews whose members run internet radio stations in different places and countries, family enterprises that document events with professional video cameras, designers of multimedia platforms, as well as individual social media users with popular Facebook and Twitter accounts.[8] Their broadcasts—also in Indigenous languages—focused on key events such as community meetings, collective construction projects, ethnic basketball tournaments, fiestas in honor of patron saints and their U.S. counterpart, *kermesses*, and dances with live banda music, all of which include cultural knowledge with a long tradition dating back to the precolonial era.[9] At the same time, these manifold expressions point toward the future. Indigenous migrants from the Sierra Norte exported them translocally and transnationally—not least through their media activities—adapting them in the process to the living standards of new places of residence, including megacities like Los Angeles, as well as to their home villages, which made great strides in a similarly dynamic way. Hence, these mediatized Indigenous lifeworlds transformed both rural and urban milieus.

Each year I spent time in two Sierra Norte villages, the Zapotec Villa Hidalgo Yalálag and the Ayuujk village of Tamazulapam del Espíritu Santo, and in satellite communities in the Central Mexican Bajío region and notably in Los Angeles, fourteen months all told. It was important to me to carry out research on the ground since digital media have a material dimension, on the one hand, and are embedded in the everyday lives of people in concrete localities, such as the association I mention in my field notes, who were preparing food together in a backyard. Creatives also pursued their work on personal computers and mobile phones in private homes in the villages of the Sierra Norte or in Los Angeles, and in the makeshift studios they set up in gyms and banquet halls. On the other hand, the on- and offline dimensions to these practices tended to merge almost seamlessly, as in the case of Pam, who was chatting with me and simultaneously checking her Facebook inbox. Occasionally, however, users kept the content and style of their on- and offline communication strictly separate—and consequently their respective spaces and times—as a strategy to reserve selected information to only one of these two spheres.

With the aid of broadcasts via cell phones and Facebook Live, autonomous mediamakers made communally lived experiences standard procedure for the first time for an audience that lived on both sides of the border. Communication in real time (which means experiencing time at the same pace as events happen, as if it were the present) raises questions about the significance of direct participation for people who reside at a great distance from each other and about their ability to live as a community—in other words, what is the role of immediate interaction in generating a collective sense of belonging? Real time also underlines Indigenous people's demand for recognition of the basic right to share the same time frame of the present against a colonial temporal logic that seeks to freeze them in the past. Such coevalness, however, was once denied to the "Other" in anthropological writing in line with hegemonic exclusion strategies (Fabian 1983).[10] It is precisely this categorical denial of an affinity to digital technology and mass media, and thus to "modernity" and "future," that still serves as a tool to colonize and dominate Others classified as Indigenous (Schiwy 2009, 13; Kummels 2017a, 15; Budka 2019, 168; Gómez Menjívar and Chacón 2019b, 8–10). In a troubling way, the "migrant" category also frames mobile and displaced peoples with the chronotope of a "migration background" and with a past that can never be shaken off, separating them permanently from the population constructed as nonmigrant (Çağlar 2018). As described in my field notes, self-determined mediamakers used livestreaming as part of their redefinition of times and spaces. Through media and citizenship practices, they extended a rural, communal way of life transnationally to urban centers, transforming them in the process: for example, by organizing cross-border support that begins by chopping vegetables, but also by reporting about those efforts as part of an exchange of political ideas on cross-border collectivity and Indigeneity. Activists and intellectuals in the Sierra Norte region refer to these communal practices of everyday life as Comunalidad. In Los Angeles they are associated with a transborder community called Oaxacalifornia and fresh interpretations of the American Dream. I will discuss these political ideas in more detail below.

I examine in this context how Zapotec and Ayuujk mediamakers produce communicative spaces and synchronize temporalities between two nation-states with the intent to reduce transnational inequality regarding ethnoracial and gender hierarchies, economic disparities, and uneven media structures. From various localities and perspectives, these actors took on the challenge of connecting audiences whose working hours and incomes differ greatly—workers and the self-employed in the United States earn up to ten times as much as those in Mexico.[11] Moreover, migrants of the first, 1.5, and second generations differ in terms of their cultural knowledge, their relationship to the village of origin, and their residence status in the United States. Residence status, in turn, determines eligibility for citizenship, educational opportunities, and adequate working conditions. These factors influence the degree to which people are able to use and shape media technology and knowledge: depending on place of residence, occupation, migrant generation, and gender, access is highly unequal. Young, academically trained Zapotecs and Ayuujk ja'ay who live in big cities gained political influence for the first time with digital tools. Their social advancement contrasts with the principle of social climbing based on age and lifetime experience in their parents' villages of origin. We will explore this aspect under the concepts of visual divide and digital divide.

This study traces how stakeholders turned to their own communication technologies and knowledge repertoires and converted them into digital formats: these include storytelling and oratory in Indigenous languages, village costumes, communal labor, sporting events, live brass band music, and dance group performances.[12] The persistence of these knowledge repositories was not guaranteed, given their deliberate suppression—as occurred with twentieth-century education policies in Mexico that dispelled Indigenous languages. Media operators and users brought their creativity and agency to bear on activities they termed *revitalización* (revitalizing) or *recuperación* (recovering), not because they want to return to past lifeways but rather as a way of committing themselves to invigorating their own culture in the present and future. At times, "recovering" includes talk of *decolonización* (decolonization) and autonomy as a *nación* (nation).[13] Comunalidad could be characterized as a decolonial approach, but since it has its own genealogy in Sierra Norte Indigenous philosophies, calling it an "epistemology of the South" seems to be more appropriate (Santos 2009 in Aquino Moreschi 2013). Comunalidad is a locally embedded way of acting, thinking, and feeling that counteracts categories imposed by present neocolonial relations. In the Mexican-U.S. context, Indigenous peoples from the state of Oaxaca often face racial discrimination (exacerbated by hierarchies in the agricultural fields and urban settings); Oaxaca is even conflated with Indigeneity as an epitome for backwardness. Asserting one's language, food, music, and dance has become a conscientious process of resisting this denigration. By way of these expressions, mediamakers and users thought deeply about their own migrant histories, the gaps emerging between home villages and satellite communities as a result of globalization, and the market structures and legal frameworks for mass media that frequently marginalized them.[14] Throughout my years of fieldwork, the act of converting locally crafted media into digital formats was always a reference to political ideas calling for action in the interests of shaping a better present and future. These ideas of Comunalidad, the American Dream, and Oaxacalifornia all pointed beyond exclusively ethnic demands.

At the same time thoughts, actions, and feelings were mediatized from concrete localities ranging from a Mexican village plaza to the backyard of a private home in Los Angeles.[15] We can see this in the stories of two Sierra Norte villages and the ways they developed autonomous media practices along different cross-border routes.

## DIVERSIFIED TRANSBORDER PATHWAYS BETWEEN MEXICO AND THE UNITED STATES

The transnational outreach of Indigenous community life has its roots in the crisis of migration and displacement; tackling this crisis via self-determined media relied on cultural resources anchored in numerous small villages, among them those of the Oaxacan Sierra Norte. I chose the Zapotec village of Yalálag and the Ayuujk village of Tamazulapam, located in the Sierra Norte some sixty miles apart, as the starting points for this exploration since they represent part of the culturally diverse spectrum that is distinctive of Oaxaca. This state has the highest percentage of Indigenous peoples in Mexico and officially recognizes sixteen ethnolinguistic groups.[16] Their homeland, the Sierra Norte, is a region of particularly rich cultural and linguistic diversity. Each of the sixty-eight municipalities emphasizes their local and ethnic specificity with their own language variant, costumes, masks, dishes, and craft traditions and a sacred relationship to the land of the respective municipality[17]—their media practices and migration strategies also address and shape these features of their home villages.[18]

The histories of Yalálag and Tamazulapam illustrate the dramatic changes that international migration has brought to the Sierra Norte in recent decades. As a key marketplace, Yalálag dominated the region culturally and economically in the mid-1960s. Peasants in the wider surrounding area journeyed by foot up to a whole day to sell their coffee and other produce to merchants in Yalálag. The same was true of peasants from Tamazulapam, most of whom earned their living from petty trade of self-produced pottery and from carrying heavy loads of coffee. Because of their economic standing, the Zapotecs claimed ethnic superiority over the Ayuujk ja'ay. Once a road network began connecting most Sierra Norte villages to Oaxaca City, Yalálag forfeited this privileged position. It then turned to agriculture and crafts, such as the manufacture of leather sandals. People from Yalálag migrated to the state of Veracruz, Oaxaca City, and Mexico City in search of economic alternatives; to compensate for village depopulation, Ayuujk ja'ay were hired as farmhands. Zapotec Yalálag gradually evolved into an ethnically mixed village of Zapotecs and Ayuujk ja'ay.[19] Meanwhile, still a mostly agrarian pueblo in the 1960s, Tamazulapam began to diversify its economic activities, with some villagers now becoming coffee traders themselves. Others took advantage of enhanced opportunities to work as teachers in the state educational system. Beginning in the 1990s, inhabitants began to take the self-employment path, first working in transport and construction, and later as managers of taco restaurants and food trucks in migrant destinations. These decades saw a 180-degree turn in the hierarchy between the two villages: today Tamazulapam is the bigger and more prosperous townlet that boasts multistory buildings in its center because its migrants in the United States plan to return and invest greater sums in their home-town. In contrast, Yalálag has not grown and its character remains that of a rural, loosely built village.

But first, we need to go back to the dawn of Zapotec and Ayuujk migration to the United States, which began with the Bracero Program (1942–1962), the bilat-eral agreement created in response to U.S. government interest in recruiting Mexican men as farmhands in labor-intensive crop agriculture, primarily in Cali-fornia. Among those who signed up were men from Tamazulapam and Yalálag.[20] When the program ended, people from the Sierra Norte continued to cross the border into the United States, albeit now unauthorized, with the aid of a border smuggler or *coyote*. Apart from the large number of men, women for the first time engaged in chain migration and set new trends (Cruz-Manjarrez 2012, 92). The gendered migration flows were not exclusively determined by economic dispari-ties, since young, single women expressly sought to escape family control as exer-cised by their parents' insistence that they marry the spouse they had chosen for them. Fellow villagers recruited each other informally for work in certain eco-nomic sectors, men and women often relying on different networks. Men found jobs in the agricultural and construction industries and the catering sector, women mainly in domestic labor and child care. The 1990s saw a substantial increase in Indigenous migration to the north in terms of numbers; those involved put their own cultural, economic, and political stamp on both the target and the sending country (contributions in Fox and Rivera-Salgado 2004; Velasco Ortiz 2008). The structural neglect of agriculture, the economic crisis, and the systemic shortage of schooling and health care in Mexico were key reasons why Oaxaca became one of the country's main sending regions to the United States.[21]

Migrants from Yalálag and Tamazulapam formed their respective "satellite com-munities"—as I call them—by exporting to Los Angeles (and other settlement areas) basic organizational forms from their villages of origin, such as communal governance, patron saint fiestas, brass bands, dance groups, and basketball tourna-ments.[22] In the process, they developed social arrangements with the respective home village. Significantly, Yalálag and Tamazulapam initiated their mass migration movements to the United States at different times.

In the case of Yalálag, a strong wave of migration to the United States surged in the 1970s and focused on work in the Los Angeles restaurant industry and private service sector. Nevertheless, as early as the 1950s, Yalaltecs were incited to cross the international border by North American evangelicals proselytizing in nearby tiny villages, so-called *pueblitos*.[23] Between the 1960s and 1980s, migrants from Yatzachi El Bajo, an evangelical stronghold, took up jobs in Hamburger Hamlet, a Los Angeles burger chain, through the mediation of a Zapotec born-again Christian.[24] Men from Yalálag worked informally in the catering sector, while women primarily found employment as housekeepers and babysitters. Yalálag migrants formed their satellite community in Los Angeles by reproducing the usos y costumbres governance of their hometown, that is, its organization in four *barrio* (neighborhood) communities whose members elect a committee in charge of the barrio's patron saint celebrations. In the 1990s, mediamakers from the Los Angeles satellite community began to specialize in documenting these fiestas called kermesses. Approximately half the migrants from Yalálag living in Los Angeles qualified for legal residence status under the Immigration Reform and Control Act (IRCA), passed in 1986.[25] Today, around two thousand persons reside in the Mexican hometown, while the majority of transnational Yalálag, roughly four thousand people, live in Los Angeles.

In contrast, mass migration from Tamazulapam to the United States started in the late 1990s. The pioneers were dwellers of agrarian hamlets (*agencias*) in search of work on West Coast crop farms.[26] Others sought opportunities in Los Angeles in the catering, construction, and service sectors. A group of men and women, the majority of whom had toiled in taco restaurants in the previous phase of migration to Mexico City, began setting up their own *taquerías* in the Central Mexican Bajío region at the end of the 1980s. Following in their footsteps, several migrants from Tamazulapam opened taco trucks in Los Angeles; most, however, were employees rather than owners. Since they immigrated too late to qualify for legalization under IRCA, the majority remain undocumented and plan to return to their hometown in the near future. Unlike Yalálag migrants, who operate a kind of parallel governance through hometown associations, those from Tamazulapam are more closely integrated into the system of their home village. Hometown membership requires them to serve as village officials in Mexico on a regular basis every six years or alternatively to support the hometown with a financial contribution. For several decades, approximately five hundred migrants from Tamazulapam have been living in Los Angeles; this comparatively small group attracts a larger group of villagers on the U.S. West Coast to joint celebrations and basketball tournaments. In addition, young Tamazulapam migrants take short-term jobs in taco trucks each year after graduating from secondary school.

Hence the paths adopted by Tamazulapam and Yalálag in journeying to the United States provide insights into differences that are partly shaped by local history, ethnicity, and their homeland region. But these are by no means the only factors that influence their contrasting transnational strategies, patterns of mediatized sociality, political alliances, and visions of the future. The contingencies of an incoherent U.S. migration policy likewise had an impact: the 1986 Immigration Reform and Control Act, commonly known as *la amnistía*, gave undocumented migrants a onetime option to have their stay legally recognized under certain conditions. While roughly half of the Yalaltecs were granted legal residence status, most of those from Tamazulapam remain unauthorized and confined in their mobility. This is another reason why the transnational communities of Yalálag and Tamazulapam differ when it comes to centers of gravity, distribution of responsibilities between home villages and satellite communities, and degree of cross-border cohesion. At the same time, the diasporas of both Sierra Norte villages have had a lasting impact on the megacity of Los Angeles, with its everchanging mosaic of ethnic communities.

Self-determined media initiatives have made a major contribution to these dynamics, a dimension of transnationalism and urban life that has so far been underestimated. Zapotec and Ayuujk ja'ay established transborder communication installing their own infrastructure. Their broadcasting promotes Indigenous languages, cultural forms, epistemes, and political organization by interactively involving an audience at home in multiple locations. Beginning in the 1940s, inhabitants of both villages used letters, telegrams, and landline telephone calls to stay in touch with relatives, friends, and business partners in the course of internal migration. They later extended these forms of communication to include photographs, audio and VHS cassettes, digital videos, cell phone calls, Skype, and eventually social media.

Media creatives experimented with audiovisual technology and aesthetic styles to forge a communal way of life on a transnational scale. Using radio broadcasts and video films, they designed formats that for the first time used Indigenous languages as a matter of course and spoke assertively about ordinary life in their villages. They developed specific film genres to document community events and the dynamics involved between Mexico and the United States. *Tequio* (communal labor), *fiestas* (like patron saint celebrations), and *conflictos* (mostly internecine land and political disputes) are some of the genres they created. These chronicles of transnationalism—initially on audio and VHS cassettes—quickly circulated among people scattered across two countries. With this culture-specific appropriation of audiovisual media, both Yalálag and Tamazulapam—and other Sierra Norte villages—play a pioneering role in transnational or diasporic film production worldwide.[27]

This study examines how these rooted media schemes evolved from 2016 on and formed a networked cluster, a kind of "virtual Oaxacalifornia," using digital tools and platforms. Their media practices centered on celebrations and fundraising at kermesses, on food sales and dance evenings for the respective hometown, and on music and dance repertoires from the Sierra Norte. The internet stations Radio Cantautor, Radio Gobixha, and Super Antequera Radio HD, which are based in Los Angeles but also have reporters in other U.S. cities and in Oaxaca, specialize in the announcement and live broadcast of events in Zapotec satellite communities. By logging into the internet page of one of these outlets, one can navigate through a torrent of interconnected Facebook pages that showcase Zapotec migrant communities and their numerous hometown associations, as well as their dance groups, bandas, and DJs. An Ayuujk cluster, on the other hand, is constituted by multimedia platforms such as Tamix Multimedios, Multimedios Jën mëⁿëny, and AR TV. The latter are based in Mexico and report with a focus on culture from the hometowns and the wider Sierra Norte region with its (ethno)political organizations. It was in the media spaces and time frames opened by these clusters and their formats that users debated common concerns and worked on projects with a transnational reach. The respective clusters did not organize strictly by ethnicity, although preference for the village language and music, whether Zapotec or Ayuujk, influenced networking patterns. At the same time, each cluster connected users who differed in age, migration generation, gender, education, occupation, language, ethnicity, legal status (which even varied within so-called mixed-status families), place of residence, and political orientation, as well as in terms of their lived realities on both sides of the international border.

As a rule, coverage by internet radio stations, multimedia platforms, and videographer Facebook pages was directed not only at inhabitants of the hometowns and their satellite communities in the United States, but also at migrants who have lived for decades in Oaxaca City and Mexico City as well as those who moved on to Bajío's industrial zone. Second-generation immigrants with family roots in Yalálag and Tamazulapam are now more acquainted with these urban milieus than with the agrarian hometowns of their parents. In the course of adapting communal practices such as patron saint fiestas, ethnic basketball tournaments, autochthonous dances, and brass band music to their new living and working environments in various urban settings, migrants and their descendants have forged new alliances. Traditional resources from the Sierra Norte have proved useful and attractive in the superdiverse urban context, also as a means of interacting more closely with people who do not belong to the same hometown or ethnic group. Several migrant communities living next to each other in Los Angeles share an interest in transnationalizing communitarian practices and ideas to enhance their recognition as Indigenous peoples with special citizenship rights and needs for social protection.

One larger alliance in Los Angeles concerns those who manage their own food trucks, shops, and restaurants and are part of over one hundred Oaxacan businesses forming a corridor along Pico Boulevard. The latter is one of the main traffic axes running through the districts of Mid City, Koreatown, and Pico Union, where neighborhoods once dominated by immigrants from Greece and Korea are now heavily populated with people from Oaxaca, El Salvador, and Guatemala. For decades, entrepreneurs who are members of Indigenous organizations have requested that the Los Angeles City Council officially recognize this area as a Corredor Oaxaqueño de Los Ángeles or a city landmark called Oaxacatown, as it is known informally. An estimated two to three hundred thousand from Oaxaca live in the city, most in Oaxacatown.[28] These mainly Indigenous migrants have a reputation for building powerful alliances, having modeled their hometown associations on their villages' communal governance.[29] Political activists and businesspeople orga-

Banda Descendencia Yalalteca, second-generation musicians at the Santiago Apostle food fair, Harvard Heights, Los Angeles, July 2019.

nized in umbrella organizations first created newspapers, bilingual radio programs, and later websites as press organs, thus addressing a transnational audience (Mercado 2015, 2019; Corkovic 2017). The marketing strategies of early Oaxacan immigrants laid the groundwork for the city's popular basketball tournaments and the Guelaguetza Festival, both of which now shape the generally positive image of Mexican immigration among the public in Los Angeles.[30]

Throughout the book I examine the way the Mexican home village is being assigned a new role in this process, one of facilitating the exchange between communities living at a distance. In several cases it is no longer numerically the largest settlement; many satellite communities in Los Angeles have surpassed it in population size.[31] At the same time, the hometown has acquired an enhanced significance as a spiritual center, a source of cultural authenticity, a holiday destination, and a sanctuary. The home village serves as a blueprint for mapping out how communal life should look in the future. For this purpose, it is codesigned from Los Angeles as the source of an "ethnic" or "village brand" (see below). Hence local embeddedness in the hometown is by no means a matter of nostalgia in the sense of looking back to the past but is instead geared to a political vision of the future.

In sum, the current study explores why, how, and with what results for community building, media actors disseminated their own cultural expressions, knowledge, and political ideas in new interactive formats by means of internet radio, videography, multimedia platforms, and ethnic influencing. They gave voice to and rendered visible previously marginalized Indigenous languages, economic activities, religious notions, and communal forms of organization in newly opened media spaces. They claimed rights concerning the daily practice of Indigenous lifestyles and cultural citizenship in their transnational scope: the interactive promotion of Indigenous languages such as Zapotec and Ayuujk; the public presence of live music performed by bandas—philharmonic brass bands with up to fifty musicians—and dances with a long tradition, all of which are forms of organizing collectively that bolster social protection in times of acute uncertainty. Consequently, the access to and design of new media for these specific concerns became key political demands. Claims arising from Indigenous lifeways with a transnational reach were discussed both internally and externally in a twofold movement. Internal debates involved the community and its alliances with Indigenous and non-Indigenous activists; at the same time, these claims were also voiced externally vis-á-vis state and federal governments in Mexico and the United States.

Against this background, self-determined media have a decisive impact on state and general public notions of who is considered Indigenous. Indigeneity is best understood as "a relational field of governance, subjectivities, and knowledges that involves us all—Indigenous and non-Indigenous—in the making and remaking of its structures of power and imagination" (De la Cadena and Starn 2007, 3). As a field of power Indigeneity shapes mobility across the Americas (Castellanos 2017, 222). In Oaxaca there is an ongoing tension between the state's definition of Indigeneity, which is used to harness a number of well-defined "ethnic groups" to its political interests,[32] and a defiant movement from below that emphasizes the communal logics of village and ethnic collectivities. The nation-state's Othering of Indigenous peoples developed from a colonial tradition of subordinating the colonized within a binary hierarchy to the dominant Spaniards and later mestizos. Twentieth-century Mexican ideology and policies called *indigenismo* consisted in implementing and justifying "assimilating" measures such as imposing the Spanish language in public schools with the explicit aim of erasing Indigenous lifeways for the purpose of converting Mexico into a "modern" (i.e., homogenized) mestizo nation. In Mexico only speakers of an Indigenous language are recognized as Indigenous. By transferring communal practices to urban spaces self-determined media outlets destabilized the once clear-cut "Othering" of Indigenous peoples that confined them to rural areas and considered merely their folkloric "ingredients" as enriching the Mexican nation. Beginning in the 1970s, when social movements in Mexico reappropriated the label Indigenous, they reinterpreted it as a unifying term for their common battle against neocolonization. Cutting-edge media initiatives played a crucial role in advancing the demands of the largely Indigenous uprisings in Chiapas in 1994 and in Oaxaca 2006 (Cleaver 1995; Stephen 2013; Schiwy 2019). An outcome of the first was legislative recognition of village governance, termed usos y costumbres, which has also strengthened hometown associations organizing according to these principles in the United States. The state of Oaxaca courts the favor of its migrant community in Los Angeles and surroundings—dubbed the Ninth Region of Oaxaca—now that migrant remittances have become the state's most important source of gross domestic product. It cooperated closely with the Frente Indígena de Organizaciones Binacionales (FIOB), the first transnational Indigenous organization founded in California, to create the Instituto Oaxaqueño de Atención al Migrante (IOAM), which was launched in 2004.

In contrast, the field of Indigeneity in California is influenced by the long-term effects of settler colonialism. This different form of state coloniality sought not to assimilate its native population but rather to reap its territory by dispossessing, removing, and eliminating it (cf. Wolfe 1999). Despite federal legal recognition of tribes as sovereign nations—which is the case for over one hundred tribes in California—Native Americans continue to experience exclusion and erasure for different reasons well into the twenty-first century. State Indigeneity mainly used "blood quantum" (ancestry being reckoned in halves, quarters, and smaller fractions by the ascription of a person's ancestors to a "race") as the standard to legally define tribal membership.[33] Defiantly, Native American communities retained divergent criteria, like kinship and political alliance, when identifying as a collectivity (White 2017). Today California has the largest Native American population in the United States. In addition to numerous historic state tribes, it is now home for people from far-off reservations who were displaced by the 1956 Relocation Act to cities like Los Angeles. Despite these differences between state Indigeneity in Mexico and the United States, some historical continuities overlap so that Indigenous peoples in Los Angeles face a field of power shaped by multiple neocolonialities (Speed 2017; Blackwell 2018), such as California's history as part of colonial and independent Mexico before the Mexican-American War of 1848. Moreover, for decades the array of Indigenous peoples in Los Angeles has included migrants from beyond Oaxaca, among them the Yucatec and Guatemalan Maya, who are also concentrated in the Pico-Union and Westlake districts. To tackle these multilayered colonialities, they organize to exchange political ideas and collaborate in their quest for visibility and citizenship rights. During public events, FIOB and other Oaxacan Indigenous organizations regularly acknowledge that they dwell on the territory of the original inhabitants of Los Angeles, the Gabrieleño/Tongva, Chumash, and Tataviam. They have allied with Native American councilmen and the Los Angeles City-County Native American Indian Commission, as they did in 2017 when they jointly supported a successful motion to establish Indigenous Peoples' Day as a legally recognized holiday instead of Columbus Day.

Since Indigenous migrants from Mexico and other Latin American countries now have a strong position within the larger community of Mexican-origin Hispanics, as they are officially categorized, they contest earlier Chicano/a versions of Indigeneity. Seen critically, those versions adopted the argumentative figure of indigenismo by imagining Indigeneity as past Aztec grandeur, in an effort to assert collective identity separate from the U.S. melting pot ideology. When they negotiate and redefine notions of Indigeneity from below, Indigenous migrants from

Oaxaca also situate themselves by discussing Native American histories, relationships to land, and displacement. In particular, the second generation with roots in Oaxaca also participates in the self-determined media that Native Americans and First Nations have launched. For example, #Nativetwitter is popular among those who engage intensely in discussions of multilayered Indigeneities and rely on English as their mother tongue (see chapter 6).

## THEORETICAL APPROACHES TO DECOLONIAL MEDIA SPACES AND TEMPORALITIES

> Thank you, my friend, for this transmission. It allows me ... not to miss the events, I mean, not just the fiesta, but the climate, the people, everything. So, I feel as if I were there, even though I'm far away.
> —User comment during a livestream of the patron saint fiesta in Tamazulapam on the Tamix Multimedios Facebook page[34]

Between 2016 and 2021, members of the transnational communities transformed digital mass communication. Self-determined media outlets such as Tamix Multimedios assumed protagonism by acting as a "social glue of migrant transnationalism" (Vertovec 2004). At the beginning of the millennium, Steven Vertovec applied this social diagnosis to migrants working far from their country of origin due to global work chains and their increased use of affordable mobile phones to stay in touch with relatives at home. The user's comment above draws attention to a dimension beyond family interconnectedness: the cultivation of an affective relationship with the locality of the hometown. Comparable media enable her to synchronize her experience of an event with many others—in this case through the digital platform run by a team of *paisanos/as* to broadcast the patron saint fiesta. Her opinion also demonstrates how interactive commenting now functions as a further adhesive. I conceptualize these media practices as crucial to the "affective production of community" (Kummels 2016a) because they were deliberately used in a way to create a communal spirit across the many rifts and fissures of the transnational terrain.

A previous study of mine, with "Indigenous media" in Mexico as its starting point, took a new turn when I discovered that neither the lens of ethnicity nor that of nation-state adequately captured media practices that ranged from photography and video to radio and television in an Ayuujk village in the Oaxacan Sierra Norte (Kummels 2017a). The motifs, aesthetic styles, and mode of circulation (e.g., transborder merchandising) of VHS videos and later DVDs indicated that transnational migration was an integral part of the media histories of particular Sierra Norte villages. Yalálag and Tamazulapam developed documentary film genres such as *tequio* (community work), *fiestas* (patron saint celebrations), and *conflictos*, all of which are categorized as *videos de comunidad* or the video genre of the communal.[35] Local mediamakers linked their work not only to political ideas about communal life but also to the emerging market through which videos were distributed transnationally. Sierra Zapotecs and Ayuujk ja'ay were among the pioneers of ethnopolitical movements during that decade, no longer joining existing peasant associations based on social class but instead organizing themselves independently and asserting full citizenship rights on an ethnic basis as autochthonous peoples (*pueblos autóctonos*) or Indigenous peoples (*pueblos indígenas*). Using autonomous radio stations and VHS videos as news media, they disseminated their own ideas for the first time to the broader public sphere about the cultural diversity of the Mexican nation-state and the political role its many Indigenous peoples should assume. Migrants participated in the movement from a distance. Yalaltecs who had moved to Los Angeles and set up a migrant association, for instance, bought and sent a VHS camera in 1987 to support the left-wing Grupo Comunitario that had taken over local governance in Yalálag.[36]

Migration, media, and the Indigenous movement, however, are rarely seen from a common perspective in scholarship. To put it plainly, this is because disciplines adhere to dividing lines, in this case drawn by communication sciences and media anthropology, on the one hand, and migration and transnationalism studies, on the other. In addition, media anthropology has privileged the study of media activism that claims to be "genuinely" communitarian and dissociates from commercial radio- and filmmaking designed for entertainment.

This book, in contrast, invariably sees Indigenous media as a product of plural, interwoven, and occasionally heterogeneous genealogies (cf. Schiwy and Wammack 2017, 5). It highlights a broad range of media practices from sending a cell phone snapshot at a private party or carrying out collaborative teamwork to reflecting on communication strategies intellectually via discursive practices. Creatives themselves analyzed the broad societal impact of mega media conglomerates versus their own self-determined media outlets (cf. Kummels 2017a, 10). Those involved initiated their practices not only at the grassroots level in rural villages but also in the asphalt jungles of Mexico and United States. Indigenous actors are diverse and interact with various political movements, including with non-Indigenous activists; they rely on these networks for media training and professionalization. The current study treads new ground by exploring digital technologies and their culturally specific appropriations by mediamakers in concrete localities, while paying attention to their scope beyond the respective national containers of Mexico and the United States. In addition, their audiovisual genres and digital artifacts are examined with an approach that takes into account the fluidity between political, commercial, and popular culture genres.

At the same time, my research ties in with studies on migration and transnationalism by anthropologists, sociologists, and political scientists who have taken a close look at the significant expansion of Indigenous lifeworlds between Oaxaca and California since the 1980s (see contributions in Fox and Rivera-Salgado 2004; Aquino Moreschi 2012; Cruz-Manjarrez 2013; Krannich 2017). The main thrust of their investigations, which also consider migration from the Oaxacan Sierra Norte, was frequently on the organization and political impact of migrant and hometown associations. Individual works provide valuable insights into the dynamics of gendered migration trajectories (Cruz-Manjarrez 2012, 2014; Worthen 2015; Andrews 2018). For the most part, however, they paid marginal attention to the way community members made use of mass communication, that is, newspapers, audio tapes, VHS videos, radio, and the internet. Although these media were harnessed to circulate political ideas across the international border, the authors omitted their importance for transnational political organization. It was primarily the mediamakers themselves, along with communication scholars, who illustrated how Indigenous Oaxacan migrants in California used groundbreaking initiatives to become politically active in the 1990s.[37] They show that Oaxacan people in Los Angeles drew on weekly newspapers, radio, and the internet in their struggle for migrant rights and successfully established a counterpublic, as they did in 2006 during the organization of nationwide demonstrations against a proposed anti-immigration law, the Sensenbrenner immigration bill (Costanza-Chock 2014; Mercado 2015, 2019). Meanwhile, current studies highlight how Sierra Norte villages formed an alliance with cyberactivists and installed an alternative mobile phone network to advance their media sovereignty (Bloom 2015; Bravo Muñoz 2017, 2020; González 2020).

Media anthropology studies on current uses of means of communication in Mexican Indigenous villages provide insight into the uneven distribution of skills in these communities. New imbalances are emerging despite the promise of democracy that digital media convey since they facilitate access to and rapid dissemination of information. It is primarily young people who use the internet, social media, and cell phones to keep in touch with their peer group and initiate partnerships and realign the social life of Indigenous communities via tech-savvy subcultures (Nava Morales 2011; De León-Pasquel 2018; Ramos Mancilla 2016, 2018, 2020). Other research indicates that mediamakers with academic training are the ones who employ digital technologies and social media to promote Indigenous languages in this cyber milieu. They run language apps, among other software, to foster both daily usage and knowledge production based on their mother tongues. As cyberactivists, they are combating failed policies that deeply affect Mexico's sixty-eight officially recognized Indigenous languages; these policies can be traced back to efforts beginning in the 1920s to impose Spanish on Indigenous students at public schools and that still reverberate today (Nava Morales 2019; Cruz and Robles 2019; Aguilar Gil 2020).[38]

In contrast, my approach considers additional factors that contribute to the uneven access to digital skills, technology, and infrastructure in the transnational context. People with distinct media abilities living in different localities faced the challenge of keeping in touch across an increasingly restrictive international border and a cross-border terrain permeated by inequalities. Despite these obstacles, people who live far from each other combined disparate analog and digital media technology—which I call *allomedia* (*allo* means different, opposite)—to open a transborder media space and align time regimes. This creative media work gave birth to debate in a networked publics and a transnational sense of belonging, as the present study shows. Nearly thirty years ago, Linda Basch, Nina Glick Schiller, and Cristina Szanton-Blanc (1994) interpreted transnationalism as a single field of social relations between two or more nation-states due to the regular flow of people, commodities, money, and ideas across the borders. Current research on transnational family, digital diasporas, and digital mediality puts greater emphasis on the complex ways in which actors make use of media to organize sociality from a great distance. These arrangements cover family care (Madianou and Miller 2012; Bryceson 2019; Baldassar and Wilding 2020), cosmopolitan values as part of a transnational habitus (Darieva, Glick Schiller, and Gruner-Domic 2016), and collective senses of belonging inspired by the use and consumption of new media (Karim 2015/2016; Alinejad 2017; Nedelcu 2019; Ponzanesi 2019). This book demonstrates how such arrangements across vast distances respond to recurring crises that have displaced the local population from their original homes in search of educational and job opportunities. It is argued that practices, negotiations, and debates carried out via self-determined media reconfigured Indigeneity and community life, both in the Sierra Norte region of Oaxaca and in Los Angeles.[39]

Opening a media space involved developing a "language" of images, sound, and text suited to exchanging common concerns and visions of the future in the transnational setting. The challenge was to overcome both the visual and the digital divide. By visual divide I refer to the comprehensive structures of inequality that people categorized as Indigenous have had to endure in the audiovisual field: inequality is inscribed not only in the hegemonic representations of Indigenous people but likewise in the materiality and social practices of audiovisual media, as well as in media training and work arrangements (Kummels 2017a, 15). In the digital era, neocolonialism is at work in several ways: high technologies are celebrated solely as cultural products of the "West" and juxtaposed with "Indigenous" body techniques like dancing and craft technologies such as weaving and pottery (Gómez Menjívar and Chacón 2019b, 17). Western high-tech development enjoys a privileged place in "universal" media history, while the role of Indigenous people, who de facto also act as a digital avant-garde in the global context, is mostly overlooked (see, for the contrary, Castells 1996; Aufderheide 2007; Schiwy 2019).[40]

Furthermore, Indigenous peoples and their lifeways lack online representation since they are at a disadvantage with respect to internet access and control. In the digital era, capital and power are concentrated in a limited group of corporations in the United States and China that have seized on social media as a means of harvesting and selling user data (Couldry and Mejias 2019; Zuboff 2019). A select number of leading players in the realm of social media platforms, such as Facebook, YouTube, and Twitter, increase the incongruity of knowledge structures because they are primarily interested in their use for data or surveillance capitalism, that is, in commercializing user data.[41] These social media corporations form an essential part of the media environment and global monopoly of the leading "Big

Five" companies in digital technology based in the United States (Alphabet-Google, Apple, Facebook, Amazon, and Microsoft), while in China further platforms wield power (Tencent, Alibaba, Baidu, and JD.com). These enterprises profoundly affect social life via their platform architecture, which is designed for collecting data on personal tastes and lifestyles (Van Dijck, Poell, and Waal 2018). Cyberactivists point this out regularly and warn against the pitfalls of Facebook, YouTube, and Twitter "affordances"—the properties or architecture of these platforms.[42] Decolonizing the internet calls for numerous measures that are by no means the exclusive responsibility of Indigenous collectivities but of all societies and nation-states, that is, the international global community (Bloom 2015; Bravo Muñoz 2017, 2020; Mercado 2019).

Hence, this book adopts a decolonial approach by placing its main focus on the historical continuities of colonialism in Latin and North America, while not losing sight of new structures emerging from the present era of digital-driven globalization. In the contested field of Indigeneity, the social classification of people according to a colonial racial scheme has been constantly renewed by persistent dominant elites as a means of exercising power. A case in point is Trump's White supremacy ideology—not least fueled by his Twitter demagogy (Fuchs 2018)—relying on the affect-charged vilification and racialization of Hispanic migrants (Berg and Ramos Zayas 2015; Hochschild 2016).[43] The way actors use counterstrategies based on cultural technology to change neocolonial relations (Schiwy 2018, 1) helps us analyze how cultural values are attached to media technology, knowledge, and practices as a result of the coloniality of power (Quijano 2000; Mignolo 2000). Decolonial approaches acknowledge the existence of a wide range of locally embedded egalitarian conceptions and practices in the Global South (Mignolo and Walsh 2018).[44] At the same time, the coloniality/modernity framework cannot explain all the complexities of today's multipolar world order and its capital flows. Their deepening of inequalities cannot be all attributed and related to historical colonialism and its forms of violence. Therefore, we also need to explore new dynamics of inequalities such as the surveillance carried out by those extracting data for profit and the ways transnational communal practices deal with the market aspects of culture circulated via digital technology (see the next section).

I refer to counteractions to present inequalities with historical continuities as "audiovisual decolonization" (Kummels 2017a, 17) to show that grassroots approaches have their own genealogies, even while entwined with non-Indigenous theories. This is the case of Comunalidad (communality; see the next section). Few media actors I talked to use the term "decolonization." Nevertheless, they challenge neocolonialism when conveying in sound, imagery, and discourse what they consider "our own" (in Spanish, lo propio or lo originario; in Zapotec, da wlhall; and in Ayuujk, këm jä'). The Ayuujk ja'ay, for instance, refer to themselves as "those never conquered" (in Spanish, Los jamás conquistados; in Ayuujk, kamapyë). Self-determined media also rely on this self-image when circulating, for example, a meme that became extremely popular in 2019 as a comment on strained international relations between Mexico and Spain. The meme portrayed the Spanish king Felipe as complaining, "I request the Mixe (Ayuujk ja'ay) to apologize to Spain, because they never let themselves be conquered."[45]

Simultaneously, the "coloniality of gender" (Lugones 2010) is an integral part of subordinating Others. Gender identities are fraught with historical continuities, like the ubiquitous enacting of binary femininities and masculinities. In this field too, there is a tension between "Western" feminisms that became hegemonial and a diversity of "homegrown feminisms" that challenge the specific conditions of Indigenous and Afro-American peoples in different places based on their own knowledges (for a discussion, see Hernández Castillo and Canessa 2012; Castellanos 2017). Migration and gender studies uncovered how migrants were often conceived as bounded male categories. This book focuses on Indigenous feminist practices or "homegrown feminisms" shaped by actors who nevertheless avoid the term "feminism." The main reason female creatives reject this label is their perception that feminism was initially defined by White women who failed to take the situation and concerns of rural and migrant Indigenous women into account. The latter engage in communal issues and claim rights via media like photography as is the case of second-generation Yalaltec Citlali Fabian (see Solis Bautista 2021) and radiomaking as reflected on by the Ayuujk intellectual Carolina Vásquez García (2018). The community influencers and other mediamakers I followed are not declared feminists but seek more balanced and diverse gender relations in "virtual Oaxacalifornia." They publicly document the situated Indigeneities of their family lives by harnessing social media's propensity to blur private and public (Baym and boyd 2012). In following their stories, I also trace how men tended to report on matters considered "genuinely" public while women have brought education, motherhood, family life, and their rights as community members (*comuneras*) to the foreground, overcoming the private/public divide. When organizing and livestreaming Zapotec and Ayuujk cultural expressions, media actors would therefore situate their Indigeneity differently: what some condemned as a break with Indigenous lifeways, others defined as a change in existing gender biases to promote a truly egalitarian form of Indigeneity.

Mediamakers and their communities are treading new ground in developing digital technologies and media practices that contradict the hegemonic version of history. Their efforts can be considered part of a long tradition of audiovisual decolonization dating back to the colonial period (Kummels 2017a, 17, 116). Despite the Spanish rulers' calculated annihilation of knowledge recorded with autochthonous technologies such as pictographic writing and figurative art (Gruzinski 2001), precolonial media strategies were continued in secret or in new hybrid formats (Ruiz Medrano 2011). On the one hand, politicized actors in the 1980s deliberately drew on these rebellious media traditions—including those from Yalálag and Tamazulapam—at a time when they also self-identified for the first time as "Indigenous peoples" to forward political aims. This study shows, on the other hand, that existing institutions of Indigenous life such as local governance, the organization of celebrations, and forms of mutual assistance were both mediatized and transnationalized in the course of migration. One example is how an essential tool of reciprocity, *gozona* account books, was transferred from written bookkeeping to VHS video format (see chapters 2 and 6). Indigenous theorists have thought deeply about these media genres of the communal way of life. As a result, mediamakers in Tamazulapam conceptualize video filming as part of the Ayuujk cosmology and as a sacred space (*espacio sagrado*) and archiving as *exta'n* (memory, testimony; see the next section). On this basis they have made political demands to the federal government for the infrastructure and broadcasting frequencies that self-determined media work require.

By carrying out media practices in a self-determined way, the creatives I accompanied were able to wield them for decolonial aims despite relying on corporate-owned social media mainly interested in "colonizing" users' data. Shaping institutions of Indigenous life with the aid of communicative practices, such as family celebrations, community festivities, association meetings, and ethnic basketball tournaments, counteracts the neocolonial inscriptions mentioned earlier, as this study shows. Media actors use alternative formats and aesthetics precisely to expose the power structures of existing hegemonic means of communication and their attendant organization, language, and images. In this process they trigger reflection and rethinking. Recent scholarship highlights various aspects of decolonization via the use of digital technologies; with their seminal contributions, Indigenous mediamakers rewrite the genealogies of existing technologies and open cyberspaces to communicate in Indigenous languages and tell their own stories (Ramos Mancilla 2018; Nava Morales 2019; Risam 2018; Bird 2020). Hence, they have the potential to go beyond a mere democratization of the digital archiving of knowledge and "create space for something different and anti-universalist" (Martens et al. 2020, 9).

## BROADCASTING THE FUTURE: ZAPOTEC AND AYUUJK WAYS OF COMUNALIDAD AND THE AMERICAN DREAM

Experiencing a broadcast was often like stepping into a world under construction in which one could catch a glance while also hearing about promising times to come. Whenever I accompanied staff from Radio Cantautor, Video Aries, Tamix Multimedios, or other organizations, they were reporting on communal projects brought to fruition thanks to migrant money and solidarity from the home village: helping someone in need, providing equipment for a youth band, or developing infrastructure for the Mexican hometown. This entailed documenting how cultures and polities of the Sierra Norte are lived in many places, among them Los Angeles. Thus, self-determined media outlets were all about futuring—that is, interpreting the present in terms of its value for times to come. Futuring is inherent to migration dynamics; it influences the decisions taken by those willing to or forced to migrate (Griffiths, Rogers, and Anderson 2013). The aspirations for one-self, one's family, and one's community are expressed in figures of speech for migration such as *cha wilh yel nbán* (in search of life) in Zapotec, *nyëpëjtëjkëp* (to seek a fortune) in Ayuujk, and *viviendo el sueño americano* (living the American Dream) in Spanish. Texts, audio, and images from diasporic media integrated the home village, as well as migration sites, into imaginative spaces that interact. Projections into the future called for critical reforms in order to fulfil these ambitions. This evokes a similar use of mass communication during the 2006 Oaxacan uprising, when activist videos showed how political subjects—encompassing rural teachers, Indigenous women, urban poor, and the educated left—built horizontal social relations in an accessible time frame (Schiwy 2019, 8–9, 33). The media actors under review here also formed broad alliances by jointly envisioning an immediate future in which they overcame the restrictive international border. Using digital tools, they fashioned utopias that seemed just a few mouse clicks away.

Along migrant media circuits the political ideas concerning Comunalidad have been taken on a journey to multiple places. There they have entered into a dialogue with other ideas that address the transnational extension of communal life: notions about Oaxacalifornia and the Guelaguetza. In addition, migrants often refer to the concept of the American Dream in order to reconcile their aspirations for economic advancement and development with communitarian principles. To examine the current interpretations of communality by Indigenous mediamakers, first let us review its intellectual history.

The term "Comunalidad" was coined in the late 1970s by Ayuujk intellectual Floriberto Díaz and Zapotec scholar Jaime Martínez Luna, founders and leaders of early ethnic organizations in the Oaxacan Sierra Norte and trailblazers of Mexico's first nationwide Indigenous movement.[46] Floriberto Díaz ([1995] 2007, 38) argued that a common territory, history, language, and organization—defining politics, culture, and social life—and the village's own legal system were the core elements of Comunalidad. He attached particular importance to the territory of the *pueblo* or municipality, since land lies at the center of cosmology and collective identity and is therefore constitutive of community (Díaz [1995] 2007, 51–53, 132–134). Both he and Martínez Luna stressed that communal organization was based on different forms of work, such as the activity invested in General Assemblies, a political office in local governance (today generally known as usos y costumbres), and tequio or joint labor. In the agrarian villages of the time, work of this kind was performed on-site for all to see and could thus be witnessed face-to-face. Martínez Luna (2010, 33, 44) later shifted attention to festivities and their enjoyment as essential for Comunalidad. Fiestas are based on a shared rural economy that ensures redistribution and equality within the village.

From the very beginning, Comunalidad emerged as a hybrid concept from the dialogues with left-wing academics at workshops hosted in the villages. Not only did politicized Indigenous mediamakers network among themselves, they also worked closely with non-Indigenous supporters, including anthropologists, linguists, and Liberation theologians—whom they had met while pursuing higher education.[47] Writing in the Zapotec language and its dissemination via leaflets, posters, silk screening, photography, and video was conveyed in workshops such as those organized by linguist Juan José Rendón Monzón in Yalálag. Díaz and Martínez Luna had studied anthropology in Mexico City, Díaz at the Escuela Nacional de Antropología and Luna at the Universidad Autónoma Metropolitana. They countered the prevailing anthropological lens on community studies by analyzing communal life from both an internal village viewpoint and the external perspective of academia.[48] In this context, Comunalidad emerged as an "intercultural utopia" from a critical rethinking of local theories and methodologies as well as those taken from "Western" knowledge institutions before applying them to Indigenous lifeworlds (cf. Rappaport 2005).

How were media harnessed for Comunalidad, and how was the latter redefined in Oaxaca between 2016 and 2021? *Comunicadores* or community mediamakers exchanged ideas on Indigenous epistemes at the Second International Congress of Comunalidad held in the Ayuujk village of Tlahuitoltepec on March 5, 2018.[49] I witnessed how many media outlets are run by a second generation, some of whom have been educated at local universities such as UNICEM (Universidad Intercultural del Cempoáltepetl), which offers a bachelor's degree in communal communication. Lilia Héber from Radio Jënpoj (in Ayuujk, wind of fire) explained to this group—which included non-Indigenous media experts like myself—how topics of concern at the radio are developed from village lifeworlds. These topics are at the same time part of a transnational Indigenous media space:

> The issue of women's participation has been gaining ground because we've also been able to put it on the table through Jënpoj communitarian radio. This is something we put into practice from our context; for example, it's part of the topic of participation in the local governance of our village. As well as the social organization of communal fiestas, communitarian sociability. At the radio we focus on broadcasting the diverse communal fiestas. We've been establishing relationships between other villages and also providing feedback on the process of strengthening these festivities and their sociability, including the exchange of brass bands between villages. That was already going on prior to our community project, but has been strengthened by our use of this medium. We've also been told that other villages have started speaking Ayuujk again and revived its use after hearing about the issue on our radio station. They began to create songs in Ayuujk. The self-recognition of migrants has indeed greatly helped our medium to put concerns such as language use, culture, and who we are on the table. Migrants listen to our station, migrants from other states and other countries, and reclaim their culture, their identity, and their language. All this is part of our reason for being a means of communication. We need to keep on building up what we conceive as communitarian communication.[50]

Radiomaker Lilia Héber went on to stress that women's participation in usos y costumbres governance is a precondition for fiestas to operate as the key organizational form at the heart of Comunalidad. She highlighted how the agency of female villagers paved the way for the mediatization and export of fiestas in the course of transnational migration, including to Los Angeles. Disenfranchised migrants ensure political participation "from below" when organizing celebrations at hometown association meetings, where they engage in mutual aid inspired by tequio and other practices of reciprocity typical of an agrarian village. As a community facility located in the Sierra Norte, Radio Jënpoj addressed these topics daily in its Facebook transmissions.[51] As a result, listeners living far from the hometown have become familiar with the way principles of community life are conceived in the Sierra Norte and reflect on them when taking part in this wider audience.

Radio Jënpoj operates with village volunteers and receives support for its infrastructure from the Tlahuitoltepec municipality, which is governed according to usos y costumbres. Conditions for mass communication, however, vary from place to place and are rapidly changing in the transnational context. Self-determined media outlets were therefore in search of further possibilities for securing independent digital infrastructure and producing content autonomously. More than eighty media organizations (e.g., radio stations, cell phone networks) from ten Mexican states came together to discuss this key issue, at the Fourth Encounter of Communitarian Communication hosted by Ojo de Agua Comunicación in San Luis Beltrán near Oaxaca City in September 2019.[52] Eliel Cruz from Tamix Multimedios based in Tamazulapam was there to learn more about the latest methods of internet self-engineering and independent platform management, and to network with alternative media experts and hacktivists. Tamix Multimedios operates on a company Facebook page because it's the most popular platform for his audience. Eliel kept himself informed at the meeting on the affordances he has to buy into. He is careful to avoid the attention economy of likes in his media work. Instead, he makes a point of ensuring that Tamix Multimedios distinguishes itself through its genuine community-based content. Historical material from the village's own video production is added to the platform. In collaboration with Rosita Román (who graduated in communal communication at UNICEM), Genaro and Hermenegildo Rojas from Tamix Multimedios conceptualized these historical audiovisual recordings as a community archive and in Ayuujk as *exta'n*. They explain the concept as follows: *Exta'n* are memories, messages, or testimonies of culminating life events to which audiovisual recording pays homage and thus contributes to their lasting effect.[53] Hence the Tamix Multimedios Facebook page curates content composed of memories that are gripping and enduring; it also disseminates them to an ever-widening community that cocreates these memories online.

Change of scene to California: internet radio stations set up in Los Angeles also uphold the long-standing Sierra Norte tradition of community media in line with the directive to "be assembly-based and collective, foster programs that deal with social topics and revenues independent of public or commercial institutions; . . . in harmony with local traditions, highly democratic, aligned to human rights and horizontal [in structure]" (Castells i Talens 2011, 135; my translation). Accordingly, they offer broadcasting services for migrant communities free of charge. In this urban milieu, however, numerous Mexican Indigenous media outlets operate as part of the "Los Angeles Oaxacan fiesta economy," a business enclave tailored to needs of migrant communities. Zapotec shopkeepers in Los Angeles advertise their transnationalized Sierra Norte products via newspapers, radio, video, and social media pages. In addition to food supplies and services for celebrations, the fiesta economy includes audiovisual documentation and live transmission of the festivities. It takes on a political dimension for transnational communities: through business models that engender visibility and recognition, shopkeepers and self-employed vendors and service providers play a crucial role in visibilizing Indigenous cultures and combating their discrimination in Los Angeles. In this context people in and from Yalálag and Tamazulapam applied village and ethnic branding strategies to their cultural expressions and products without fully submitting to a market logic (cf. Comaroff and Comaroff 2009). In Los Angeles they attempted to shape the transnationalized community into a village, Zapotec, or Ayuujk brand by acting as what some specialists have termed an "immigrant" or "ethnic economic enclave" within the capitalist market (Wilson and Portes 1980). But in this case entrepreneurs did not rely exclusively on coethnic social networks but instead expanded them via their ethics of reciprocity. Indigenous migrant shops and restaurants—as well as their clients—are able to forge a collective identity via their products, food items, furnishings, and decor, since in the process they jointly "disrupt and challenge narratives of racialized Indigeneity" (Castellanos 2015, 67).

Facing distinct conditions in the United States, the Oaxacan Indigenous movement there rarely uses the term "Comunalidad." That said, however, members and leading figures of Indigenous-migrant umbrella organizations such as Frente Indígena de Organizaciones Binacionales (FIOB), Organización Regional de Oaxaca (ORO), and Federación Oaxaqueña de Clubes y Organizaciones Indígenas de California (FOCOICA) likewise highlight the validity of Oaxacan communitarian principles. But they have to be adapted to new parameters: Migrants from Yalálag and Tamazulapam work in the United States for the most part as employees in the restaurant sector, in construction, and as housekeepers and nannies in private households, frequently for two employers simultaneously. A few are self-employed, some with great success, as in the case of a number of restaurant owners and owners of taco food truck chains or grocery stores. Odilia Romero, who comes from Zoogocho in the Sierra Norte and migrated with her family to Los Angeles at the age of eleven, was the first female general coordinator of FIOB from 2017 to 2020.[54] In 2016 she cofounded a nonprofit organization, Comunidades Indígenas en Liderazgo (CIELO), which engages in philanthropic aid for Indigenous migrants in Los Angeles. She explained that Comunalidad under these new urban conditions is primarily practiced by hometown associations and migrant communities when hosting fiestas on the weekends:

ODILIA: Everything changes [in Los Angeles]. You migrate and you change your food habits, you change the way you dress, the way you talk, but you preserve some things. Even if people from over there [the Oaxacan Sierra Norte] say that only residents of the villages can truly appreciate and feel what Comunalidad is, we have a different perspective on Comunalidad here. In the end, what we do *is* Comunalidad because we work together, we live together, there's a lot of solidarity involved. . . .

INGRID: The term "Comunalidad" seems to be less in use here [in Los Angeles] than over there [in Oaxaca], right?

ODILIA: Well, no, because it's more of a practice. It's like the Guelaguetza. Everyone knows about the dances, but most people don't know or behave according to the Guelaguetza concept.[55] In one of the many workshops that we organize for government employees I raise the question: "Do you know what the Guelaguetza is?" "Yes, that dance event, that restaurant . . ." But the Guelaguetza is much more than that, right? And the same happens with Comunalidad. Academics use it a lot, they refer to that label. Some Indigenous intellectuals use it, too—but the community just puts it into practice.

INGRID: And do you think it's also practiced in Los Angeles?

ODILIA: Oh, sure, day in, day out. Every weekend you can sense there's Comunalidad.[56]

A term that characterizes the communal way of life in its transnational scope was coined in Los Angeles: Oaxacalifornia. Sociologist Gaspar Rivera-Salgado, founding member of FIOB and project head of the UCLA Labor Center, closely monitored the process in the 1990s, when anthropologist Michael Kearney (1995) gave currency to the term "Oaxacalifornia" for the "deterritorialized transnational space" unfurled by Indigenous migrants from Oaxaca, including Mixtecs, Chinantecs, Triqui, and Zapotecs. The concept of a transborder communality is now predominantly voiced by members of the politicized second generation in Los Angeles (see chapter 6; see also Chávez 2020; Nicolas 2021). These descendants of unauthorized migrants from Yalálag explained Oaxacalifornia to me as a space that percolates through all of California where they can practice their own culture, rooted in Oaxaca, in a vibrant way on U.S. soil. Indigenous lifeways in this setting are no longer primarily oriented to the hometown of the first generation. Instead, they combine cultural knowledge ranging from community-specific brass band music to the panethnic *folklórico* dances of Los Angeles to transnational citizenship. According to Rivera-Salgado, by broadening Comunalidad to include Oaxacalifornia, Indigenous communities updated their concept of autonomy by detaching it from a bounded territory:

Comunalidad goes beyond simple territory, it includes a process that, according to anthropologists, produces a sense of belonging and identity. In other words, it has a dual nature that exceeds mere territory and refers to what other intellectuals have termed a "political community." The message conveyed [by Comunalidad] sort of interrupts migration, since not all Indigenous people remain in their territory. It subverts this idea that we have to fight for our territory and guarantee full control of it.... It used to be a highly traditional issue, so migrants in the Mixtec language were called the *na syika nda'vi,* meaning "those wandering faraway lands." And later on, there was talk of us being in Oaxacalifornia. This other concept advanced the idea that: "Well, perhaps we are not that separated after all!" How should we describe our reality: Are we wandering about on foreign soil or do we share a common space? ... Some villages handle it flexibly and others don't, declaring instead: "If you are not here [in your hometown], you lose all your rights, everything." I think it's interesting that this concept is not a given, but negotiated in the context of political practice. There are groups of organized migrants who want to continue belonging to the village of origin—and that's why they engage in institutionalizing the practices that allow them to do so.[57]

The Guelaguetza festival is precisely such a site of political and media practices negotiated in a transnational setting. In Oaxaca the state government was the first to control the mass event now called Guelaguetza. Since the early 1930s, it has presented the folkloric costumes, music, and dance of its regions (in the meantime eight regions) as a vehicle for integration and a highly profitable tourist attraction.[58] Oaxacan migrants, on the other hand, conferred a thoroughly new meaning to the Los Angeles Guelaguetza (as part of a series of Guelaguetza events in California), while using the same name: migrants from small villages like Macuiltianguis (Valles Centrales), Yatzachi el Alto, Yatzachi el Bajo, Xochixtepec, and Zoogocho (Sierra Juárez) who, since the early 1960s have been immigrating to Los Angeles in large numbers to escape abject poverty, were among the pioneers who organized the first festival displaying Oaxacan migrant dance, music, crafts, and food in Normandie Park in 1987. In Los Angeles the Guelaguetza is managed by the migrant umbrella organization Organización Regional de Oaxaca (ORO).[59] The annual city festival has evolved into a showcase for the public visibility and recognition of the numerous communities from Indigenous Oaxaca, something unauthorized migrants are otherwise denied.

Indigenous visibility requires constant negotiation with various stakeholders, as was explained to me by Isaí Pazos, director of ORO from 2014 to 2019, and Dalila Castillo, a member of the board.[60] Together they introduced a new element in 2014, the Calenda, a procession of dance groups and brass bands down Pico Boulevard a few days before the main Guelaguetza event. Both pointed out the necessity of "adapting and modifying" the cultural roots from the Sierra Norte villages to Los Angeles. To launch the Calenda they consulted and convinced as many migrant communities from Oaxaca as possible for the purpose of mobilizing their forty-three brass bands and numerous dance groups.[61] Just as vital was the process of lobbying and forming alliances with communities from El Salvador, Korea, Bangladesh, Greece, and the African American community. With their support they began to apply for permits. Furthermore, they discovered that declaring

The Guelaguetza Calenda parades through Oaxacatown with Flor de Piña dancers, Los Angeles, July 2019.

the procession a "parade" was the way to obtain city approval, in addition to working closely with the Los Angeles Police Department. Finally, Isaí, who runs his own video and media company, ensured coverage by Hispanic media, in this case the Telemundo 52 TV station, a key move when it comes to fostering a positive public image.[62]

Isaí belongs to the 1.5 generation of the Yalálag migrant community. He is a prominent advocate of what could be termed a policy of "dancing for recognition." Indigenous dances allow children and second-general youth to learn about the history of their parents' hometowns ludically. After founding the youth dance group Nuevas Raíces (New Roots), Isaí pursued a policy of recognition primarily via the Guelaguetza festival. Claiming visibility by performing folkloric-style dances contrasts with the tactics of organizations such as FIOB, which primarily rely on explicitly political discourses. In addition, Isaí and Dalila draw on the slogan of the American Dream or Sueño Americano often mentioned in migrant communities. The classic aspirations of the American Dream refer to immigrants' hope for economic advancement based on hard work and determination and better educational opportunities for the next generation; depending on the broad spectrum of political perspectives, the dream is viewed alternatively as a desirable and attainable goal or as an illusion, given that structural inequality prevents its fulfillment. In contrast, Isaí and Dalila interpret empowerment through dance and perceive the renewed pride in Oaxaca as an "indigenized" American Dream that migrants have managed to advance on communitarian terms:[63]

The young people of the first and second generation here in the United States now admit that their parents are from Oaxaca or even declare "I'm from Oaxaca," and that didn't happen thirty years ago. That's why I think the work of the Organización Regional de Oaxaca has changed our mindset and the way Oaxacan people are presented today. We know that a person from Oaxaca is a fighter, hardworking, and sustains the family with two or three jobs. Why? Because they want to live the American Dream. But the real question is: What is the American Dream? We don't know, because everyone lives it their own way.

Other migrant groups take a more radical political stance where the American Dream is concerned, such as the Dreamers, unauthorized young people who are supported but not granted citizenship by the U.S. government.[64] Attorney Lizbeth Mateo, who originally comes from Valles Centrales, is one of the Oaxacan community's prominent Dreamers. In March 2018, she became the first undocumented migrant appointed to a Los Angeles City Council advisory committee as an expert on college access for low-income students. With her high-profile activism, she and other Dreamers challenge hegemonic U.S. notions of migrant upward mobility, by denouncing how it is exclusively granted to "deserving" migrants who silently adapt to the mainstream (cf. Abrego and Negrón-Gonzales 2020).

At the Guelaguetza Festival, the communitarian ethos is more strongly linked to the cultural and business aspirations of the Oaxacan community: "We are indeed fighting to uphold the name Oaxaca in business, culture, music, and cuisine," Isaí claims. Dance, brass band music, and cuisine are thus intertwined with the notion of economic advancement that on U.S. soil is pursued by relying precisely on these cultural resources. As a way of "conveying our history," dances and the symbolism of their costumes are thoroughly explained to children who perform them, according to Isaí. And then there is, as Dalila explains, "our sociability and they see that constantly because celebrations are held all the time. There's really no need to say to the children 'That's what you need to know' because they're absorbing it little by little." Dalila's own daughter is passionate about culture from Oaxaca: "She began dancing when she was two. She wasn't interested in Barney or Sponge Bob videos. She preferred to watch a video of me dancing *Flor de Piña* and imitated me in front of the TV without anyone telling her what to do. She used to ask for the video and dance all by herself."

The communal conviviality that abounds when dance groups and migrant associations from Oaxaca come together is linked to a market strategy evident at the Los Angeles Guelaguetza. In 2014, ORO registered Festival Guelaguetza as a trademark for "organizing community festivals featuring primarily art exhibitions, musical performances, ethnic dances and the like, and also providing ethnic food and dining."[65] A debate on the commercialization of the event had already erupted in the political organizations that represent migrants from Oaxaca in the United States. Criticism was leveled, for example, at high rents for exhibition stands ($2,800). During my research, members of the FIOB, who otherwise work closely with ORO, voiced their disapproval of the trademark registration. Isaí Pazos, who was president of ORO at the time, defended his action, claiming it was a countermeasure against outsiders who threatened to profit from the Guelaguetza organized by ORO:

> We found out that some people were doing business with photographs. They used to sell a photo for 30, 40, 100 and more, but none of it was for ORO. And that's why we began to protect the rights and reserve them. The same applies to the name Guelaguetza, which is now protected by ORO. That was an issue we coordinated with the Oaxacan state government, because the Guelaguetza was getting out of hand. People were holding a "Guelaguetza" here and a "Guelaguetza" there and even business owners organized their own Guelaguetza to make a profit. Which is why we began controlling it. It's not about doing business, because the Guelaguetza belongs to the community. We simply protected it by registering it as a brand. There are people from Jalisco, from Zacatecas, who want to host a Oaxacan Guelaguetza even though they're not Oaxacans.[66]

The link to entrepreneurship in Los Angeles is partly intended to ward off external economic interests but serves at the same time to maximize profits in favor, for example, of raising funds for the transnational communities. The wider community of people from Oaxaca, therefore, is also defined in terms of who as a member is permitted to profit from the "musical performances, ethnic dances, ethnic food and dining" mentioned in the trademark registration. In Los Angeles, these economic activities are an integral part of a Oaxacan fiesta economy that revolves around private and community celebrations that are not purely market-oriented and remain to a large extent profoundly communitarian. According to Martínez Luna's concept of Comunalidad, fiestas constitute an enjoyable center-piece of communitarian life—and remain key even in the distinctive setting of the diaspora.

## ITINERARIES OF THE BOOK

Setting out along several transnational paths, this book follows itineraries on which Zapotecan and Ayuujk media outlets pioneered cross-border communal life. Chapter 2 first explores "Histories of Mediatic Self-Determination: Pioneer Oaxacan Videos Go Transnational" for providing insight into how Zapotec and Ayuujk digital outlets build upon local histories of self-managed media. These histories are based on traditional oratory, music, dance, and crafts as well as the appropriation of analog mass media such as photography, radio, VHS video, and television broadcasting since the late 1980s. The chapter traces the diversified media histories of Yalálag and Tamazulapam in the Sierra Norte during initial waves of migration to Mexican and U.S. cities as well as the political engagement of these villages over audiovisual decolonization. Village mediamakers recurrently

created facilities and genres tailored to community needs and transborder networking. At the turn of the twenty-first century, adapting digital technology to
community affairs takes center stage. This allows for transnational communication in real time and aligning a sense of belonging for those on both sides of the
restrictive international border.

Chapter 3 focuses on "Zapotec Dance Epistemologies Online" and the everyday practices of documenting and archiving knowledge shaped by Mexican Indigenous peoples. With their Facebook pages and YouTube uploads they have created
an alternative archive of videoclips of traditional Zapotec dances hosted on the
internet: the largest audiovisual collection of such dances in the world. Migrants
and villagers dedicate themselves to recording and publishing Zapotec dances
that originate from the Oaxacan Sierra Norte, but are now intensively cultivated
by second-generation immigrants born in Los Angeles. Using the example of the
Los Angeles dance group Nueva Generación Krus Yonn, the chapter shows how
in particular mothers/*comuneras* engage as "ethnic" or "community influencers."
They renegotiate gender equality and the relationship between Yalálag and its
satellite community in Los Angeles by organizing performances of dances that
previously were staged only by men and by communicating about them on digital
media. When livestreaming these innovative performances for a transnational
audience, media-savvy experts anchor Zapotec dance knowledge and Indigeneity
to new territory and adapt it to contemporary interests that include those of
second-generation immigrants.

Chapter 4, "The Fiesta Cycle and Transnational Death: Community Life on
Internet Radio," delves into illness, death, and mourning in the context of transnational life at a time when caring for family members at home on the other side of
the international border is impeded by Trump's "get-tough" anti-immigration policies in the United States. Community videographers and internet radio teams
engage in organizing a "good death" in this context by adapting traditional care
and death rituals to several localities of Oaxacalifornia. This chapter closely follows negotiations in Zapotec, Spanish, and English concerning the "Graveyarders," a novel migrant association in Los Angeles, in their effort to renovate and
extend the cemetery of their hometown Yalálag—a project that would prove
visionary in the context of the pandemic. It analyzes how they handled disagree-
ment with the hometown with the help of an internet radio broadcast live via
remote hookup in a Los Angeles backyard. Internet radio stations get involved in
crisis communication; they also promote the fundraisers of Oaxacan Indigenous
migrant associations. These media outlets contribute to an intensified transnational fiesta cycle, expanding its spatial outreach and combining time regimes.
This provided increased social protection for Mexican Indigenous peoples and
extended their sense of belonging transnationally during the Trump era.

Chapter 5 embarks on a journey to examine "Ayuujk Basketball Tournament
Broadcasts: Expanding Transborder Community Interactively." It follows a legendary ethnic basketball tournament hosted by the Ayuujk ja'ay or Mixe in their

Oaxacan homeland and how it was exported to migrant destinations in Central Mexican cities and in Los Angeles. Media practices carried out by game promoters and sponsors are crucial for organizing and disseminating the games. At each venue these actors support a transnational digital infrastructure that connects people and teams from dispersed satellite communities with very different living conditions. Media creativity at the three tournaments enhances participation and allows people to experience Ayuujk basketball from afar. Ethnic identity and gender are redefined in the course of media work. For example, at the Copa Mixe Bajío Tournament Ayuujkness is construed as grounded in the taco business of Central Mexico and its gender division. Despite economic and infrastructural disparities among the localities of the three tournaments, the Ayuujk media outlets shape basketball as an "Ayuujk sport" and unifying force based on Comunalidad. Interactive community media and audiences are key to this process of centering an expanding transnational community on Ayuujk basketball as an antidote to marginalization and oppression in urban settings.

Chapter 6 examines "Turning Fifteen Transnationally: The Politics of Family Movies and Digital Kinning" by analyzing media use at quinceañera parties celebrated by migrants from Yalálag living in Los Angeles. At first sight these are "shockingly" exuberant parties with elaborate dance shows dedicated to the coming of age of a fifteen-year-old daughter. However, videography, live broadcasting, and cell phone posting have converted the parties into a site where transborder digital kin work takes place. This chapter focuses on a mixed-status family and follows their daughter Francis's coming of age in 2018 from initial preparations to the afterthoughts of family members. Community videographers who specialize in making "Yalálag style" quinceañera videos and party guests who broadcast live with their cell phones are key media actors who record, comment on, and disseminate different layers of an extended family for a transnational audience. The fifteen-year-old girls belong to a young, politicized second generation that negotiates Indigenous identity, Oaxacalifornian belonging, and citizenship in the United States, while they also bridge the digital divide and connect the satellite community in Los Angeles with the Mexican home village.

The epilogue deals with "Reloading Comunalidad—Indigeneity on the Ground and on the Air" and assesses the influence these media initiatives have on a transnational community in constant flux due to crises sparked by incoherent U.S. migration policies among other factors. To advance their own interests, Zapotec and Ayuujk people have created cutting-edge media facilities that serve as forums of communication and debate between home villages and satellite communities dispersed in two countries. They highlight cultural perspectives, social needs, and political demands of decolonization that otherwise receive little attention in the dominant public spheres of the United States and Mexico.

# 2 · HISTORIES OF MEDIATIC SELF-DETERMINATION

## Pioneer Oaxacan Videos Go Transnational

"No video, no fiesta!" is a phrase doing the rounds among the enormous fan base of the transnational fiesta video industry. Between 2013 and 2019 and again in 2021, I traveled through the Sierra Norte of Oaxaca in shared taxis, in minibuses, and by hitch-hiking. Each time I attended a patron saint fiesta, I came across at least one professional videographer from the region—frequently several—in the throes of recording the festivities, recordings they sold there and then in rapidly edited versions burned onto DVDs.[1] Meanwhile, even more DVDs (or a master copy of the film) would be dispatched to migrant communities in the north. My inquiries revealed that fiesta DVDs usually had a circulation of several hundred copies and were mostly sold in the United States. Apart from community fiestas, other events made video documentation almost indispensable: during my first visit to Yalálag in August 2015, I was unexpectedly invited to a wedding and witnessed two local videographers filming over several days. They were hired by the couple's families to record every detail of the occasion in the bride and groom's households, respectively. As a result of the high demand in Yalálag and Tamazula-pam, four or five videographers from each of these villages specialized in the work. DVD discs from this self-determined production were regularly on sale at the village weekly markets throughout the region; in many instances they were presented on widescreen television sets to attract customers.[2]

Some DVDs became bestsellers because they had captured an outstanding performance by a brass band or a dance group or a superlative sports competition. In Los Angeles, the other side of the transnational communities, I also came across these Mexican DVDs and similar films portraying kermesses hosted by the migrant communities there. The production, circulation, and consumption of this genre provides unique insights into the sheer dimensions of migration to the United States and transnationalism, and at the same time into communitarian lifestyles, their impetus on modes of reciprocity, cultural expressions, and organizational forms. Audiovisual documentation mediatizes and transnationalizes them in the process.

These highlights show that movies depicting communal or private fiestas, sports tournaments, construction projects, or even political disputes are meanwhile an institution in the Sierra Norte and its transnational derivatives. This chapter analyzes how these and other media forms such as hybrid internet radio stations and multimedia platforms have emerged from local initiatives and their cross-border arrangements. The introduction outlined the various migration paths and strategies adopted by the Sierra Norte villages. Media practices have always been a key element of these processes. In radio programs, films, video clips, and social media postings, mediamakers reflect on the idiosyncrasies, specific needs, and transborder life in general of the respective communities. Divergent village and migration stories have found their expression in village governance and patron saint fiestas. Mediamakers record local affairs with varying aesthetic languages and culture-specific preferences. On the issue of whether to involve community members in the United States in the *usos y costumbres* governance of the home village, each municipality in the Sierra Norte has therefore sought its own solution (see also Kearney and Besserer 2004; Robson et al. 2017). The media formats and motifs of Tamazulapam and Yalálag vary according to their differential inclusion of migrants in the United States as active citizens by their village of origin. Community members living outside of Tamazulapam must assume a religious or political office locally on a rotating basis or compensate for this duty by contributing financially to a festivity—which is why sponsorship of home village fiestas is a major issue in audiovisual recordings and live broadcasts. Tamazulapam also places great emphasis on hosting a basketball tournament, which draws teams from the Ayuujk villages throughout the region (see chapter 5), as part of its patron saint celebrations. Yalálag, in contrast, does not involve migrants in governance of the hometown. Most migrant community members, however, have set up parallel organizations in the United States that participate in their common culture and politics from there. Yalaltecs are particularly proud of their Zapotec dances, and the hometown prides itself as being "the cradle of dance." Recordings and livestreams of these dances, which are passionately cultivated in Los Angeles, are used specifically to transnationalize this dance knowledge and socialize the second generation with it (see the next chapter). When mediamakers portray the fiesta cultures of their communities on either side of the border, which are closely linked to their usos y costumbres governance, they are creating transnational versions of Comunalidad.

Newly emerging high technology was resourcefully adapted and combined with age-old knowledges and technologies. The latter include the dances of Tamazulapam and Yalálag that commemorate historical watersheds such as the Conquista, the Mexican Revolution, and mass migration to the north, which are passed on performatively.[3] Against this backdrop, the comprehensive recording of long dance performances in Yalaltec fiesta VHS and DVD formats and the video clips currently posted on Facebook and YouTube can be understood as continuing while at the same time shifting the meaning of and updating older performative

Videographer Leonardo Ávalos Bis recording a brass band at a marriage for the bride's family, Yalálag, August 2015.

media formats. Mediamakers produced VHS cassettes, DVD discs, and online video clips to serve several purposes. Their clients often consumed them as entertainment but would also use them as didactic tools in, for example, teaching dance. Thus, an understanding of the history that is deeply rooted in Ayuujk and Zapotec culture would be passed on to second-generation children growing up in the United States. Dance, digital videos, and social media exemplify the multimodal strategies that span the transnational media space.

A broad spectrum of media actors shape these cross-border solutions by virtue of their media practices and products. Small video enterprises in Mexico circulate and market the DVDs in close cooperation with their clients, including migrants living in the United States; they are constantly in touch with fiesta donors, distribution networks, and videographers, all of whom belong to migrant communities there. Consequently, this web of media actors creates a transnational infrastructure through which hometown villagers and migrants concentrated in certain neighborhoods of Los Angeles communicate regularly. Furthermore, despite adverse political conditions such as the systemic disadvantage of Indigenous people in the context of both countries, these people engaged in knowledge transfer and cultural translation; they formed economic and political alliances at the local and transnational levels. All this activity opened up a media space that by far exceeded the interpersonal level of communication. An audience, for instance, that consumes a newly released DVD around the same time (in the style of a television or Netflix program) and exchanges views on it constitutes a community of viewers. Multiple scattered audience groups and current social media users could imagine themselves as a viewer community (cf. Anderson 1991; Appadurai 1996) since they are the main consumers of self-determined genres and can empathize with the events being shown. This mediatized reality is commented on and exchanged and becomes an emotionally shared experience.

These insights motivated me to examine other village-specific trajectories and entanglements of migration, Indigenous political movement, and mediatization. The villagers of the Sierra Norte have forged their own media histories. During the latter half of the twentieth century, they began on their own initiative and for various reasons to use mass media such as photography, video, radio, and television. The many ways in which they integrated self-determined media formats into community politics and religion, social life, reciprocity systems, and the economy can be traced from the perspective of the media operators themselves. The pioneering solutions with which they wrote universal media history are now examined.

## COMMUNAL LABOR AND PATRON SAINT FIESTAS ON VHS

The following section introduces the perspectives of creatives such as photographer Juana Vásquez and videographers Pancho Limeta in Yalálag, Genaro and Hermenegildo Rojas in Tamazulapam, and Arturo Vásquez and Salvador in Los Angeles.[4] Their ideas and actions have served to decolonize media history, since they contributed to shape Indigenous media in independent, locally based and transnationally extended ways. Ironically, this media history would later be accredited to a homogenized field called "Video Indígena" whose momentum, some have suggested, emerged from a Mexican state program for the promotion of Indigenous media.[5] Nevertheless, the story goes the other way around: "Video Indígena" was able to capitalize on these preexisting initiatives in Indigenous villages which continue to evolve according to their largely autonomous dynamics.

Meanwhile, I cannot overlook the fact that as a non-Indigenous academic my writing on the media scenes described here also prompts feelings of uneasiness. My research subjects repeatedly addressed this issue with me during our conversations. In an ongoing dialogue, I regularly reflect on my engagement in a critical light, precisely as an antidote to the imbalance that has privileged me as a non-Indigenous person in educational opportunities and has not only placed my interlocutors at disadvantage but also, to some extent, even deprived many of their mother tongue.[6] My interest in Indigenous media arises from its potential for empowerment and dates back to the beginning of the 1990s. That the protagonists of this book allowed me to gain insights into their lives and their work and generously shared their profound knowledge with me had to do with my accompanying their daily lives, listening to, and learning from them, gradually adopting a collaborative research methodology, and taking part in citizenship practices, including the communal mediamaking of the communities portrayed in this book. In search of what unites us, we identified our endeavor to give voice and visibility to cultural diversity as a means of overcoming inequality based on discrimination and erasure. While media actors prefer to articulate their positions directly via their own outlets, which use Facebook, YouTube, Twitter, and other social media, many appreciate the academic format of a book like this one. I gained their approval to write about them by sharing my texts showing my ability to express myself in this format.

Mediamaker perspectives make clear the crucial agency of these people, who simultaneously absorbed ideas from various external currents in the course of internal migration in search of education or work: hometown villagers became familiar with photography and video as practices of left-wing media activism in Mexican cities and universities in the 1980s, on the one hand, and adopted these media for documentation and family-based memory work during international migration to the United States, on the other.

First of all, I will briefly summarize how the production of patron saint fiesta movies in Tamazulapam got under way in the early 1990s (see Kummels 2017a, 197–213, for more details). A collective of young men from this village launched their own local television channel, TV Tamix, to promote the Ayuujk language and culture. The patron saint fiesta was one of their first motifs. They broadcast from the celebrations for the Holy Spirit and produced one of their first edited analog videos in 1994, a twenty-two-minute documentary titled *Fiesta Animada* (Animated Fiesta). The backdrop to this venture was their close collaboration at the time with the Centro de Video Indígena of the National Indigenist Institute (INI). *Fiesta Animada* was edited strictly according to film festival standards, which stipulated a maximum length of twenty-two minutes for short films. When they screened *Fiesta Animada* in Tamazulapam itself, the local audience was not impressed by its breathless rhythm of editing. Viewers felt that everything of interest to them at the five-day-long fiesta was merely portrayed in short fragments and therefore piecemeal. Hence this documentary was not a fiesta film in today's sense of its characteristic epic length simulating real time. Genaro and Hermenegildo Rojas explained this to me in an interview I recorded in 2013. Their perspectives take center stage in one of my documentaries portraying their work, *The Very First Fiesta Video* (2021).

In contrast, self-determined videography in Yalálag—which I will discuss in more detail here—saw the light of day in the context of internal disputes between two political factions, the Comunitarios and the PRIistas. The former was keen to help Comunalidad achieve a breakthrough and the latter intent on preventing it. This at least is Francisco "Pancho" Limeta's version. He is one of the oldest regional videographers (in Sierra Zapotec, *benhe bxhin xhena*) and has been documenting patron saint fiestas, weddings, and funeral ceremonies since 1987 with his enterprise Pancho Video, and meanwhile publishes and archives historical and current videos on social media.[7] He promotes his video business using the logo of a Negrito mask, the mask being an age-old communicative device to enact a persona, human, animal, or spirit. He learned the media trade in a period that saw radical political change and paradigm shifts locally—and helped to make this Indigenous media world happen.

Pancho gave me an account of the background: up until the 1970s, *caciques* dominated his village, which had once been a key marketplace in the region for coffee. These strongmen unilaterally pushed through the interests of a prosperous local elite that saw itself as "progressive" and "modern," and distanced itself from the majority of local peasants and their Zapotec culture. By the late 1960s, opposition to the PRI cacique had begun to grow in the community. The socialist and Marxist-oriented Grupo Comunitario succeeded in removing the local PRIistas from power in the village governance in a democratic election in the early 1980s. It then proceeded to revive communal forms of organization and implemented social programs to promote Zapotec culture, not least to boost their political base in the village. As a member of the Grupo Comunitario, Pancho Limeta helped to reorganize the village governance according to usos y costumbres (as the civil-religious system of yearly rotating officials was later called), which had not been practiced in Yalálag for decades. The General Assembly was reestablished as the highest political body, as was communal labor or support, *tequio* (in Sierra Zapotec, *llin lhao*), in which every man and women was required to participate.[8] Based on tequio, the Grupo Comunitario tackled the extensive renovation of the municipal building. Pancho codesigned the 1983 Communication Program of the Comunitarios, which included the targeted use of media to engage villagers in a positive reassessment of their traditions (such as tequio). Means of communication here included verbal debates at community meetings, megaphones (*altavoces*), leaflets (*volantes*), silk screening, photography, and videography using the Zapotec language (Estrada Ramos 2001, 37–38).

Pancho Limeta trained in audiovisual media in order to support the political project of the Grupo Comunitario. In the aftermath of the devastating earthquake of 1985, he left for Mexico City to learn photography with other interested people from the Sierra Norte. Ricardo Montejano, a radio journalist and left-wing activist living in the capital, instructed the group in socially critical photography. In Yalálag, anthropologist and linguist Juan José Rendón Monzón organized cultural dialogue workshops in cooperation with Grupo Comunitario. Based on the collaboration of villagers and Salesian liberation theologians, he later published a book titled *Comunalidad. Modo de vida en los pueblos indígenas* (Comunalidad. Indigenous Peoples' Way of Life).

Juana Vásquez, a Comunitaria from Yalálag and a founding member of their women's organization, the Union of Yalaltec Women, also learned how to take photographs in the 1980s. She was taught by her brother, who had migrated to Mexico City and studied photography there. Some of the vital tools they used were writing, analog photography, and VHS video in order to advance, as she

Pioneer videographer Pancho Limeta, filming at preparations for a marriage luncheon, July 2016.

explains, the "preservation" of Zapotec culture. And yet these actors did not pri-marily refer to Zapotec heritage as something past, but rather revived cultural tra-ditions selectively to realign them with the present and project them into the future (cf. Hill and Bithell 2014, 5). They actively opposed attitudes denying Zapo-tec people a place in present and future (cf. Fabian 1983; Speed 2017, 788). As an antidote to a homogenizing modernity, the spoken Zapotec language as a local medium was promoted and disseminated with contemporary media forms acquired by the village vanguard at the time, as Juana points out:

The Communitarian Group we formed ran the project to preserve our culture, lan-guage, agriculture, and costumes. The project included regaining the language, the dances, everything. At the same time, we were confronted with modernity, because people used to say to us: "All this is part of a past long gone, everything to do with the language, the attire, all of that. A council of elders has no meaning," they alleged, "that's history, it shouldn't exist anymore." They were always talking about modernity, about new inventions. And that's why we began to promote something different: how to write in our own language. And then fortunately a professor from UNAM arrived, a linguist, Juan José Rendón . . . with him we began to write in Zapotec. In those days we used posters to explain tequio, gave reasons why we should provide tequio. Posters informed the village about agriculture too, everything was written in Zapotec. This was a form of creating awareness among people that they could indeed write in Zapotec. And we produced booklets about health, agriculture, and the language. . . . All of that was recorded on video as well. Pancho was in charge of filming and I would capture things in photographs.[9]

At the same time, the Comunitarios in Yalálag collaborated closely with villagers who had migrated in large numbers to Los Angeles. Their communal organization in the Californian megacity played a major role in reinforcing the position of the left-wing faction in Yalálag. Supporters in Los Angeles founded La Comunidad Yalalteca de Los Ángeles, something I learned from Israel Monterrubio, one of its founding members; he had migrated to the United States as early as the 1970s.[10] In exchange with the Comunitarios in the hometown, he helped with the groundwork to establish a mode of reciprocity that attempted to level out the economic imbalance between the north and the south: more affluent migrants in Los Angeles raised funds for construction projects in the home village and in return the hometown villagers performed communal labor as their contribution to the arrangement. Based on this division of labor, ambitious construction work was carried out in Yalálag: the elaborate renovation of the municipal building and the expansion of the church of San Antonio compound. The saint became extremely popular with migration and was the focus of devotion by the transnational community (see below).

It was against this background, Pancho explained, that the tequio videos (*xhen ke llin lao*) were invented as a first transnational genre. In 1987, La Comunidad Yalalteca de Los Ángeles donated the first video camera to the hometown; it was one of those *agigantadas* (giant size ones) with large batteries. It was specifically destined to document communal labor in Yalálag. The images were supposed to prove to migrants in Los Angeles that the money they raised had indeed been invested in the intended construction project—and to encourage them to make further donations. According to Pancho,

> Our countrymen in Los Angeles . . . used to send information to us in Mexico and the municipal building was renovated with their help. . . . The work was carried out, for example, after a General Assembly had agreed on the number of working days required. And everyone complied either by doing the work or paying a certain amount to compensate for tequio. . . . In the past everything was done with manual labor because we had no machinery. People would shovel gravel and sand, and make adobe or bricks by hand. That began to change in the 1980s and in the 1990s we got machinery. When I photographed or videotaped communal work, I mostly had to capture who was present and gave their service. Yes, that was the most important thing. I had to record it because they [in Los Angeles] especially wanted to see who had participated. Women also had to provide tequio. Tequio usually meant four working days and women did two days, half of what the men did.[11]

Seeing who took part in the work—the video captured the public performative aspect of communal labor and allowed migrant community members to experience this visually and audibly from afar. Progress in construction, such as at the municipal building, was also recorded: all of this meant dreams coming true—at least for one political faction.

On the other side of the border, the *paisanos/as* in Los Angeles likewise documented their community service, borrowed from the village of origin but realigned to the urban setting; they organized saint fiestas and dance events in the private homes and backyards of community members, events at which they raised funds for the home village. Videotapes confirmed who in Los Angeles had been active for the hometown and given a donation. Everyone present was portrayed in their respective activities with long shots and slow pans.

These tequio videos became part of the citizenship practices of cross-border reciprocity and crucial to paving the way for Comunalidad across the uneven transnational terrain. The use of video as a new audiovisual technology expanded existing *Guelaguetza* or *gozona* booklets (*libretas de Guelaguetza* or gozona) and remediatized them (De la Fuente [1949] 1977, 147; Cook 2014, 100–101). Gozona or *gzwun* (in Sierra Zapotec) refers to a system of mutual aid between households that involves reciprocal gifts or labor contributions. The receiving household jotted down in a notebook the names of those who contributed goods, money, or labor. This frequently long list of names and contributions on different occasions is to this day still written down and read out loud in Yalálag. It is customary at community fiestas to announce the names and the donation amounts collected by each member over a loudspeaker system in the village for all to hear. Videotaping and sending or delivering videocassettes to the other country was understood as gozona; similar to the handwritten notebook entries, audiovisual records of contributions made and to be returned were kept on large VHS cassettes. While gozona was extended in transnational scope via new video practices, video as a modernized accounting system was integrated into communal activities of cross-border range.

The production, circulation, and reception of video images essentially enabled tequio and gozona to be practiced and experienced together in the new division of tasks framework between hometown and satellite community. Hence communal forms of organization were not "revived" in the old sense but de facto reinvented in their first ever transborder outreach. In Yalálag, Comunalidad—a term first in circulation in the early 1980s—was closely linked from the outset to international migration and this transnational allocation of duties. Juana Vásquez, who notably photographed women's communal work at the time, described the function of photographs and videos to me as "testimonies" and as "compelling proof" in the cross-border context:

Records on video were originally introduced because people living in the United States supported communitarian work. In those days we renovated the municipal building ourselves, since the federal government didn't give us any funds. Much of the work was provided by tequio and with the help of those living in the States it progressed. Those of us living here did tequio when people over there, for example, financed a handrail. We would get a receipt for expenses and send them a copy. Videotaping became popular as a way of showing how the money had been used. When the boundary wall enclosing it was being erected, they [images of the wall] were sent. That's how we used to work. The construction work that migrants set in motion was significant, since there were no other financial resources to do it at the time.... During the seven years of renovation, only half the village [participated in the work]. The other half didn't do anything due to a serious political problem we had [internal factionalism]. But together with those living in the United States those of us here in Mexico, in Oaxaca, managed to complete the improvements. The testimony of tequio captured on videos and photographs was extremely important since highly compelling proof of what was being done here was then sent to them.[12]

Video production was diversified in the course of the pioneer years. It was also employed in the documentation of conflicts within the village. One of Pancho Limeta's first recordings was of a four-hour court session held in the municipal building in 1987 (Estrada Ramos 2001, 67). At this court session, village officials affiliated with the Grupo Comunitario attempted to reverse the split of the municipal brass band. Bandas are political power factors and key elements of the communal fabric in the Sierra Norte.[13] In 1986, a group of approximately twenty musicians formed the independent Banda Autóctona. In his role as community videographer, Pancho was to record the outcome of the dispute for the ruling Comunitarios, a document that at the time was to be kept in the municipal archives along with the written protocols. These conflict videos, not unlike tequio videos, were consumed by the viewership according to their own criteria. As part of a new way of cultivating transnational sociability, they satisfied the need for more news about the home village, entertainment, political debate, and/or sensationalism. Migrant viewers in Los Angeles were interested in the people shown, their appearance, their moods, their social interaction, and many other details, so as to discuss them—in the words of my interlocutors—in the context of gossip. The viewing of conflict videos frequently stirred up a range of feelings, including concern, compassion, and anger (Gutiérrez Nájera 2007, 161–166).[14] Supporters of both political factions used them as a source of information on political disputes in the hometown, to show solidarity from afar and to mobilize more supporters. The production, circulation, and reception of videos corresponded to affective media practices; that is, they were intended to specifically address viewers affectively in order to gain their political support. It meant arousing feelings such as nostalgia for the home village, but also triggering perturbing sentiments such as anger, all of which were conjured up by videos of local disputes and political struggles (Kummels 2016a, 2017b).

Pancho divides the development of village videography into three stages: the boom of tequio videos was followed by the upswing of social event videos and eventually by the commercialization of moviemaking, which in the past had been practiced free of charge as a service to the community. Around 1995, the portrayal of joint work and village assemblies gradually gave way to curiosity and enjoyment in the recording of community fiestas (in Sierra Zapotec, *lni*) with Zapotec dance performances and parodies. As Pancho recounted, "Tequio was set aside and what people now support most are religious issues, it's what they have faith in most."[15] This shift took place at a time when the satellite community from Yalálag began to establish itself in Los Angeles. In the Californian megacity, migrants likewise organized in line with their affiliation to one of the four *barrios* (neighborhoods) in the Mexican village of origin. This facilitated the hosting of patron saint fiestas for the respective saints that had taken roots on U.S. soil. At this point, hometown political conflicts were coming to a head and 1998 saw the Grupo Comunitario lose its dominant position. A coalition of renegades and PRIistas accused the left-wing faction of now even indulging in *caciquismo* (local despotism) and of using state funds to cement its own power in Yalálag. Violent clashes, which last broke out in 2001, claimed one villager's life (Cruz-Manjarrez 2013, 88–89). To this day, there is still much animosity between the supporters of each faction. Alarmed by the extent of the internal violence, however, both factions agreed to a truce in Yalálag in 2001. Since then, they have been careful to maintain a balance of power. The village kept to the communitarian system of electing new village officials on an annual basis at a General Assembly. At elections, supporters of each faction alternate for the highest office of municipal president.

As part of this pacification process, the Comunitarios began to actively support the religious fiestas at the end of the 1990s. Migration to the north saw a surge in devotion to San Antonio de Padua, although the official patron saint of Yalálag is San Juan Bautista.[16] San Antonio was seen as a miracle worker in the context of unauthorized border crossing (Cruz-Manjarrez 2013, 79). La Comunidad Yalalteca de Los Ángeles collected financial donations to enable the extension of the church of San Antonio and the surrounding facilities in Yalálag. The Comunitarios in office at the time were less in favor of fostering festivities as manifestations of Catholicism. Instead, they saw them in a new light as truly communitarian institutions and pillars of the grassroots way of life: after all, fiestas were based on mutual assistance and communal work and were a platform for Zapotec cultural expressions, particularly banda music and dance performances. Community members in Mexico and the United States thus agreed across factional lines that the San Antonio fiesta on June 13 would unite them in the spirit of Comunalidad.[17] This fiesta approval was also vital at the time in attenuating the division of villagers into Catholics and Evangelicals, given that the latter reject Catholic celebrations.

In the mid-1990s, Pancho Limeta, Víctor Monterrubio, Héctor Bis, Leonardo Ávalos Bis, and other videographers began to focus their self-determined media production on movies of patron saint fiestas for the four barrio saints and San Antonio, each of which lasted up to five days. They were recorded on VHS cassettes with large analog video cameras. Leonardo Ávalos Bis described their aesthetic style as *videos de comunidad* (in Zapotec: *xhen ke yell*), which he specifi-cally characterized as the endeavor to capture "what is real," using long sequences in real time and avoiding any kind of "distorting effect," such as time-lapse shots, fades, and numerous cuts.[18] The community videographers also recorded the con-struction work at the churches of these saints, to which further facilities were added step-by-step, including a basketball field, a kitchen, a dining hall, and a rehearsal room for dance groups. Construction work was financed by migrant donations from Los Angeles. It is no accident that the videographers are members of different barrios; in other words, every barrio relied on its own filmmaker. There is no simple explanation why until then mainly men had become videogra-phers;[19] Juana Vásquez took up photography, and there are a few other examples of women engaging for a short time as videographers. But women back then still had to conquer areas of village life denied to them, for example, membership as a banda musician.[20] Marriages were arranged by the parents in most cases and women in general had to submit to patriarchal norms restricting their movement in public life—escaping these local norms often motivated their migration (Aquino Moreschi 2012, 120–124).

In Los Angeles, a comparable media scene emerged around the same time: Arturo Vargas and René Fernández specialized there in VHS kermés movies.[21] An identical communal distribution model for these videos was set up in the 1990s in the context of both countries: videographers taped the films on behalf of the com-mittee that organized the fiesta and did their best to follow their desire for docu-mentation of the barrio dances in real time, with a long shot if possible. Each barrio claims authorship of certain dances, and learning them is considered both a privilege and a service to the community (see the next chapter). The videogra-phers edited VHS magnetic tape old-school style, fast-forwarding and rewinding to identify the beginning and end of the shots they required. They made copies from an edited master and handed over the agreed number of VHS cassettes and later DVD discs to the committee, which reimbursed them only for the material costs. The committee sold the videos primarily to the respective barrio members (in Los Angeles and Yalálag), collecting money to cover the cost of the cele-brations or to finance the next one. Arturo Vargas reports,

> I didn't charge [the barrio committee members], because I'm from Yalálag and work nonprofit, not for my own benefit. So back then I invested my time and my work in producing a video and recorded the entire kermés. All that had to do with the sacred dances, the food, ballroom dancing, everything involved in that event. Finally, I would edit the tape and include the names of people on the com-mittee, the date, the barrio they belonged to and then I handed over my produc-tion. It was an entire set . . . consisting of fifteen to twenty cassettes so that they were able to make money based on the time and work I had invested by selling those videos. I made a bit of profit, too, when they sent them to the barrio they belonged to, like Santa Catarina or Santiago. And I collaborated with them like that

for many years up to 2005. I used to help out at almost every event, because each barrio [four in total] would host three or four celebrations a year. . . . I also helped out with a sound system as the popular DJ they called upon to provide music and entertainment. They would contract a banda and I was the one in charge of the sound. That wasn't my contribution alone, my entire family was involved. . . . Me too, I supported San Antonio. There's a saying in Yalálag about this saint: "San Antonio belongs to the entire village." I supported San Antonio with my videography.[22]

Arturo explained the content of the 3 or 4 two-hour VHS cassettes documenting a kermés:

The most important thing for the committee in charge of the kermés is to record the people working when they're busy preparing food, right? And the people who sell things, some would mix cool fruit beverages or the *pozontle*, others would prepare *tlayudas*, *mermelas*, *quesadillas*, or any other snack sold at the event.[23] They want absolutely everyone working to be taped so that when a copy is sent to the home village the residents will see who contributed and who made the event come to life. In other cases, everyone who participated in construction work in Yalálag has to be recorded. It is important to them that we record the dances, because those who dance los Negritos, la Malinche, or any other sacred dance are also part of this performance, so they have to be documented as well, right? And besides, the whole environment and the excitement can be appraised on video, how many people attended, especially what the ballroom dancing felt like. It's a way for people to remember what that particular event was like.

But beyond that, VHS videos allowed for cross-border socializing, as Arturo points out:

In those days video was the only way people could see some family relative living here. That's because children sometimes stayed in Yalálag or the other way around. A wife living here in the United States could see her father and her children who stayed back there. . . . We're talking about the period before digital communication. When a tape from Yalálag arrived here, it was the only way for relatives to see their mother, their father or their kids who had remained in Mexico. Some had left their wives or husbands to take care of the children.

Hence, with the help of videos portraying a particular fiesta, residents in the hometown and in the satellite community in Los Angeles got a good impression of each other's community lives. Ideas and practices of Comunalidad, which had been adapted to the different situations in each country, were shared. In addition to the similarities between U.S. kermesses and hometown patron saint fiestas, the audience also noted differences. The Los Angeles fiestas were shorter and took place indoors in banquet halls, and they borrowed some cultural elements from migrant neighbors. In the Los Angeles videos, children and youth took center stage in music and dance performances, which at the time was still largely an adult domain in Yalálag. The dance performances of hometown fiesta videos also circulated in Los Angeles as didactic tools to learn music and dances from the village of origin, where they were considered to be performed authentically. Videos were used to debate the degree of "authenticity" of the different cultural versions performed either in the village of origin or the satellite community (see the next chapter).

At the beginning of the 1990s, fiesta videos were produced in a self-determined way in a number of Sierra Norte villages. Migration led to a high demand for videos by people in Oaxaca who wanted them as gifts for relatives and friends in the United States and by those who worked and lived in the north but longed for recordings of the fiesta as *the* central event in their hometown. Furthermore, community members adapted the new audiovisual media to their needs for transnational socializing. Juana Vásquez remembers how audio cassettes and "video letters" were adopted with great enthusiasm: they allowed for long-distance communication in the Zapotec language, without having to learn how to write it.[24]

As early as the 1990s, local videographers in the Sierra Norte fitted into the regional market system as typical itinerant merchants (*comerciantes ambulantes*). One of the pioneers in this trade was Ingeniero Fernando Sánchez, who traveled in his motor home from one patron saint fiesta to another, week in, week out, throughout the year to record videos and sell them locally. Zapotec entrepreneur Sánchez, who was based in Guelatao and had learned how to make movies in the United States, established this business model with his enterprise Video Líder (which he later renamed Video Rey; Kummels 2017a, 210–211). With videos titled *La fiesta de mi pueblo* (followed by the name of the village), he tapped into new local markets. He documented the festivities in such a way that key elements or mini-events of the patron saint fiesta were shown as chapters, among them the reception of the brass bands and dance groups, preparations for the main feast, catering of the fiesta guests, a church mass, and much more. Sánchez narrated his films on the spot as a reporter. This culture-specific genre was distributed at the patron saint celebrations themselves and sold at the markets that villages hold on a particular weekday. Kermés videos in Los Angeles were circulated in much the same way, notably in the niche of migrants' "Oaxacan fiesta economy" (see chapter 4).

At the same time, videography in Yalálag was linked to the explicitly political field of the regional Indigenous movement (Cremoux Wanderstok 1997, 125–130; Estrada Ramos 2001). In Mexico, Indigenous organizations such as the Servicios del Pueblo Mixe (SER), founded in 1988, set up their own media departments, ensuring that Indigenous protagonists, community meetings, and other hitherto unconventional images and voices were circulated in public. As of 1994, SER distributed its own news programs. Indigenous media were further established through the CLACPI (Latin American Coordination of Cinema and Communication of the

Indigenous Peoples) film festivals where cinematographers contributed to the sense of belonging to the autochthonous Americas they called Abya Yala (Salazar and Córdova 2020). Videographers like Pancho Limeta moved seamlessly between the two fields, filmmaking that was strictly political and, on the other hand, videos de comunidad, which were also merchandized via a market circuit and had entertainment value. The year 1995 saw Pancho gradually professionalizing his filmmaking craft in workshops run by Ojo de Agua Comunicación, which came into being when staff split from the National Indigenist Institute (INI) in 1998 as a result of differences over the political orientation of Video Indígena. It organized workshops in Oaxaca in the 1990s (including one in Tlacolula), where they actually taught film along the lines of existing ethnographic models.[25] The cinematic stylistic devices that were taught there, however, did not correspond to the taste of village viewers; that is, they rejected the protagonism of individual film actors and the dynamic pace of various camera angles and rapid cuts. Pancho pointed out that this was also true of Yalálag: "A course is supposed to teach you how to make documentaries, but here [in Yalálag] nobody wants documentaries. [A documentary] is short, only five or ten minutes long. And nobody here is interested in ten minutes. This is what they want: if it's [an event is] eight hours long, they want a video that lasts eight hours and if the event takes ten hours the video should also be ten hours long." Videographers like Pancho thus deliberately "unlearned" much of what they had been taught in workshops on documentary filmmaking. Most people in Yalálag and other Sierra Norte villages were keen on the wholeness of the event, wanted to discover details for themselves in long, unedited scenes, and preferred long shots of collectives that allowed them to follow social interactions. These preferences cannot be generalized, but they corresponded to the majority taste of the generation of that time. In addition, culturally specific genres such as the analog fiesta video continue to shape current digital versions. They are precursors of the present-day multimedia formats of patron saint fiestas and kermesses, which are now archived in chronological threads on multimedia platforms after streaming on Facebook Live.

## VILLAGE VIDEO GENRES: FROM GHOST TOWN TO SPONSOR TAPES

"We refuse to let our village die," said Antonio, a man in his mid-sixties, during our first conversation.[26] I had traveled the short distance from Yalálag to Santa María Xochixtepec for the three-day fiesta of the Virgen del Rosario at the end of September and beginning of October 2017. Thanks to the intervention of a friend in Los Angeles, I was able to get in touch with the *agente suplente* (deputy mayor) of Xochixtepec, Antonio Hilario. From his house on a hill, we looked down at the hustle and bustle of the fiesta, a sight that seemed to contradict this threat of abandonment. I arrived at the festivities just as a group of sixteen children and youths were in the midst of an impressive performance of La Danza de la Malinche in

Dance moms and Bene Xhon Video recording at the Virgen del Rosario Fiesta in Xochixtepec, Mexico, October 2017.

front of the church. Emanuel Pérez Morales, a local videographer in his late twenties, was recording it and followed the dance group meticulously with his camcorder and a drone over the next few days. Antonio pointed to an inflatable castle where children were enjoying themselves bouncing up and down and quietly remarked, "All these children speak English." Xochixtepec is currently home to a hundred people, only ten of whom are school-aged children, so the community no longer has its own public school. Many like Antonio are retired and have returned from the United States; he himself had lived in Los Angeles since 1968. When he retired last year, he made a pact with his children in Los Angeles that he would go back there only if he needed long-term care. Antonio preferred to spend the winter of his life in Xochixtepec; after all, "my land is here, my maize plot is here." As a village official, he is in charge of organizing the fiesta. Most of the original residents of Xochixtepec, two hundred fifty people, live in Los Angeles and pay a regular contribution, which was used to refurbish the church and the *agencia* administrative building and helped to finance the fiesta.

Xochixtepec is seen as one of the many "ghost villages" in the Sierra Norte. In Los Angeles, on the other hand, the Xochixtepec migrant community is famous—and consequently Xochixtepec itself—because it introduced the very first Sierra Norte style brass band there in 1977. With single-mindedness, it financed the unauthorized border crossing of an outstanding composer and conductor from Yalálag, Alberto Montellano. In return, Montellano created a high-profile migrant banda and was actively involved up until his death.[27] As a result of their great artistic skills, the two hundred fifty migrants living in Los Angeles have the biggest say in the cultural affairs of the hometown's patron saint celebrations since most of the dancers and musicians performing in Xochixtepec fly in from Los Angeles. In addition, the Mexican hometown receives substantial local support from neighboring villages. The Virgen del Rosario fiesta I visited was attended by Yalálag's Banda Autóctona, other brass bands from Santa María Tavehua and San Andrés Yaa, dance groups from Xochixtepec and Santa María Yohueche, and finally Bene Xhon Videos run by Emanuel and his wife from Yatzachi El Bajo. The woman who baked tortillas nonstop in Antonio's house for the fiesta visitors had also made the journey from San Melchor Betaza specially for the event; tortilla preparation at various saint fiestas is her new line of work. A whole regional network compensates for the absences caused by migration and displacement. "Ghost villages" is therefore a misnomer; they are very much alive, and video is part of making their present and bright future.

Videographers take on a key role, as Melissa Pablo-Hernández from Los Angeles clarified.[28] She began to visit her home village of Xochixtepec regularly with her husband when her two children were growing up. The family enjoys watching fiesta DVDs from Yalálag and the neighboring villages at weekends in Los Angeles, which is one reason her son became a Zapotec dance enthusiast. She has much praise for videographer Emanuel, who year after year faithfully records the fiesta, thereby relieving her of having to do so; apart from that, "He does it so well." Emanuel Pérez Morales began to take an interest in videography in 2007, inspired by a local initiative to revive Zapotec culture in Yatzachi El Bajo.[29] In reality, he prefers documentaries with fast cuts and a dense atmosphere, where close-ups, camera drives, and drone shots constantly alternate, while a presenter comments live on these scenes.[30] For the sake of the Los Angeles migrants, however, he focused on producing the lengthier fiesta movies. He is impressed by the cultural impact they have on his municipality Yatzachi El Bajo, the U.S.-born dance groups, for instance, that are so highly skilled in Zapotec dances. He gives his patron saint films a dynamic touch, a compositional film device he learned from tutorials on the internet. For the Virgen del Rosario fiesta, he produced eight DVDs of two hours each, which he sold locally and in addition sent as digital files to the United States on demand. A number of videographers in the Sierra Norte specialize in "ghost villages," including Edmundo Ambrosio in Lachiroag. After his return from a work stay in the United States in 2002, he began to record family celebrations, construction projects, and patron saint fiestas in San Cristóbal Lachiroag. The self-determined video industry made it easier for him to reestablish himself in the tiny village, greatly depopulated by migration. His movies have brought him wide recognition as a videographer, both in the Sierra Norte and in Los Angeles.[31]

The case of Xochixtepec and Lachiroag, which are considered "ghost villages," illustrates the vibrancy of Comunalidad and how it is organized transnationally based on a cross-border division of labor—likewise the merit of community videography as an indispensable component. In the words of Antonio Hilario, "All of us provide service here, those living in Los Angeles as well. We are not governed by the laws of the city."

Let us now take a look at another video variant invented in the transborder context, self-determined documentation catering to the needs of migrants working as farmhands, which I would dub "the peasant-style video." Many residents of Tamazulapam's rural agencias began to migrate to the U.S. West Coast before those from the hometown's urbanized center. People from the agencia of Maguey preferred to work in the labor-intensive crop agriculture of the states of California, Oregon, and Washington. Although they earn less than they would by working in the construction and restaurant sectors of Los Angeles, those involved see an advantage in having to spend less on food and housing. This shows the diversity of transnational migration flows, even from one municipality such as Tamazulapam to the United States, and how these follow different routes and labor markets as destinations. Accordingly, the demand for particular styles of self-determined videos is organized differentially in the transnational setting. I became aware of the videography of "the peasant-style video" when I attended the change-of-office ceremonies in Maguey on January 2, 2019. A young videographer couple, Erik and Fernanda, were at work there and told me their job was to send their unedited footage to an Ayuujk video entrepreneur in Woodland, California (near Sacramento).[32] The editor in Woodland specializes in recordings that primarily spotlight events either in Maguey or in its satellite community in Woodland. He has close connections with the Los Angeles migrant community and visits some of its fiestas and basketball tournaments. Because I was featured in this change-of-office video, a number of Woodland residents on a visit to Los Angeles recognized me and to my surprise treated me like an old acquaintance, although we had never met in person.

Finally, I would like to talk about the *mayordomo* videos, a further variant of saint fiesta videos I discovered in March 2018 in San Pablo Güilá in Valles Centrales, south of the Sierra Norte. I was motivated to visit this village for the first time when Jesús Ramón García, a videographer from San Pedro Cajonos, told me he would be filming there at the Fourth Lenten Friday because people from numerous Sierra Norte villages worship the Christ of Güilá. On March 9, 2018, I was amazed to see that the fiesta attracted such a vast number of pilgrims, Sierra Zapotecs, Ayuujk ja'ay, and Chinantecs, all recognizable by the distinctive women's attire of their villages. A happy coincidence saw me invited to the semiprivate feast of the mayordomo couple. As was typical for many villages in Valles Centrales, patron saint fiestas in Güilá were primarily organized not by the municipal authorities (as in Tamazulapam) or a fiesta committee (as in Yalálag and its satellite communities), but by the mayordomo. During colonial times, prosperous landowners or big farmers were responsible for the organization and cost of the patron saint fiesta as a service to the Catholic Church (Cordero Avendaño de Durand 2009, 65–79).

Currently in Güilá, the General Assembly appoints a mayordomo couple, who decide whether to take on this service and cover the high expenses involved. Sponsorship expenses are often shared by family members, especially those who

DVD cover of a *mayordomo* video, a genre typical of San Pablo Güilá, Oaxacan Valles
Centrales. Courtesy: Antonio Cruz, Video Richi.

earn a good salary in the United States. Around 2008, the local outlet, Video Richi,
began to specialize in the production of mayordomo videos in Güilá.[33] Its entrepreneur, Antonio Cruz, gave me a fair idea of the ins and outs of this genre. For the
mayordomo couple of San Pablo's patron saint fiesta in January of that year, he
produced a series of seventeen DVDs, totaling thirty-four hours of footage. Cruz
was contracted by the couple for three days at 2,500 pesos per day. His task was to
meticulously record the community *topiles* (police officers) helping to decorate
the fiesta venue, and men and women preparing the tortillas, the corn *atole*, and the
cocoa drink—all of them sacred dishes. Other feast highlights with the mayordomo couple as the protagonists were also filmed, such as the presentation of *velas
de concha*, meter-long wax candles with elaborate decoration, the celebration of
mass, and a *jaripeo* (Mexican bull riding) competition specifically held in honor
of the saint. Documentation is preferably entrusted to the local videographer, as
he is familiar with the important details and ritual acts. His clients, the mayordomo couple, could rest assured that all of the ideas and effort that went into making the fiesta a success and the help received in solidarity would be obvious in the
video. Thus, mayordomo videos in the case of Güilá reinforce the protagonism of
the sponsor couple and their personal networks. On the other hand, Jesús Ramón,
who traveled from San Pedro Cajonos, produced DVDs overnight of the more
public aspects of religious devotion and fiesta attractions and sold them as souvenirs to the numerous pilgrims on-site.

## COMMUNITY LIFE ON DVDS

Pancho Limeta describes the third stage, which saw a boom in the commercial production of an extended assortment of fiesta videos: "They suddenly wanted recordings of social events, quinceañeras and funerals. Our *paisanos* introduced the quinceañeras from the United States and birthday parties, too. This third phase we're in now began around the year 2000." At the turn of the century to the new millennium, family celebrations were held for a fifteen-year-old daughter, a quinceañera, and in Los Angeles elaborate parallel wakes (*velorios*) for relatives who had died in Yalálag. By this time, a second generation had grown up in Los Angeles and the satellite community was thriving. Nevertheless, the economic situation of migrants should not be generalized; there were significant differences in the educational and work opportunities available to those with documents as distinct from those without. One indicator of the increased prosperity of the migrant community of Yalálag in Los Angeles was the growth of their self-determined media industry. Audiovisual documentation of events on both sides of the Mexican-U.S. border was now part of the enormous effort that went into hosting family celebrations. People who lived at great distances from each other strengthened their communal living (*convivencia*) in this way, as Juana Vásquez explains:

> Videographers are commissioned to film all the festivities, like weddings, christenings and quinceañeras, which we meanwhile celebrate here in Yalálag, too. Even when someone wants testimony of a burial, they will ask Pancho to film it. And later on, this is sent to the United States so that those who are unable to travel here can see it, the burial of his or her parent, of a father, mother, brother, or sister.... A very interesting solidarity situation with the family has arisen. If someone passes away here [in Yalálag] and the children can't return, they organize a rosary for the mother, grandmother, father, or brother over there [in Los Angeles] and people go there and support them with a financial contribution. They raise money to send the recording to the family living here. As I'm told, people who go to a wake contribute gozona, a form of mutual assistance. If they don't attend, then there will be no return contribution if somebody in *their* family dies. So, a lot of thought is given to communal living (*convivencia*) when somebody is in need.... It's also fascinating how it's organized there.[34]

One dimension of this media boom involves the shift from analog to digital videography: Around 2000 digital camcorders with AVCHD technology, PCs, and film editing software were on the market for the first time at affordable prices.[35] Established video genres based on analog signal recording were gradually replaced by the electronic representation of digital camcorders and recordings distributed on DVD discs. These could be duplicated and circulated in large quantities much more quickly. They sold like hot cakes at local patron saint fiestas, were sent to the United States via a self-managed parcel service (*paquetería*), and found a niche among the broad selection offered by the flourishing market in pirated videos, which primarily traded in Hollywood films and blockbusters from the Mexican film industry; pirated versions of films dealing with social movements and the Indigenous movement were also sold.[36] Several videographers began their careers as distributors of such pirated DVDs and then developed videography skills.

Community videographers, particularly in Los Angeles, altered their business model around this time and no longer filmed on a volunteer basis free of charge. They began to film private parties commissioned by families who either could afford their services or paid for them through donations from *padrinos y madrinas de video*. For the first time, videographers in Los Angeles captured individual successful migrants and their offspring, the opulence of their celebrations, and their consumer goods (see chapter 6). They charged the going rates for social event productions in Oaxaca City or Los Angeles but at the same time were part of the Oaxacan fiesta economy in Los Angeles, whose participants sought to support their compatriots by combining market orientation with the logics of reciprocity. Apart from maximizing their profits, these mediamakers were concerned with maintaining a communal alignment and occasionally filmed kermesses free of charge.

Salvador, a videographer in his early fifties from Yalálag, is an example of this paradigm shift from communal filmmaking toward marketing profit-oriented quinceañera films, which are currently his main source of income. After several migrant stages in Mexico and the United States, he finally settled in Los Angeles in 2000 and began to produce kermés films on DVD for the barrio committee of Santa Catarina (see also chapter 6). One afternoon, Salvador told me that only a few years ago he was still filming for barrio committees almost free of charge "in order to support the community."[37] In 2011, however, an incident occurred at a kermés in honor of Santa Rosa de Lima. The so-called *burla* or parody is for many the kermés highlight: community members dress up and imitate their compatriots who were talk of the town the previous year. Topics range from lapses by community officials and "blunders" in the choice of partners to personal preferences that deviate from majority "standards." Everyone eagerly awaits the parody, even the videographer, for whom filming the *burla* is a must. While he was filming it, Salvador suddenly realized that he and his then-fifteen-year-old daughter were the target of the parody. His teenage daughter was his film assistant and a Rockabilly fan who wore flared skirts and petticoats, and a flower in her hair. The parody publicly ridiculed her taste in fashion. Salvador was deeply hurt because young people are usually exempt from public mockery. According to Salvador, "I got angry and after that I started charging them . . . they poked fun at me in the parody and I didn't like it because it's not supposed to target children." In other words, he attributes his adoption of the business pattern and price policy of market-oriented videographers in Los Angeles to his disappointment with the community.

A sharp dividing line is drawn between communal and private-sector initiatives in Mexico and the United States, particularly by explicitly political, activist media outlets. Their quest for autonomy and the sovereignty of self-determined communication modes challenges neoliberal media policies: neither the state nor private mass media companies should be allowed to dictate media content. On the other hand, photography, filmmaking, and livestreaming that meet the specific needs and communal lifestyles and are produced for profit have also emerged in the villages of the Sierra Norte and their satellite communities. Mediamakers in the Sierra Norte since long travel from one village fiesta to another and are part of an itinerant trade traditionally organized in weekday markets and fairs requiring legal authorization to celebrate a patron saint fiesta (Acevedo Conde 2012, 34–37). Up to a point, this market dynamic has been exported to Los Angeles, where a fiesta niche economy developed around kermesses and other fundraising events held throughout this sprawling city. The controversy surrounding communal versus private-sector initiatives also has a local dimension: the bone of contention in the home village concerns the threat of commodification of village culture. While it is considered appropriate for officials to showcase village culture as a "brand" at fiestas, marketing it on tape or in cyberspace—even if carried out by villagers or on their behalf as consumers—is controversial. The officials in each barrio, agencia, or municipality claim what could be called community copyright on their cultural forms and public presentation at fiestas. They usually allow only their own community videographers to record them on video and subsequently sell them. Outside videographers, on the other hand, are charged a fee—sometimes substantial—for permission to film. This process shows the tensions and efforts to reconcile commercial media activity with communal guidelines: usos y costumbres governance has the final say when it comes to the media work of private entrepreneurs, since the latter are pushed to comply with their obligations as community members (*ciudadanos/as*).

In daily practice the fields of communal and commercial filmmaking constantly overlap and are often pragmatically balanced. Media operators like Pancho were often active for a time as *comunicadores* in the communal media scene and at other times as *videógrafos* on the private commercial sector. The uncompromising dividing line is more likely to be drawn by radio producers and filmmakers more formally aligned with the political Indigenous movement. They network in NGOs and umbrella organizations such as the Mexican state-run National Institute of Indigenous Peoples (INPI) and their communal radio stations, the Latin American Summits of Indigenous Communication of Abya Yala, the Coordination of Cinema and Communication of the Indigenous Peoples (CLACPI), and the World Association of Communitarian Radios (AMARC). These organizations strengthen media collectives by actively supporting only what they define as strictly communitarian outlets, which they assist by developing community-run infrastructure, including cell phone networks and intranet facilities (to which only local people have access), and training in the know-how to operate them. At the same time, international migration to the United States has brought media actors into close contact with its less regulated, liberal media market, one that has fueled private-sector Indigenous media in the Sierra Norte villages since the late 1980s.

## INDIGENEITY IN REAL TIME: MULTIMEDIA PLATFORMS, INTERNET RADIO, AND ETHNIC INFLUENCERS

As a rule, the processes of community building triggered by online platforms and social media differ greatly—depending on their initial motivations, current mission, and the way they mobilize their audiences. In the case of Yalálag and Tamazulapam, it was the regular flow of people, goods, money, and ideas across the international border that led to transnational socialities. In other words, those who were communicating knew each other from local settings and had formed a community before those contexts were expanded through digital forms of sociality (cf. Hepp 2015, 209).[38] Distinct causes and media actors were involved in the online communalization of Yalálag and Tamazulapam. In the case of Yalálag, its satellite community in Los Angeles began networking to raise funds and organize assistance when natural disaster struck the home village in 2010 (Gutiérrez Nájera 2012, 9). As for Tamazulapam, a politically ambitious member acting from the hometown created a Facebook page in 2013 that presented itself as the village General Assembly; it became a sort of "virtual General Assembly" operating parallel to local governance and was popular with migrants (Kummels 2015). Hence Zapotec and Ayuujk people from the villages of Yalálag and Tamazulapam created a transnational online community at different times and for different reasons. Both processes relied on Facebook or *el feis*, since it had become the most commonly used platform for interpersonal long-distance communication. In both cases, a community-based cluster comprising a large number of users who first communicated privately now generated a transnational "networked public" (cf. boyd 2010).

From 2016 to 2021, self-determined mediamakers creatively used social media and livestreams, for instance Facebook Live and FaceTime, to attract larger viewer communities. Against the backdrop of a gradual increase in the number of hometown residents communicating via Facebook privately, internet radio stations such as Radio Cantautor were launched in 2015, multimedia platforms such as Tamix Multimedios in 2018, and streaming providers such as AR TV in 2019. Common to all of these digital media outlets is their use of Facebook pages to communicate interactively with users and accumulate the social capital accruing from a vast networked community, which is mirrored in announcements such as one by AR TV: "Like and share. It helps us to generate more content."[39] The Facebook Live streaming function, which has been available since August 2015, is the preferred mode because it conveys the sensation of physical distance being removed. Streamed events trigger a sense of copresence, of "being there," notwithstanding the user's constant awareness of distance, as the quote from the Tamix Multimedios user suggests (see the introduction). Yet for the many people who now consider their cell phone "an object so intimate that it feels like an extension of one's body" (Miller et al. 2021, 7), it is precisely the typical forms of digital long-distance communication that allow them to experience this strong sense of close-ness (cf. Mollerup 2017). Short messages, even emojis alone, can be highly effective in eliciting empathy, agreement, and belonging—or antipathy, dissent, and dis-tancing (see, for example, Winocur 2019). The age-old analog art of puns and word play (cf. Kummels 2007b, 350–353) has been remediatized this way. Occasionally the lack of comments by livestream followers is also experienced as copresence, for example, at a basketball final where everyone seems to hold their collective breath when they are not posting emojis.

That said, for the self-determined media that wanted to span a bridge across country borders, the actual digital divide of the transnational terrain posed a huge challenge since it limited their ability to livestream and reach all potentially inter-ested parties. To understand the magnitude of the problem, we need to first look at digital infrastructure in the Oaxacan Sierra Norte. Mexico's Indigenous regions in general still had the highest poverty indicators in the country, and settlements of fewer than five thousand inhabitants the least amount of digital infrastructure (Cave, Guerrero, and Mariscal 2018; Gómez Navarro and Martínez Domínguez 2020). Since the sparsely populated Sierra Norte was not a lucrative option for cell phone and internet service providers, they were slow to develop the necessary infrastructure, if at all. It is no secret that the expansion of national and multinational telecommunication corporations, such as large platforms and search engines like Facebook and Google, is subjected to their economic interest in harvesting and sell-ing user data. They extend their business activities around smartphones and inter-net connections first and foremost where profit is greatest. In addition, these companies have little or no interest in the key issue of the content that media users wish to communicate and access (Bravo Muñoz 2020). In Tamazulapam and Yalálag, the villages that take center stage here, that content broadly concerns the citizenship practices of sharing a communal way of life across the border grounded on culturally specific knowledges expressed in Indigenous languages, dance, music, sports, rituals, and fiestas.

On the U.S. side, in contrast, most migrants from these villages live in urban areas such as those of Los Angeles, and in the agro-industrial zones of the West Coast. Almost all of my interlocutors in Los Angeles were extremely well con-nected and had internet access via cell phone or a tablet. In addition, office work-ers and high school students often had a PC at home. This is consistent with analyses of the overall situation of Latinas/os in the United States, for whom a narrowing of the digital gap was noted in 2016 in relation to Whites and people with professional training, the latter having previously been way ahead in terms of digital equipment and know-how (Brown, López, and Lopez 2016). My interlocu-tors had acquired digital competence in professions where at one time we would not have suspected to find them: digital media skills are now part of the activities of housekeepers and fast-food restaurant employees.

There are therefore vast differences between the United States and Mexico and between urban and rural areas within transnational communities when it comes to accessing digital communication. It is precisely this big picture and the daily experience of its cracks and fissures that spurred media actors on both sides of the border to bridge the gap in the interest of family, communal, and/or entrepreneurial communication. In many instances it was the local radio producers, videographers, and IT experts who, also motivated by their business interests, laid the foundation for the digitalization of their underserved communities. In Yalálag and Tamazulapam, they set up antennas on their own initiative, arranged cooperation with external private internet providers, and established cyber rooms in tandem with video services. In Tamazulapam it was a local businessman who opened the first cyber room, after returning to his home village following completion of his computer technology studies. This first cyber room was a hugely popular meeting point for village youth. In collaboration with Yin Et Radio from Tlahuitoltepec, he also broadcast the Copa Ayuujk basketball tournament for the first time at the Santa Rosa patron saint fiesta in 2013 (Kummels 2017a, 76). Tamazulapam was first equipped with a 4G antenna by the Telcel Group in 2020. In the case of Yalálag, the General Assembly held an in-depth debate on the pros and cons of cell phone network coverage by multi Telcel and has currently voted against it.[40]

These early projects forged local media history and created pioneering infrastructure, media formats, and distribution channels. The digital divide was also narrowed by transferring technology along the migration circuits. Media experts in the Sierra Norte often told me how the gift or purchase of affordable cell phones and PC hardware in the United States for relatives and friends in Mexico had greatly inspired them during the pioneer period (Kummels 2017a, 212). And in the end, media actors in both countries jointly created internet radio stations and multimedia platforms run by transnational teams. They combined various formats and networked their outlets. Useful skills in the cross-border context were effectively passed on within the community, also between young and old: although social media savvy predominated among those under thirty, older people were happy to be instructed by them when motivated by family or political interests to develop these abilities.

Several of the vanguard mediamakers made the transition of combining the firmly established video trade with a new trend toward more personalized social media formats, when broadcasting patron saint fiestas, for example. A key component is the personal address, whereby the mediamaker concerned appears on camera or/and audio commentary and tries to come across as spontaneous as possible. A variety of creatives have specialized in this off-the-cuff method of addressing the cultural expressions and ideals of the Zapotec or the Ayuujk way of life, particularly suited to mobilize a large number of like-minded "friends." I call these media actors ethnic or community influencers (see the next chapter). A concrete example of this is Kanzio Lize, a thirtysomething videographer from Yalálag who lives for the most part in Oaxaca City. In 2015 Kanzio set up a Facebook page titled KanzioLizeFilms, which is now extremely popular and has over a hundred thousand followers.⁴¹ He mainly posts photos, video clips, and short texts on his page, which focuses innovatively on classic motifs such as portraits of young and older women in traditional costumes, dance formations and dance couples, food, rituals, fiestas, and landscapes of Yalálag. Unlike traditional community videographers, however, Kanzio regularly uses compositional film devices such as highlighting the subject against a blurred background or adding dramatic lighting effects with Adobe Photoshop and Lighthouse software. The digital artifacts he posts frequently combine these attractive photos and short poetic texts. Users often express delight at such explicitly affirmative image-text combinations of Zapotec culture and the nobility of its people—especially against the backdrop of discrimination that results from the imposition of Whiteness as the standard of beauty. Although the Kanzio Lize Facebook page is simultaneously his business page, where he acquires new video commissions, most users perceive it as a showcase of Yalaltec life in general. In addition, he posts these digital artifacts almost in real time from the cyber room his family runs in a grocery shop in Yalálag. When I was in Pam's Los Angeles apartment during Easter of 2016, her adult son launched a YouTube search for Yalálag on a free afternoon. The algorithms offered my hosts up-to-the-minute news on their favorite subject, namely, video clips of the ongoing Easter celebration in their hometown posted by Kanzio Lize. It was now in vogue for migrants to be pictured on this much-visited site, as it drew a large viewership: whoever commissioned Kanzio to make a fiesta video was guaranteed a huge resonance among the networked publics. This dynamic reinforced the function that his Facebook page took on as a showcase of village life.

The new multimedia outlets brought this multimodal combination down to a fine art by creating Facebook platforms that integrate a varied content: from live broadcasts via Facebook Live to historical photographs and videos digitalized for publication. In 2018, former members of the pioneering TV station in Tamazulapam launched Tamix Multimedios in collaboration with a new generation of mediamakers; in the same period, media operators from Tlahuitoltepec created Multimedios Jënmë'ëny. Eliel Cruz, who is in his early thirties, works as a primary schoolteacher in one of the village's agencias. He told me how Tamix Multimedios came into being and how the content he coselected or produced from the start essentially defines its communal character:

I had just finished my [communal] service as a *teniente* [police officer] and a number of things had happened that really made me think. What's going to happen now to this community's history? How are we going to share it? And looking for information on this I couldn't find a media outlet that was doing exactly that. . . . I don't want to brag, but nationwide [on social media] I couldn't find the kind of communal outlet I had in mind. We began looking for a name for our page and decided: "Well, let's call it Digital TV Tamix." We thought of lots of other names. But then we pondered, "What are we going to share?" "We are going to upload photos, texts, videos, audios, podcasts. We can publish anything digitally." . . . To do that I have to enter a name, right? And although I had never thought of it before, on the spur of the moment I came up with, "Why not call it Tamix Multimedios?" The multimedia issue allows you to cover infinite options. . . . It also had to do with political issues and what's happening in our villages. But we also wanted to put them aside sometimes and ask in other ways: What's going on in our community? We also have a cultural life and maintain traditions. That's the path this page has taken. Our content has to be from our own village culture and its region.[42]

This media outlet targets a transnational audience. Eliel also streams seemingly trivial elements of village life with his cell phone, such as sales at the market, a heavy rain shower at a major traffic junction, or images of the Mexican hometown in a fog. He adds a personal touch to the recordings by briefly commenting on them via narration and/or text, letting people know how he feels at that moment. Hence the content goes hand in hand with a personalized media language. For the locals this can be uninteresting at times, but for the migrants who cannot be there, it translates to *nostálgicos*, as Eliel says: "The idea is for people living outside to witness what is happening in their hometown, to long for it and say: 'Aaay! I'd like to go there.' This content is also part of the cultural revival and enrichment of Tamazulapam."

Similar to the pioneer television station TV Tamix when it was founded in 1993, Tamix Multimedios first focused on covering the hometown patron saint fiesta in 2018. Because of financial constraints and shifting viewing habits, however, the staff did not broadcast it in full length. Instead, they divided the livestreams into chapters, which remain permanently archived on the Facebook page and can be accessed at any time. A vital aspect of the new social media format is its interactivity: while viewers/users experienced community life online, they intervened with likes, emojis, and short comments and followed the postings of other viewers/users. Eliel devoted much time and effort to setting up antennas, for example, to optimize the live character of broadcasts with a stable connection. There was also an economic dimension to the enormous technical effort and gathering of expertise: both required financial investment that the usos y costumbres governance was not willing to cofinance. The village media outlet now faced the challenge of looking for sponsors, which in turn influenced the content of what was broadcast. Even though the mediamaker himself was not a fan, up until 2019, Tamix Multimedios, had devoted a lot of space to basketball because "that's something people living outside are interested in" and "basketball has attracted countless followers to the page."

I will briefly discuss the digital format of the Santa Rosa de Lima patron saint fiesta and the Copa Ayuujk basketball tournament that Eliel of Tamix Multimedios livestreamed in August and September 2021.[43] In his own analysis, he sees his personal presentation of and (albeit brief) commentaries during the live broadcasts and his coverage of fiesta events based on personal invitations and preferences as innovative, compared to the more established fiesta videos. In his twenty-five posts, mostly livestreams ranging in length from four minutes to just over an hour, he nonetheless produces chapters similar to those of traditional fiesta videos.[44] Eliel wanders around the fiesta and its various happenings, and—just like a regular visitor—spontaneously accepts invitations from basketball tournament sponsors, for instance, who invite people to dine and dance to a brass band in their homes. In other words, when Eliel is recording, he "eats, drinks and sometimes gets drunk" in the style of many other fiesta visitors. This is something videographers would have avoided in the past since they had to tape the events for hours as completely as possible. In addition, livestreaming with a cell phone requires Eliel to get as close as possible to his motifs; this contrasts with the former stylistic preference for portraying large collectives with long shots. He also records many motifs on the spur of the moment—unlike established fiesta moviemakers, who basically take up a fixed position at the plaza or some other large venue. While livestreaming at the home of a sponsoring couple, where the San Isidro Huayapam brass band of around forty children and youths performed, Eliel noticed that his livestream was being shared on their Facebook page. During the band's intermission he began to read out private messages from friends and parents intended for their page. Many of them were from the United States, for example a message from a mother in Phoenix, Arizona, to her son. Amid much laughter—and many tears—a strong sense of copresence with these absent friends and parents emerged. In contrast to his broadcasts two years ago, Eliel rarely streamed from the basketball games. AR TV, a streaming service in operation since 2019 and run by Pablo and Rocksi, a couple from Sierra Norte and Valles Centrales, had taken over the job at these festivities. AR TV now has over three hundred thousand followers and its transnational dimension has become a multipronged enterprise in the Sierra Norte region; if the need arises, this outlet hires other regional creatives to cover the event. Whereas Tamix Multimedios is more into cultivating the realm of transnational community life with regard to Tamazulapam, AR TV has shifted to serving the vast audience of the entire Sierra Mixe region and its transboundary foothills that is interested in sports (see chapter 5).

   In summary, it can be said that self-determined media are now actively producing transnational affiliations under new conditions. In doing so, they are essentially building both on traditional and on mass media that have long been anchored in the hometown. These include the patron saint fiestas themselves with their dances, live music, and sports performances, and their analog remediatization, from which genres such as patron saint fiesta VHS videos originally emerged. Mediamakers in the digital era are ultimately looking for ways to pursue community interests that defy constraints (such as the affordances) imposed by social media like Facebook. Eliel remarks thoughtfully that this is why he keeps an eye on the number of Tamix Multimedios followers and likes, and the exponential growth of content sharing as a new currency. Despite his constant search for alternatives, for the time being he has opted for appropriating what commercial social media have to offer: "Because I livestream with private-sector software, I received a lot of criticism from them [non-Indigenous activists]. But I told them that we need to experiment with these tools and harness them to our common benefit. I made them understand that many *paisanos* engage in social media, since it's still new for them, right? We are striking out in new directions for using social media, uploading our content so viewers will be able to see it."

The next chapter focuses on the mediamaker perspective in the satellite communities of Los Angeles. Ethnic or community influencers are likewise attempting to reconcile media innovations with a communal ethos and at the same time overcome the transnational divide—albeit under the conditions of an urban environment and distinctive national policies.

# 3 · ZAPOTEC DANCE EPISTEMOLOGIES ONLINE

The Zapotec people of the Oaxacan Sierra Norte have a rich dance heritage on which they base their own knowledge.[1] An example of this is La Danza de los Negritos: it commemorates a pilgrimage that men from Yalálag undertook in the mid-nineteenth century to venerate the Black Christ in Esquipulas, Guatemala. According to one widely diffused account, they adopted the dance from Maroons who guided them when they lost their way. One of the most striking changes in recent years concerns the protagonism that women and girls currently assume when performing such sacred Zapotec dances once reserved to men. At the heart of this chapter is the issue of how Indigeneity is embodied through dance; it specifically explores the way Zapotec Indigeneity was negotiated in a transnational outreach while introducing a female version renamed La Danza de las Negritas in 2016. Anyone looking for audiovisual records of Sierra Zapotec dance in general is unlikely to find much in the established research archives that specialize in collecting audiovisual materials on Indigenous cultures of Mexico and the United States, such as the Cinematographic and Video Archive Alfonso Muñoz and Photographic Library Nacho López of the National Institute of Indigenous Peoples (INPI) in Mexico, the Smithsonian National Museum of the American Indian in the United States, or even the prominent archives of Oaxaca City.[2]

However, anyone who searches for these dances on the internet—for example, typing "danza de los negritos oaxaca" in Google—will come across hundreds of YouTube and Facebook videos. The oldest published video clips date back to 2008; some are a few minutes long, while others last for over two hours. These materials document the staging of these dances in the context of a patron saint fiesta in one of the many Zapotec villages in the Oaxacan Sierra Norte, or a similar kermés fiesta organized by the Oaxacan migrant associations in Los Angeles. Sacred dances such as La Danza de los Negritos are key to patron saint worship in any Zapotec village—and are now also practiced intensively in Los Angeles and other U.S. towns and cities. At the same time, recordings focusing on Sierra Zapotec dances are published on personal as well as company Facebook pages and on

YouTube. Once I became aware of the enormous dimension of this content and started following the performances both on-site and online, I noticed how extensively Yalaltec women engage in organizing, documenting, and publishing the dance activities of their children, both boys and girls. Lisvelia Hilario for example, a Los Angeles dance group leader in her early forties, launched a Zapotec dance initiative for the purpose of redefining Yalaltec lifeways in a transnational setting. She and others make these expressive forms visible and accessible to the public above all on digital platforms, which they have in part created to publicly share their family life.

## COMMUNITY INFLUENCERS' ARCHIVING "FROM BELOW"

My Los Angeles host Pam, whom I presented in the introduction, is an example of a mother and *comunera* engaging as a transnational community influencer. She is well aware of how much time she spends documenting, collecting, and sharing digital materials through her Facebook page, which she jokingly refers to as her "part-time job." A native of Yalálag, she has been living in Los Angeles for around thirty years and works as a housekeeper for two American landladies in Beverly Hills. With her cell phone, Pam regularly takes snapshots, records video clips, and creates posts to "share beautiful things with my *paisanos*," because "what if they never get an opportunity to come and walk around here?"[3] Via Facebook Live she transmits extensively from kermesses, while she also disseminates other dimensions of her family life. When she was able to afford her first trip to Las Vegas in 2017—accompanied by her husband, brother, and adult son—she was eager to share this experience with her followers—around four hundred "friends"—and livestreamed their visit of the Hotel Venice casino. Acquaintances in Yalálag were excited to follow them and commented on a migrant from their transborder community having fulfilled the American Dream. One villager posted the following enthusiastic comment: "Oh, blessed be God for all the marvels you let me see! Who would have thought of that. . . . When we were both in Yalálag we would play *polaca* betting beans and corn grains.[4] Now you are in a huge casino and play with money." In the weeks that followed, images of Pam in Las Vegas that she had stored on her page became part of a "mini-archive" of Facebook snaps and livestreams that this group of users frequently visited (cf. Garde-Hansen 2009, 143).

Why refer to Pam and others in what follows as "community" or "ethnic influencers"? "Influencer" is used to designate "everyday, ordinary Internet users who accumulate a relatively large following on blogs and social media through the textual and visual narration of their personal lives and life-styles" (Abidin 2016, 3). They influence the behavior of consumers based on their strong presence and reputation in social media. The term "ethnic influencers" also refers to self-taught specialists in this kind of performance, with a large network of "friends" and an interest in experimenting with everyday technologies and searching for new, attractive themes. However, here they use their narrative skills to influence follow-

Community influencers recording La Danza de los Chinantecos, Harvard Heights, Los Angeles, July 2019.

ers in terms of cultural forms and ideals considered to be rooted and to express particular Indigenous identities—in the Yalaltec case, one that revolves around communal dances, brass bands, and fiestas, mobilizing them as ethnic discourses on "the Zapotec way of life" (*lo zapoteco*). Since unauthorized migrants' routines in the United States are disrupted as a result of the immobility forced upon them, community influencers used digital media to bridge geographical distance between the United States and Mexico and generate a form of temporal copresence (cf. Madianou 2016). They strategically used narratives and archival skills to incite a larger audience to "be communicative" and "get into a bigger conversation"[5] regarding cultural issues and engage in a larger debate, thereby opening a media space for a transnational community (Kummels 2017b, 135). In Zapotec thought, this method of "doing affects" implies "doing knowledge" as well.[6] Performing Zapotec dance always requires the collaboration of colleagues who will play the accompanying music. When reflecting on these practices as corporeal knowledge, my interlocutors did not engage in Cartesian dualism. They consider that determination to engage for a cause depends on a close coordination between one's heart and mind.

I argue that these practices of narrating developments online as they evolve and curating them on social media for an audience (including people who do not ethnically identify as Zapotec) can be conceptualized as archiving knowledge "from below." In this way, people living in distant places with distinct migratory statuses visibilize, share, and compile personal experiences—including dreams come true—often embodied in actions and performances that transmit knowledge and function as an episteme (Taylor 2003, xvi). In the present case women who explicitly define themselves as mothers and comuneras are the main persons storing this bodily wisdom on Facebook and YouTube "mini-archives," therefore shifting archival power relations. Unauthorized immigrants live in fear of potent state archives such as the one managed by the U.S. Immigration and Customs Enforcement (ICE). This repository of penal records stemming from various federal agencies since the Trump era includes even civil law violations. Border patrol agents and immigration officers use this archive to prevent the entry of undocumented immigrants or to deport them. In contrast, actors like Pam invest their time and creativity in everyday media practices that allow them to "piece our story together" as a way of overcoming the increasingly impassable border. One of my interlocutors used the expression *armar la historia* to refer to the way in which she made use of her cell phone at a church wedding in Los Angeles. She spontaneously connected the bride with her father in Yalálag, while her husband posted a picture of this touching moment on Facebook, thus involving a wider audience. The father was not able to travel to the United States since he "has a record." By connecting them at a decisive moment, my interlocutor managed to include him in the wedding narrative as it evolved—and shifted power relations toward building community across an uncertain transnational terrain.[7]

Michel Foucault (1969) and Jacques Derrida (1995) pioneered the analysis of aspects of the control, monitoring, and governmentality exercised by state archives that claim a monopoly on knowledge production. By privileging written knowledge, such archives have served to substantiate the universality of the (Western-centric) world of science that operates along dualisms that exclude oral and corporeal wisdom (Santos 2018). On the other hand, recent scholarship has also demonstrated how new, diverse ways of archiving seek to decolonize existing repositories either by developing their democratic potential or radically departing from archival affordances that buttress state control (Basu and De Jong 2016). Arjun Appadurai (2003, 16) in particular elaborates on the concept of the living or migrant archive and points out that "the personal diary, the family photo album, the community museum, the libraries of individuals are all examples of popular archives and, of course, oral archives have been repositories of intentional remembering for most of human history" while they are "also a part of everyday life outside the purview of the state." In a similar vein Stuart Hall (2001, 89) has emphasized that the diaspora archive's vibrancy rests on its "on-going, continuing, unfinished open-ended" quality geared to the future.

In this chapter, Yalálag migrants and villagers' engagement with social media attracting a transnational audience is scrutinized through the introduction of a controversial and innovative dance. In 2016 the female dance group of Nueva Generación Krus Yonn performed La Danza de las Negritas in the hometown as an act of female empowerment vis-à-vis an "outdated" gender structure and unequal access to corporeal knowledge within the transnational community and beyond.

The premiere made me reflect on how the media practices of cell phone recording and collecting and assembling images, sounds, and textual messages concerning the novel dance, as well as the users' way of accessing and publicly commenting on these postings, help to diversify and decolonize knowledge. Currently, several researchers have taken notice of the specific characteristics of Facebook, YouTube, Twitter, and Instagram, as well as the potential they offer to individuals who seek to create varied archives on the web; due to interactivity they are coproduced by a great many users (Abidin 2016; Featherstone 2010; Garde-Hansen 2009; Geismar 2017; Kaun and Stiernstedt 2014; Kaun 2016; Lange 2019). The "media archeologist" Wolfgang Ernst (2013) stresses that the interactivity and temporal qualities of online repositories lead to a new archival regime. In the words of Anne Kaun (2016, 5397), "The long-term, stable archive . . . is today converted into an archive of procedural temporality based on permanent updating and real-time processing." That is, the online management of memory is no longer primarily concerned with preservation but instead is reconfigured in view of an economy of digital circulation. The actors shape memory toward immediate accessibility. Manipulating temporality allows for transforming the hierarchy of knowledge within an archive. Conventionally, the documents and artifacts were valued and carefully stored because of their antiquity and degree of conservation; the collection of keepsakes related to "important" (often male) historical personalities was privileged.

In contrast, archives "from below" focus on contemporary dynamics concerning Zapotec dances and their potential for constructing a different future: they provide a platform for the leading role that women and girls play in shaping dance knowledge. Throughout this chapter, I show how women within emerging transnational communities combined their narrative skills as mothers and comuneras to develop innovative archival practices. Mothers extended their habit of collecting family memories in private photo albums to the digital cocreation of community events for a "networked publics" (boyd 2010; see "How Users Coproduce the Online Archive of Zapotec Dance"). As comuneras they now cater to an audience and their sense of collectivity deriving from interconnected social media pages and digital platforms. Being a comunera means engaging as a village member who assumes regular duties and accomplishes service on a committee, for example. When organizing patron saint fiestas and kermesses the interaction between two generations is crucial in making these celebrations come about; they are hosted to collect funds for their respective hometowns. The first-generation parents engage as officials in charge of the committees, volunteer to prepare the meals, act as DJs on-site, and visit as consumers. Most of the dancers and musicians are second-generation youth and children who are socialized at these get-togethers and receive instruction from dance teachers and band directors who often developed their skills in Los Angeles.

In the following section, I explore the characteristics and motivations of such community influencers who create "living archives" of Zapotec dance on social media by publishing and collecting their personal aural and visual experiences. In the course of their archival activities from below, actors transform knowledge with respect to its access, management, and storage. I assume that they displace the hegemony of existing archives that ignored and therefore silenced the wisdom transmitted by dancing bodies and oral histories. The main questions that arise from the Sierra Zapotec dances that I accompanied on-site and online are the following: What do media actors communicate in terms of gender and Zapotec culture? Who is their intended audience? In relation to the interactivity of these practices, I inquire as to what users contribute when commenting on and shaping online archives disseminated publicly. Finally, I examine a wider issue: do these emerging archives decolonize knowledge and subsequently contribute to the transnational community's sustainability?

While I follow a media anthropology perspective, I avoid a media-centric approach that tends to ascribe substantial changes in archival practices primarily to the emergence of novel technologies in the digital age. Instead, I assume that actors in general adapt media technology—in this case social media's so-called affordances—and invest it with cultural resources such as their narratives and aesthetics spurred by cultural desires and needs (Williams 1977; Martín-Barbero 1987; Miller at al. 2016; Kummels 2017a, 7, 32). Therefore, I accompanied people engaging with dance, music, and social media on the ground in the course of their everyday lives. With regard to mothers' creation of family albums, Gillian Rose has emphasized that analyzing the effects of collected images requires not only looking into the family snaps themselves but also examining what "mini-archivists" actually do with media when interacting with family members and others. This reveals how "women work . . . through their own desires, pleasures, fantasies and melancholies, at least partly on their own terms" (Rose 2010, 9). My interlocutors reflected on their practices and affects precisely when they managed and organized media such as their Facebook page. For this reason, conversations that took place on my interlocutors' PC or cell phone whenever they would log onto social media proved particularly fruitful. This allowed them to create a certain copresence with their relatives and friends in different places during our exchange (see "How Mothers and Comuneras Craft Dance into a Media Event").

## TRANSMITTING ZAPOTEC DANCE KNOWLEDGE VIA THE BODY AND VIDEO

Whenever I glanced across a Los Angeles living room or the patio of a house in Yalálag, large framed photographs of family members wearing spectacular dance costumes, often with dramatic masks, would attract my attention. It is not fortuitous that bodily dance performance was among the first motifs to be photographed by local amateurs, later recorded with video and now preferentially disseminated via Facebook and YouTube. Yalaltec people consider their hometown "the cradle of dance," and its inhabitants are indeed well-known for their mastery of a great number of them. Los Huenches (the Ancient Zapotecs), La Danza de los Cuerudos (the Dance of Those in Leather Jackets), La Danza de San José, and La Danza de los Negritos are considered emblematic for the village's four barrios. Each barrio claims specific dances as its intellectual property and cultural heritage.[8] As a major attraction of patron saint celebrations, dances with live banda music are a key element; a committee that forms part of the usos y costumbres governance assumes responsibility for their organization. In most cases a personal vow is at the heart of participating in a dance and taking on the financial burden of purchasing the elaborate costume and mask. At the same time, those who are involved with the dances demonstrate their fulfillment of duties as a community member or *comunero/a*. To some degree, the Los Angeles satellite community has adopted the organizational pattern of the village of origin: four neighborhoods, each with its respective dances. These socioterritorial units have been adapted to the urban setting.

Zapotec dances are a field ridden by tension and cultural creativity in the transnational setting: the debates often triggered by their performance revolve around issues of their origins, intellectual property, and authenticity—and by extension around wider concerns for the future of Zapotec Indigeneity. At the same time, they are constantly being reinvented: dance teachers, composers of *son* music, experienced and/or aspiring dancers, and now ethnic influencers—in their role as community documentarists and archivists of the dance—intervene in these creations and the controversies they provoke. One of the most striking changes concerns the public protagonism that women and girls currently assume in Zapotec dances, particularly sacred dances once reserved to men. I argue that the way photography, VHS video, and digital platforms have been used to remediatize Zapotec bodily dances (cf. Bolter and Grusin 2000, 5) plays an important part in altering the social and gender relations constantly being renegotiated and inscribed in the epistemic field of dance.

For this reason, we need to examine the history of the Zapotec knowledge system of dance and how it was organized, performed, circulated, and stored before 1987, that is, in the era before the appropriation of VHS video. Malaquías Allende, a resident of the Santiago barrio in Yalálag born in 1933, is a local historian who chronicles the history of Zapotec dances.[9] He was commissioned by local officials to transcribe oral testimonies because of their interest in clarifying rivaling neighborhood claims that specific dances were their exclusive cultural heritage. As for La Danza de los Negritos, the historian traces a fascinating story of its many authors: a Yalaltec man named Cirilo Poblano Cano is credited with "copying and creating" the dance during a trip he undertook in 1851 in veneration of the Black Christ of Esquipulas, Guatemala. A dance, however, also requires the composition of several *sones*, which, according to Allende's informants, was carried out by two men from the Santa Rosa neighborhood, the barrio that today claims the dance as its intellectual property. A woman from the neighborhood of San Juan, however, also contributed two of the seven sones ascribed to the dance. Finally, two women pioneered sewing the elaborate costumes by hand. The history of this dance in Yalálag therefore illustrates that women were involved in dance from its beginnings, although not on equal terms. Some key expertise remained exclusively in the hand of men: male dance teachers memorized the complex steps and figures and taught them via their bodies to the rhythm of a son melody that they whistled (as a substitute for the banda music during rehearsals), a teaching method used to this day. The Negritos dance characters were assumed by men; membership in the municipal brass band accompanying the performance was also exclusively male up to the turn of the millennium.

Diana Taylor (2003, 36) has coined the term "repertoire" for the mode of transmitting and memorizing knowledge via the body. She juxtaposed it to the "archive" and emphasized that throughout history the archive was used to record and determine knowledge through writing and images. These media formats were privileged because of their durability, while the supposedly ephemeral corporeal epistemologies were marginalized. However, when Yalaltecs refashioned the mode of transmitting dance knowledge in the context of extending their community transnationally, they did not juxtapose the body "repertoire" and the "archive." Rather, people began combining transmission of the dances via both the body and videocassettes: creatives pioneered analog moviemaking in 1987 because they were eager to capture the dances as the main fiesta motif. Local videographers devised the fiesta video genre to send these VHS tapes to the growing satellite community in Los Angeles. This implied much more than a simple change of medium when documenting and archiving dances: videomaking altered dance knowledge itself. The execution and appreciation were no longer solely dependent on a dance teacher; a competent videographer able to produce images and sound apt for learning bodily movements was also required. To allow viewers to appreciate a dance as if they were on-site, fiesta video aesthetics rely on camera setting: a frontal long shot to capture the entire group of eight dancers and enable viewers to judge the accurateness of the steps and figures. For this purpose, the performances are documented from beginning to end, that is, during the recital of eight pieces of son music that can last for an hour.[10]

Fiesta videos were therefore not only used to entertain a transnational audience. Parents residing in Los Angeles began applying such videotapes as didactic tools to socialize their children with the cultural heritage of their hometown. Second-generation children, born in Los Angeles, frequently mention that they became fond of Zapotec dances and music because the genre was consumed for pleasure in their homes.[11] Almost every family collects numerous fiesta videos, from traditional VHS cassettes to modern Blu-rays, in dressers or closets or underneath a bed. Videographers generally store all videotapes and DVDs at home, hoping for future sales. This and later remediatizations of Zapotec dances played an important part in altering the social and gender hierarchy negotiated in the epistemic field of dance. People currently use cell phones to pursue dance for all the various reasons mentioned above, including family entertainment, the cultural education of children, and citizenship tasks in the context of patron saint festivities and kermesses. Since Facebook has become the most popular forum to socialize with relatives and friends living far away, users often resort to images depicting themselves and relatives engaging in fiestas as community affairs to provide visual and aural testimony of their participation as citizens in this transborder Yalaltec commitment.

In Los Angeles women and young girls first became involved as dancers by assuming the role of female characters formerly performed by men disguised as women. Women and young girls have successively taken on traditional male roles as well, and in recent years some have even become dance teachers. When I interviewed first-generation parents about their reasons for seeking more gender-equal dance participation, they emphasized how dances had been a privilege reserved to wealthy people and adults in the Mexican hometown during their youth. In their opinion, Zapotec dances were "democratized" for the first time in Los Angeles since migrants from families that previously had been less wealthy were finally able to afford costumes that cost up to a thousand dollars. At the same time, Zapotec dances have also become popular as an antidote to gender and racial discrimination firmly rooted in Los Angeles. In the megacity's world of employment, first-generation women mainly found jobs in care chains as illegalized and therefore poorly paid and exploited house cleaners, babysitters, and care workers. They often achieved better working conditions but had to negotiate them on their own or by forming alliances to search for employers who would treat them fairly. Discrimination was also experienced by second-generation children at school, where their Indigeneity was excluded in curricula, invisibilized by their sweeping categorization as Hispanics, and even compounded by the actions of teachers (Alberto 2017). In everyday life the second generation often experience how citizenship is denied them despite their birth in the United States, for example, when peers at education facilities denigrate them as racial "Others" and foreigners (see chapter 6).

In contrast, Zapotec dance rehearsals offer an opportunity for meeting with family members and friends living dispersed throughout the city with similar experiences and the common quest of changing existing conditions. Backyard practices also serve for keeping children "off the streets" in the problem districts where many live. Moreover, the dances themselves enact the realities of transnational migrants and their aspirations (Cruz-Manjarrez 2013, 153–189). *Chusca* or parodic dances stage the crossing of the border without papers from the 1960s (the Dance of the Wetbacks); they document shifts in gender role models since most men work in restaurants in Los Angeles and take pride in their cooking skills (the Dance of the Cooks). Currently, empowering idols such as Spiderman and Captain America appear in the dances (the Superheroes Dance; see also Peña 2017). The innovative nature of these dances is promoted both in Los Angeles and in Yalálag: the hometown has hosted an annual tournament for vanguard dances since the 1980s; the Superheroes Dance, for example, was invented there. Professional videographers from the community and spectators using cell phones regularly tape the dances. Video clips have become a key media format in capturing and storing these creations.

Nevertheless, particular Zapotec dance versions were often subject to criticism within the transnational community, precisely because Indigenous wisdom was produced and altered through recording, publishing, and archiving. Sacred dances to venerate the saints are an emotionally charged issue of debate. As is often pointed out, they have been part of the neighborhood or village heritage since "time immemorial"; there are those who are afraid that these dances may lose their "authenticity." Chusca dances, which often parody other ethnic groups or make fun of Yalaltec people themselves in the process of modernization, also trigger affective dynamics. Each barrio committee, which forms part of the system of governance and organizes the fiestas and dances, seeks to control their audiovisual representation. This is based on the idea that each dance has an "owner," that is, a person identifying with a barrio who designed the choreography, created the attire, and chose or composed the son music to which it is performed.[12] Whenever possible, committees commission specific community videographers to record and later sell videos to raise funds. Anyone else recording the dance at length arouses suspicion of "pirating." Therefore, a dancer in Yalálag who lived for many years in Los Angeles explained to me that recording dances in general "helps in some ways, but hurts in others" because "other villages see the video and copy the steps. They no longer need to come here, since they can watch it on video."[13]

In the next two sections, we look precisely into the way mothers and comuneras negotiate newly gendered versions of Zapotec culture via their media strategies.

## HOW MOTHERS AND COMUNERAS CRAFT DANCE INTO A MEDIA EVENT

In July 2016, the annual patron saint festivities in honor of Santiago Apostle took place in Yalálag, and as usual Zapotec dances were performed all day long on two consecutive Sundays. However, at this fiesta a premiere took place that was anything but typical. The female dance group of Nueva Generación Krus Yonn had arrived from Los Angeles only a few days before. For the first time, young women born in Los Angeles between thirteen and nineteen years old publicly performed La Danza de las Negritas in front of the Santiago chapel.[14] Their parents were Yalaltecs who had been living in the California megacity unauthorized for years and could not accompany them. Their performance triggered discussions on site in Yalálag and in Los Angeles, and within a transnational media space between Mexico and the United States. Photos and videos of the young women and their pioneer dance performance were recorded, posted online, and heatedly debated: Should young women be doing this dance? Did gender reversal jeopardize the "authenticity" of Zapotec sacred dances? And in what direction should Zapotec culture evolve in the future to strengthen it in the hometown and beyond?

Premiere of La Danza de las Negritas at the chapel of Santiago Apostle, Yalálag, July 2016.

When following this event online I discovered that people who use Facebook to systematically publish dances are between thirty and fifty years of age and belong to two generations of migrants: those who immigrated to Los Angeles from 1990 to the start of the new millennium and the Los Angeles–born descendants of earlier migrants. These two groups are now parents. The first group has reformulated initial migrant aspirations of "getting ahead" and "seeking a future." Initially, they were motivated by the possibility of earning more and saving money to invest when they returned to Mexico. However, after marrying and starting families in Los Angeles, they reoriented their efforts toward a permanent stay in the United States and creating a brighter future for their children. This has motivated first- and second-generation women to engage in new ways as comuneras. Migrant mothers seek to offer their children a dual education within the multicultural context of Los Angeles: they encourage them to access higher education within the American school system, while at the same time they are also concerned with their children "not losing their (Zapotec) roots," "maintaining their identity," and "knowing where they come from" by engaging in Zapotec dance and music. This formula has enabled a high percentage of members of the Oaxacan second generation to proceed to higher education (Vásquez 2019). "Dance moms" now bring their children from an early age to kermesses and barrio dance rehearsals to make sure that they familiarize themselves with dances and live music from the parents' village of origin.

Most parents of the dancers share an illegalized status and a working-class background as employees in restaurants and housekeepers. For example, my interlocutors, parents of a nineteen-year-old dancer, revealed how they promote their children's participation in Zapotec dance groups to socialize them according to values they attribute to the village of origin, but which they have in fact adapted to the U.S. setting. They negotiate these values at the intersection of intimacy and "illegality" with its "flows that both shape and are structured by gendered and familial actions and interactions, but are always defined by the presence of the U.S. state" (Boehm 2013, 4). Immigrant parents and children have differential residential status and are affected by the racial hierarchy imposed on them in their host country. The unauthorized parents commented on how during adolescence their U.S.-born daughter distanced herself from them by discriminating against their village of origin, referring to it as "your (backward) rancho," and questioning their authority. Yet the parents unexpectedly triggered a turn from shame to pride when they sent their then-fourteen-year-old daughter to Yalálag as "punishment" during her vacation. To their great surprise she returned with new admiration for Zapotec culture. From then on, the parents and their daughter jointly engaged in a new type of dance ensemble, Nueva Generación Krus Yonn (New Generation Yalaltec Cross), created in 2008.[15] While membership in barrio dance groups is based on affiliation with a Yalaltec neighborhood (and handed down by family ties), this novel troupe accepts members from any barrio or even from different Zapotec hometowns. Their dance teachers do not necessarily descend from a family famous for this tradition, as occurs in Yalálag. In Los Angeles dance teachers are frequently self-taught and rely on unconventional methods for their choreographies such as consulting video clips circulating online. Sebastián, a man of about forty and the current dance teacher of Nueva Generación Krus Yonn, explained to me that the dance video genre had impacted on the viewing habits of the second generation; their parents even use them as a didactic tool. His own son became excited about Zapotecan dances and music, and learned by watching videos and DVDs time and again at home.[16]

As for the dance group leader, Lisvelia was born in Los Angeles in 1976; a second-generation Yalaltec American, she has a high school education and works in an office. She is one of the people who devote themselves to systematically recording and posting these dances as a community influencer. Interviewing Lisvelia for some time after the premiere—while she was absorbed in archiving "from below"—was a revelation. While she successively clicked on her past postings, she described the dance initiative as a project with a political dimension that was also intended as a form of modernizing Yalaltec culture in a transnational setting. Accordingly, she planned Nueva Generación Krus Yonn's first appearance very strategically—focusing on making an impression on the village of origin and its "outdated" gender structure. She followed up on other initiatives involving female appropriation of formerly all-male dances that are booming in the context of transborder community building. Since 2014, girls whose parents had migrated from villages neighboring Yalálag and formed satellite communities in Los Angeles have been performing all-female versions of La Danza de los Negritos.[17] The dancers from Yalaltec families, including Lisvelia's own daughter, were keen on proving that this was "not solely a man's danza," as a comment on her Facebook page read. According to Lisvelia, several obstacles had to be tackled in Los Angeles, beginning with finding a Zapotec dance instructor willing to teach the men's dance to girls. Even before the first rehearsal, a machista revolt was underway. Some of the Zapotec men in Los Angeles scoffed that women's bodies were uncapable of performing ritual dances the proper way because of their "boobs" being in motion. The women were just as harsh, chiding that dancing would impair the girls' reproductive capacity. Nevertheless, she persevered. The dance group continued to train for a performance in Yalálag, in the very heart of the "the cradle of dance;" performing in Los Angeles was considered secondary.

Anticipating that the gender reversal of the dance would be controversial, Lisvelia had initially avoided publishing information about it on Facebook. However, once the staging was guaranteed she engaged intensively in online practices of documenting and archiving. Her personal Facebook page holds an impressive quantity of diverse materials and remediatizations; many digital artifacts deal with Los Angeles dance performances. Since 2009, Lisvelia has maintained the page, where she has uploaded more than a thousand video clips, an indication that "a major effect of social media is that human communication has become more visual at the expense of oral and textual modes" (Miller et al. 2016, xvi). Since she first began posting, she has perfected her skills to fashion an attractive Facebook page and regularly pioneers new features such as FaceTime and Facebook Live transmissions. Her video clips of female dancers have been seen by as many as two thousand users at a time, turning her private memories into a public archive.

Lisvelia attributes the growth of her social media archive to followers and their positive encouragement: "My Facebook is full of good memories, some are sad memories, but even that is a good thing. Some people will criticize you for what you have on your page, but most people will be like 'OK.' A lot of my daughter's and my sons' friends, they are always commenting about it, like: 'Oh my God, Mrs. Hilario, we love when you post stuff like that, it's good to know about it!'"[18] But, as she explained, this was not her intention at first. She created the dance archive by using Facebook as a sort of family album: "So, as you see I keep all my memories of my kids. Stuff that we do, like Halloween, when we went to the fair. . . . I tend to keep good memories of just different kinds throughout an event. That is something that I know my kids will later enjoy. . . . With all this technology it's something that you need, because it's more resourceful and useful and I just get memories. . . . I am very proud to share them, like every moment of my kids."

Like many other mothers throughout the world, Lisvelia believes that an essential part of her role as a mother consists of promoting family ties and values through the collection of visual memories in the form of family photo albums, scrapbooks, and the emergent "mini-archives" on social media. The custom of creating photo albums is widely practiced, both in the European context in general and among the Latin American middle class, for the purpose of handing down to

Lisvelia visiting her Facebook page and the photos of her daughter, a Las Negritas dancer, August 2017.

their son or daughter a document of their childhood (Rose 2010; Figueroa 2016). For many Indigenous migrant women from Mexico this has also become a routine practice. They are experts in designing what Pierre and Marie-Claire Bourdieu term sociograms: visual registers considered mandatory of the existent social roles and relations within a family that amateurs capture through photographs at major family celebrations. Their purpose is "to solemnize and materialize the image that the group intends to present of itself" (Bourdieu and Bourdieu [1965] 2004, 601). However, in her research on mothers' collections of family snaps in southeast England, Gillian Rose (2010, 42) cautions that we need to pay closer attention to the negotiations of the mother-children relationship and to complications that also guide the production and use of portraits emphasizing family togetherness.

I would further add that when the creation of sociograms around family events is transferred to Facebook, sociograms take on a new quality. On Facebook, media actors combine memory practices in a multimodal way when "creating photograph albums, sharing photographs, messaging, joining groups and alumni memberships, making 'friends' and staying in touch with family" (Garde-Hansen 2009, 135). Such contents are regularly shared with an audience. Memory itself is transformed, for it is increasingly archived and disseminated by individuals publishing pieces of their biography and their personal experiences to interact and network in a public way. Due to this state of dynamic evolution, archives have a "living" quality (Hall 2001; Appadurai 2003), the property of "dynarchives" (Ernst 2013, 82). The smart-phone pictures uploaded as content have new characteristics as well: in contrast to the classic family portraits captured in "sociograms," digital snaps mostly function as vehicles of the networked sociality for the person who is taking and sending them (Hjorth 2007; Gómez Cruz 2012). These snapshots are capable of generating an immediate copresence. Moreover, as digital artifacts they display a greater malleability since anyone who is a "friend" can alter them when they access, share, show, and comment on them.

In other words, unlike sociograms created for photo albums meant for intimate use within a family, the digital artifacts that Lisvelia as a mother and comunera uploads to her personal Facebook page address a much wider community, arousing sensations of intimacy and immediacy. Her page exhibits the social relations she maintains with acquaintances from various phases of her life as well as her daughter's time in high school. She has accumulated eleven hundred Facebook friends, most of whom she also knows offline. When she showed me her page, she stressed how the memorable moments of her daughter's life were part of this wider community: "I don't post videos just of her. I also will post videos of the group, you know." Her publications revolve around themes such as her family, Yalálag, Xochixtepec (her husband's Zapotec hometown), and Zapotec lifeways in general. However, these themes are always approached as part of the Yalaltec cross-border community and, in addition, as part of the multicultural society of Los Angeles. She pointed out, "It's not only about the *paisanos*.... Where my kids go to the school in Taft out in the Valley, it's a very diverse high school. So, my kids have met kids from Russia, Poland, Persians.... When they talk about their culture, my kids say: 'Oh, it's similar to what we do.'"

To communicate with this diverse society, Lisvelia publishes visual and textual narratives that I conceptualize as "futurograms": they link an important landmark of her daughter's life or of family life with the future vision of a wider community, tying it selectively to the past (cf. Hill and Bithell 2014, 5). In a similar vein, U.S. women in their quest to achieve social, cultural, and civic equality have used scrapbooking to shape their lives on a small scale "according to available resources, aesthetic preferences and as contemplations on the past and dreams for the future," as Karina Hof (2006, 381–382) has highlighted. When opening the digital photo albums on her Facebook page, Lisvelia showed me how she combined two portraits of her daughter. In these photos, she appears as both a banda musician who plays the clarinet and as a dancer in La Danza de las Negritas. In the accompanying Spanish text she underscores that her daughter is a second-generation Yalalteca in Los Angeles who is proud of her genealogy and roots in Yalálag. "My daughter Kayla ... she is my greatest pride. She has been dancing since she was five, her first teacher was her uncle Isaí Pazos, she participated in La Danza de los Malinches with him for four years and with Mis Raíces for two years. She also took part in La Danza de San José with her teachers Juan and Cleto Chimil. And these last three years.... My daughter, being second-generation born in Los Angeles will always be proud of where her grandparents are from, Villa Hidalgo Yalalag and Xochixtepec."

As we inspected her collage, Lisvelia provided me with more information so that I could better interpret the multiple messages that she condensed in this "futurogram." She explained that during her own youth in the 1990s, she, like many of her contemporaries, did not take pride in the Zapotec culture, when the migrant community was less visible in Los Angeles than it is now. In the context of discrimination toward "Oaxacans" or "Oaxaquitas" regarded as only capable of performing unskilled labor, their cultural knowledge did not enjoy the appreciation that it does today. The elaborate organization of dances in Los Angeles, their public visibility in the city, and increased pride in the dances themselves sparked a change in attitude. Hence, as a mother whose five-year-old daughter joined the dance group My Roots (Mis Raíces) Lisvelia first became interested in Zapotec culture. Isaí Pazos, a cousin who migrated to Los Angeles at the age of four, became a dance teacher and created the My Roots ensemble (from 2014 to 2019 he was director of the Oaxaca Regional Organization, which organizes the Guelaguetza festival in Los Angeles). Isaí was a pioneer in orienting dance activities toward youth born in Los Angeles, with the aim of connecting them to Zapotec epistemology and their parents' hometown. In 2010, Mis Raíces performed La Danza de la Malinche in Yalálag for the first time.

The project that Lisvelia developed in 2016 was similar, in the sense that it sought to set a new benchmark for dance that would be recorded, posted, and archived as a memento that was accessible to the networked collectivity. But in this case she seized the opportunity to livestream the event, intensifying an identification with a novel dance version via copresence in real time.

## DIGITALLY SHOWCASING THE DANCE PREMIERE

The Mexican premiere of the group's performance of La Danza de las Negritas took place in front the church of Santiago in Yalálag in July 2016, sparking a controversy that first evolved on-site in face-to-face discussions. During the second performance in the hometown one week later, Lisvelia engaged in an innovative media practice: she was the first to transmit the dance using FaceTime. This signaled the start of the dance premiere's further evolution as a "media event," that is, an event that became just as meaningful for social interaction as the offline dance premiere that took place in the physical-geographical setting of the hometown (cf. Hine 2000, 67).

Let's first have a look at the offline dimensions of the event at which I was present, since they differ from the online presentation: before the first performance, the dance group was officially welcomed in Yalálag at a reception organized by village officials. After parading down the street, the dancers entered the town hall, where the municipal president received them and delivered a speech in their honor. This type of reception, which was formerly reserved for delegations from neighboring villages, has become routine nowadays whenever brass bands and dance groups visit from Yalálag's satellite communities. One of the dancers gave

The Las Negritas dancers parading down the street before their reception at the Yalálag town hall, Mexico, July 2016.

an arrival message followed by reception speeches of Yalálag's officials. These were all delivered in a serious, respectful, and ceremonial manner. Everything seemed to run smoothly; nevertheless, I later found out that intensive negotiations were being conducted backstage to enable the troupe to perform. Lisvelia had reached a prior agreement with officials from the Santiago committee (the neighborhood where her family comes from), but when she arrived in Yalálag she was told, much to her surprise, that she also required permission from the municipal president for the premiere to take place. Thus, officials considered this novel performance a delicate matter, although ultimately they authorized it.

Its mediatization added to the legitimization of the dance group's unusual presentation at the Santiago Apostle fiesta: local videographer Pancho Limeta, a pioneer videographer in Yalálag and key actor (see chapter 2), filmed the reception as part of his normal work routine as a fiesta chronicler. His mere presence at the reception, where he recorded the female dance group, helped establish the group's credibility as an integral feature of the hometown patron saint fiesta. Images of the dancers would later appear in the main fiesta video disseminated as a DVD series, as well as on ads featured on his Facebook company page. Moreover, the dancers commissioned Pancho to produce the movie "La Danza de los Negritos performed by young ladies living in Los Ángeles California" as a keepsake for their family archives.

In contrast, another village videographer, Kanzio Lize, refused to record the performance, even though the parents of one of the girls had offered him an assignment. Kanzio filmed most of the performances at this particular fiesta and showcased them on his very popular Facebook page and YouTube channel. An informal conversation with the videographer revealed that he had a lot to say as to why he failed to post images of the dance on his social media pages, which many consider to be the leading archive of Yalálag's social events.[19] To begin with, his home barrio of Santa Rosa claims authorship of the Negritos dance, and he opposes its performance by outsiders. However, the mediamaker also stressed that the female group had failed to wear the Negrito masks the first Sunday that they performed (they wore them in defiance on the second Sunday as a challenge to criticism). He interpreted that omission as a sign of disrespect and a break with the "mysticism" of the dance. In his opinion, Los Angeles Yalaltecos/as were not doing Zapotec dances the "right" (i.e., traditional) way. Interestingly he himself deals with the dances in inventive ways when mediatizing them; moreover, he resides not in the village but in Oaxaca City. Thus, we see how creatives argue "lack of authenticity" in response to competing innovative approaches; the charge does not originate from any "hard-core traditionalists."

By livestreaming the performance, Lisvelia generated a common experience of immediacy among viewers and users. By accessing the wireless LAN of the nearby hospital, she transmitted images of the Negritas dancers sending a playful greeting to their parents, thereby creating a transnational screen-to-screen forum to compensate for the fact that many parents could not attend on-site. Her cell phone reporting therefore deviates from the more distant gaze of the videographer Pancho, who concentrates on capturing an overall view of the choreography and ceremonial aspects of the dances. During the twenty-minute transmission, the novelty of the method, as well as that of the performance itself, received extensive comments, particularly from the mothers, aunts, and godmothers of the dancers—that is, mainly by women. Lisvelia encouraged these Facebook users to publicly express their pride in this moment of female protagonism. The users congratulated the dancers with phrases such as "A proud moment for us women!!," which were recorded while the group performed. They expressed "joy" at being able to witness their daughters dancing as the event unfolded. They posted emojis as mini-icons of their affects, especially clapping hands, smileys, hearts, and thumbs-up. Lisvelia, as well as these "friends," capitalized on the Facebook setting that announces live transmissions. In turn the "friends" interactively created visual displays of popularity simply by sending emojis that then appeared next to celebratory textual comments. During the live feed, two generations of Yalaltec women communicating from two countries (and with diverse immigration statuses) experienced the dance performance in copresence. La Danza de las Negritas had intentionally been anchored in the village of origin to enhance its authenticity within Zapotec culture.

From this moment on the performance triggered discussions at multiple forums on-site in Yalálag and in Los Angeles and within a transnational media space between Mexico and the United States. The debate on the issue of whether young women should perform this dance previously considered appropriate only for men was upheld online for some time. After the performance Lisvelia invested more of her time in processing the event on Facebook, fashioning it into a web event. Christine Hine was the first to emphasize that online media events are just as meaningful for social interaction as offline incidents, which unfurl in a physical-geographical setting. Those who follow develop a "sense of engagement" with that "media event" as "an ongoing and living event" (Hine 2000, 67). Online media episodes emerge from cultural digital artifacts that many discuss; people relate to these events from many locations through their media practices. In addition to creating the livestream artifact described above, Lisvelia designed a photo album of the dance rehearsals and performances of the main protagonists in the form of a slideshow. Likewise, she remediatized old VHS recordings of her daughter practicing when she was five years old (she used her cell phone to reproduce the historic images). Through their immediate, quantifiable reactions to the web event, users, especially dance moms, encouraged her to create more digital artifacts: "There were twelve shares! I'm like: 'Who are these people?' Some people I don't even know them! And that's why my cousin always comments: 'Liz, why do you get thousands of views?'"

Through her choice of Facebook entries and comments during the interview, Lisvelia demonstrated how she, as a second-generation Los Angeles Yalalteca, actively reconstructs Indigeneity from a gender perspective. Since they are presumed to be "less Zapotec," people like her who were born in the United States are sometimes belittled as *yalaltecos gringos* in the village of origin; most, for example, do not speak the Zapotec language. At the same time, they now are at the vanguard of Zapotec cultural knowledge: they use social media to publicly discuss its gendered nature and authenticity and to publicly advocate for female empowerment. In our conversation, she relayed how she counteracted reproaches in Yalálag that the female dance performance had been a deliberate attempt to mock the sacred dance. Lisvelia took care to legitimize her initiative to reform the dance with the "futurograms" she posted on Facebook. In these digital artifacts, she links her "village of origin" with a fondness for this place and with its authenticity: this applies to the collage made with cell phone snaps of her daughter and a text that emphasizes the Yalaltec roots of a young woman commonly considered a "Latina" or "Hispanic" in Los Angeles. In offline conversations, Lisvelia takes a stance on authenticity that is widely adopted by the second generation in Los Angeles: "Nothing in this world is the original, nothing." Her response to those in the Yalaltec community who criticize her versions of Zapotec culture is, "If we [from the second generation in Los Angeles] don't do it, who will?"

Thanks to her media and archival skills, Lisvelia plays a political role within her community. In 2017, she spearheaded an initiative that successfully raised funds to refurbish the parish building in the hometown. It is in this wider context that she endeavors to document, publish, and preserve the activities of the female dance group Nueva Generación Krus Yonn as thoroughly as possible. After the female dance group appeared at four other Zapotec kermesses in Los Angeles,

Lisvelia posted the following message along with a smiley emoji next to a portrait of the eight dancers: "Whatever you set your heart and mind to, it can and will be done. Feeling proud." Gender empowerment is promoted through images, sound, and text conveying affects as an indispensable component of the unity of heart and mind. The respective digital artifacts are coproduced by the users, who enrich her archive and disseminate its contents beyond Lisvelia's personal page. Her page is therefore consulted as an archive of the dance group's performances and those of similar ensembles in the Zapotec community—even if no one explicitly refers to the page as an archive. Because of its open nature, which encourages users to coproduce and increase its elements, this emerging archive reaches toward the future. That focus on the future is conveyed by its representation in female versions of sacred dances, which are not yet a common practice. Instead, they are the outcome of a bold initiative that required the organization of an exceptional event on the ground and on the air. The archived digital artifacts on this dance call for reform of the village repertoire to ensure greater gender equality.

## HOW USERS COPRODUCE THE ONLINE ARCHIVE OF ZAPOTEC DANCE

So far, I have primarily focused on the way that community or ethnic influencers contribute to create an online archive of Zapotec dance. In this case their narratives on social media are about female identities centered upon cultural knowledge and community life. Their postings and livestreams seek to capture the attention of a "networked publics" (boyd 2010). Individual users create Facebook pages and successively include different layers of "friends," such as members of their nuclear family and acquaintances from various phases of their life. Here "friendships" can range from very intimate and lifelong to casual and temporary, and can even include people who remain strangers. The success of the postings and livestreams depends on the chord they strike with users who perform their social relations online, where success is measured by the number of visits and likes registered on the page (cf. Kummels and Cánepa 2016, 9). In the case of high numbers, a post is considered successful and therefore "archivable" since users comment on it, copy it, link to it, and share it. By including them in other files, certain digital artifacts and content are disseminated, thus ensuring their durability.

Given the interactivity of the emerging archive, it is now necessary to examine the ways in which users utilize and shape it. We need to consider that when users "read" and interact with its content they go beyond the original intention of the person who recorded and uploaded the digital items. For example, details of the images of a happening, such as the people who were present and the nature of their expressions and interactions, are often perceived as indicating the quality of the social relations depicted and are interpreted as such. What motivates viewers to visit a social media page, then comment and alter digital artifacts that convey Zapotec dances?

When accompanying users in their daily life, I learned that many visits to the online archive of Zapotec dance are connected to a mundane interest in fiestas and kermesses. When they look up the postings of their Facebooks "friends," users want to find out when and where a celebration will take place, so that they can also attend. This allows them to spend their weekend with friends and acquaintances, either meeting them and having fun on-site or communicating online. Because they are hosted frequently, it is possible to visit a kermés, food sale, or dance evening celebrated by people with ties to Yalálag or to neighboring villages of the Oaxacan Sierra Norte on any given weekend in Los Angeles. When community influencers livestream the dance performance of a kermés, their online community is immediately notified through Facebook. In addition, people who engage in the festivities on a collective basis, like barrio committees, brass bands, and dance groups, seek to transmit them live. Furthermore, DJs, photographers, videographers, and internet radio hosts who are (semi)professionally involved in celebrations operate company pages on Facebook. As mentioned in the introduction, frequently Zapotec dances are recorded so that their images can be used to announce, promote, and document a kermés that a committee is organizing as a fundraiser. In Yalálag, earnings are mainly invested in refurbishing and expanding community buildings such as those attached to a barrio church. The dances are almost always transmitted as highlights of the celebration to attract more people and sponsors.

Additionally, some people have a more specialized interest, such as the parents of the dancers, as well as those who teach dances and those who practice them. Therefore, these users regularly search among the hundreds of recordings uploaded to YouTube, such as those of La Danza de los Cuerudos (documented on YouTube since 2008). As I was able to observe, people study the dances, use them as background music during rehearsals, or look for a video clip of their own performance to assess the quality of the dance steps and choreography they executed. Furthermore, these recordings are also sought for entertainment. For example, after a kermés takes place, Pam's family would search for recent recordings on YouTube. The household members would watch the dances that were recorded on their television and would act as judges, commenting as to whether performers executed the dance well or had been adequately trained by their teacher. Spectators enjoy detecting deviations from established dance conventions, such as deliberate transgressions and (harmless) accidents. Issues regarding the origin and intellectual property of a dance are also discussed at home, as well as the legitimacy of its appropriation. Images that are the subject of intense online criticism are sometimes removed from YouTube. Emotional critiques on Facebook and YouTube, however, are often viewed positively by Yalaltecs as a form of "being communicative" and "getting into a bigger conversation" or "doing affects," and therefore spur their engagement in an affective public sphere (cf. Lange 2014). First-generation migrants consider competition, a predilection for debating and splitting in fractions typical of Yalaltec lifeways, even in its transnational outreach.

The accessibility of public comments on Facebook and YouTube encourages user contributions. Furthermore, users upload their own recordings of particular dance performances and usually give them captions according to categories already disseminated on YouTube. Consequently, they develop archival skills that allow them to become involved in Zapotec epistemology.

Most users of these "mini-archives" found on Facebook and YouTube have a common interest in the Yalaltec community and Zapotec cultural knowledge. At the same time, both the collectivity and the ways of storing and transmitting knowledge are changing rapidly as a result of migration and reconfigurations in the hometown, its satellite community in Los Angeles, and the relation between both settlements. The online dance interventions shape these transitions, for example, the emergence since 2008 of dance troupes like Mis Raíces and Nueva Generación Krus Yonn, which manage their own pages and publish their activities that seek to attract and integrate young people born in the United States. The kermesses have been reoriented in such a way that they no longer mainly focus on collecting funds for the hometown; now they also collect donations for youth brass bands and people in need in Los Angeles. The posts motivate a wider group of users to attend kermesses: in Lisvelia's case, the circle of friends and acquaintances she has built since 2009 on her Facebook page. In the same manner, the new internet radio stations attract an even more diverse and inclusive crowd to the kermesses. Their demographic composition goes beyond that of a single Mexican village of origin such as Yalálag and is reconfigured by a public interconnected through "mini-archives." Thus, people from several Oaxacan villages, their descendants, and their contacts in the multicultural city of Los Angeles are included. At the same time, however, the kermés upholds the "brand" of the original hometown by enhancing its Zapotec cultural heritage as a resource (see the next chapter).

Moreover, people in the academic world (myself included) are interested in this online archive of Zapotec dance for research purposes. The second-generation descendants of the communities in question have added their own narratives and advanced their careers in anthropology, sociology, history, and political science, among other disciplines, since the 1990s. They have published dissertations, chapters, and volumes that reveal the collective agency of the Zapotec migrant communities in Los Angeles, including their own engagement in La Danza de las Negritas (Nicolas 2021). Therefore, online texts, sounds, and images of Zapotec dances and live music are in part produced and consulted by an academic circle, which also contributes to their definition as part of a public archive.

## TURNING POINTS TOWARD REGENDERING INDIGENEITY

In line with other researchers, I propose that individuals interconnected through social media such as Facebook and Instagram are creating archives that are simultaneously visited and co-constituted by large numbers of users (Abidin 2016;

Featherstone 2010; Garde-Hansen 2009; Geismar 2017; Kaun and Stiernstedt 2014; Kaun 2016; Kummels & Cánepa 2021). From different disciplinary angles, these scholars stress that the changes implied in mundane practices are leading toward a new archival regime. They seem to agree on one point: individual users are shaping archives that are novel in the sense that they include many aspects of reality that were excluded under previous archival regimes. The state considered that only items related to its general work were worth archiving (Mbembe 2002, 19). The online archive of Zapotec dance stores cultural manifestations and components of Zapotec epistemology that have been ignored by established institutional archives. Not only has the amount of audiovisual and textual material on Zapotec dance and music increased quantitatively in an unprecedent manner, but memory and knowledge itself have also been radically transformed. The temporality of archives, the spaces they occupy, and their durability are being altered based on the culturally specific uses made of digitalization and its potential for interconnectivity. The experience of temporal copresence is generated not only by the use of digital infrastructure but also by the production of emotionally touching narratives to "get into a bigger conversation." This allows users to connect to a community when sharing events in real time despite geographical distance. The spaces that accommodate an archive have adopted new characteristics: much like the internet itself—which does not have a nucleus and interlinks very diverse technologies, contents, and actors—the online archive of Zapotec dance is polycentric. Users who upload contents to this repository may have divergent interests depending on the conditions they experience in different places and countries. And yet they jointly contribute to and consult the online archive of Zapotec dance, where value is attached not to antiquity and the quality of conservation but to constant updating and immediate access to cultural knowledge. The data in digital format are far more ephemeral: they can be altered, erased, and so on, by any user. At the same time, the ability to copy, forward, and embed these items with a few clicks makes them permanent in other ways—especially popular content that is reproduced in great numbers. What is "archivable," in the sense of what will endure, depends on popularity with users.

These "dynarchives" of Facebook and YouTube do not constitute archives in the "classic" sense; they do not display the same characteristics of state archives that were the object of analysis by scholars like Foucault, Derrida and Mbembe. Nevertheless, I argue that the online archive of Zapotec dances does not arise from a random constellation of diverse users that upload video clips and other digital artifacts and view them online. Instead, the converging political interests of the media actors who engage in this archive shape its constitution. Many of these creatives are self-taught. They play a role as emerging archivists by developing competences through cultural and political activism. In this case, community or ethnic influencers have used their media abilities to inspire other users with regard to (trans) cultural practices and ideas of "the Zapotec way of life" and to renegotiate gender structures in a transnational outreach. Through archival operations, influencers reassemble the epistemology of Zapotec dance—from which novel versions of Indigeneity and what it means "to be Zapotec" arise. Such versions imply presenting, recording, and archiving audiovisual images, sounds, and texts that destabilize criteria for the authenticity of Zapotec dance such as the nexus of dance, masculinity, and sacredness. Internet users also take part in shifting gender relations and Indigeneity when they interactively coproduce digital artifacts on personal Facebook pages and YouTube platforms. The ways of preserving, altering, and disseminating Zapotec dances today depend precisely on the combination of bodily knowledge and digital archival skills, on practices on-site as well as online.

This chapter demonstrated how self-taught specialists engage in digital documenting and storing that advance the deliberate construction of an archive. Community influencers such as Pam and Lisvelia show how much time, work, and attention to detail are devoted to digital artifacts, which include recording, livestreaming, and photographing, as well as organizing, editing, designing, and animating images, writing texts, and publishing with a cell phone (cf. Abidin 2016). While Zapotec dance knowledge depends on many groups of participants, among them second-generation Zapotecs socialized in Los Angeles, this chapter focused on media work invested by mothers. They have developed cutting-edge media activities by expanding their skills and kin work with the creation of family photo albums and documenting online as comuneras about issues with broader political interest, particularly gender and family relations. As archivists they demonstrate how mothering is not restricted to caring within their own family or caring as domestic workers for other families but is an integral part of communal work. Mothers/comuneras redefine Oaxacan Indigeneity for purposes of sustained transborder community building. By storing Zapotec epistemology in a way that creates an alternative to existing public archives, the emerging archive decolonizes knowledge. In a broader sense, it challenges the duality between the self-made archivists and professionals, between local knowledge and science, and between those who assemble and control archives and those who are able only to consult them. The emerging archive responds to current epistemological needs of strengthening and expanding a transnational community across a restrictive border between Mexico and the United States. Dance knowledge online is stored not as a tradition frozen in time but as the malleable, interactive aspiration of a future Zapotec society.

# 4 · THE FIESTA CYCLE AND TRANSNATIONAL DEATH
## Community Life on Internet Radio

In 2016, new broadcasting outlets run by Indigenous migrants began to shape the Los Angeles media environment: internet radio stations such as Radio Cantautor, Radio Gobixha, Radio La Estrella de Oaxaca, Super Antequera Radio HD, and La Voz de Yalálag Los Angeles (in Zapotec Bxhen ke Yarharj) soon enjoyed an audience of up to tens of thousands of followers.[1] I first saw Radio Cantautor in action in July 2017, when I attended a Los Angeles rosary on behalf of the patron saint Santiago Apostle hosted by the Santiago barrio committee, an informal hometown association from Yalálag.[2] Just one year before I had experienced the rosary as an intimate gathering that an onlooker could witness only on-site.[3] This religious ceremony is led by a community *rezadora* (prayer leader) during the nine-day preparations for the main patron saint festivities. When I reached the backyard of the single-family house in South Central shortly before prayer recitation, I noticed that the radio station's approach conveyed a novel, more public edge to this event. The four reporters from Radio Cantautor wearing company T-shirts with the station logo caught my eye first. Adrián Beltrán, head of the radio station, led the religious music program, at times himself playing the organ, then switching to guitar, while commenting live in both Zapotec and Spanish for a transnational audience. A reporter nicknamed La Chaparrita de la Sierra (Shorty from the Sierra) first used her cell phone to livestream the rosary as two rezadoras knelt in front of the altar, which was richly embellished with fresh flowers around the effigy of the patron saint. Walking slowly along the rows of chairs in the backyard, she took care to record each visitor. Afterward she focused on the crowd enjoying an Oaxacan-style meal and then dancing to the live music of the brass band Santiaguito. Suddenly she joined in the dance, while continuing to broadcast with her cell phone.

What made internet radio stations remarkable was this new style of close interaction between broadcasters, guests at the fiesta location itself, and—via digital technology—dispersed listeners at a distance. At an extremely trying time for

Prayer leaders (*rezadoras*) reciting the rosary in front of the altar for Santiago Apostle and livestreaming, South Central, Los Angeles, July 2019.

migrants, Radio Cantautor provided a unique media formula designed for giving the community a major boost. It courageously showcased the lively cultural production of numerous fiestas featuring Oaxacan food, brass bands, DJs, and dance groups. Internet stations relied on a staff of volunteers who, apart from their ordinary work in other economic sectors, became committed presenters and radio producers and continued training as such. These stations specialized in live coverage of weekly events organized by the numerous Zapotec migrant committees to collect funds, mostly for their villages of origin. They invited people to stop by for food, live music, and dance performances at festive or ritual ceremonies tailored to the urban context of Los Angeles: food sales (*ventas de comida*), rosaries (*rosarios*) to honor a patron saint, fairs (*kermesses*), evening dances (*bailes serranos*), Christmas *posadas*, and wakes (*velorios*). Usually held on weekends to accommodate the tight schedules of wage workers in Los Angeles, they often took place in the backyards of members who wanted to support the community by making their private property available.

From then on, whenever I attended migrant meetings and celebrations I would encounter the staff from Radio Cantautor and similar stations. Internet radio reporters would walk by the food stalls at fundraisers, asking volunteers in Zapotec, Spanish, or English about the traditional beverages and dishes they were selling, such as *pozontle*, *aguas frescas* (fruit beverages), *empanadas*, *tamales*, and *tlayudas*. The reporters also gave band members and dance groups a say during short interviews; many were young people who resorted to English as the language they spoke best. In other words, in the middle of a noisy environment, internet

radio workers gave a voice to people from different generations who communicated with one another in three languages. This new broadcasting format portrayed Zapotec lifeways in Los Angeles as diverse, constantly enacted, commented
on, and negotiated through everyday experiences. Illness and death were an integral part of these experiences; therefore internet radio stations also reported on
wakes—the rosary ceremony to commemorate a deceased person before his or
her funeral.

## TRAILBLAZING RADIOS

Radio Cantautor, Radio Gobixha, Radio La Estrella de Oaxaca, Super Antequera
Radio HD, and La Voz de Yalálag attracted a myriad of followers with their live
coverage of events in Los Angeles (and occasionally in the Sierra Norte in Oaxaca) dealing with life in Oaxacalifornia. At the same time, these internet radio stations additionally operated from Facebook pages, where they posted video clips
livestreamed with a cell phone. They published a wide range of mixed-media content on these pages and shared newspaper articles, inspiring quotes, GIFs, and
memes with their listeners; some of the content was selected from the internet
and reposted. Volunteer teamwork for the purpose of community advocacy relied
on a hybrid media formula that combined a radio station with a Facebook page
(cf. Bonini 2014; Jiménez 2020). This in turn prompted its public to engage in
coproducing radio in a novel way. Listeners and users triggered innovations: they
were now able to codetermine radio station information by sending messages,
likes, and emojis. In the course of their interventions, they linked their personal
Facebook profiles to the station page, at times interacting closely with the broadcasters, while they themselves became subjects featured on these pages. Long-
standing activist radio stations like Enfoque Latino, which had hitherto broadcast
from a soundproof studio and did not operate a Facebook page, gradually picked
up on these innovative elements.[4]

   My interlocutors brought to my attention how internet radio stations helped to
build community. Years ago, members of Yalaltec associations in Los Angeles
would advertise their fundraisers and invite guests through the conventional
media of the time: word of mouth, phone calls, leaflets, and posters in the many
Oaxaca shops on Pico Boulevard and the surrounding area. Once the committees
began to promote their events on their collective Facebook profiles, publishing
both traditional poster images and modern video clips, they were tapping into a
new audience through the grid of interconnected Facebook pages. Combining
digital images, sound, and text, they advertised delicious Oaxacan food, live Zapotec music, and dance—all for a good cause, which became a matter of survival
given the Trump administration's aggressive anti-immigrant policy. Donations
were now being collected to support Los Angeles youth bandas and members of
migrant communities who had run into difficulties due to illness, unemployment,
deportation, or the death of a relative. With their regular live coverage, internet

radio stations promoted these fundraisers, which attracted larger crowds to the venues, even people from outside the Oaxacan community. The remarkable increase of such events, their new alignment, and the dense cycle of fiestas organized by hometown associations was tantamount to a transnational upsurge in mediatized Zapotec cultural life.

My assumption is that communal practices were renewed and the transborder community expanded through self-determined media activities in the realm of internet radio during this period—this hypothesis will now be examined. I further presume that these innovative media activities responded to a severe crisis: the heightened vulnerability of migrants as a result of the Trump administration's piercing anti-immigration rhetoric and policies that curtailed humanitarian protection. Creatives comprised two generations, including a considerable number of unauthorized first-generation migrants, and tailored their media practices to their need for additional social protection and public recognition in the urban space of Los Angeles and the transnational reach. The following questions are at the heart of this chapter: What changes occurred in the self-determined media scene, which new emphases were placed on Zapotec rituals and festive organization, in what manner did the transnational community reconfigure—and how were these developments related? In what way did internet radio reporters realign media practices? How did gender-specific digital strategies contribute to bolstering the migrant community in Los Angeles and to reinforcing cross-border communality during the hostile political environment of the Trump years?

I first introduce the matter of managing death and ritual ceremonies for the deceased in the transnational context. For residents of Yalálag and migrants living in Los Angeles, coping with the illness or death of a relative presents a particular challenge owing to the geographic distance that separates them and the blocked mobility of migrants without legal authorization. At the turn of the millennium, they began to open up a new media space, initially by creating videos and later with live broadcasts, to commemorate the deceased with dignity in the transborder setting. Audiovisual documentation of wakes and funeral services and circulation of videos served as an antidote to migrant immobilization. As a way of coming to terms with this distressing aspect of social life, people in and from Yalálag expanded and realigned communal organization, the logics of reciprocity, and sociability between Mexico and the United States.

In a second step I examine Comitiva Proyecto Panteón as a new type of migrant association created in Los Angeles in 2016. It is remarkable in its organizational aspect since it deviates from the established barrio committees in Los Angeles, which follow the hometown model of neighborhood committees that exist to carry out festivities on behalf of a particular patron saint. Instead, Comitiva lays claim to representing the entire Yalaltec community. Furthermore, it assumed a task decided upon by its members in Los Angeles: the collected donations were to be invested in the renovation and extension of the cemetery in Yalálag, which put matters surrounding death at the top of a transnationally defined agenda. Moreover, these hometown association members became media practitioners themselves to mobilize transnational villagers in Los Angeles and in Yalálag and coordinate cemetery construction work. When a crisis arose with the hometown officials, they forged a strategic alliance with the internet radio station Radio Cantautor. How they sought to remedy this situation by negotiating community across the border in real time will be explored in more detail.

The third step outlines the contributions made by these innovative media outlets to a dense, year-round cycle of Zapotec fiestas intermeshed between Oaxaca and California. The bustling activity invested in fundraisers has enhanced the cultural, economic, and political position of the Oaxacan community in Los Angeles. Hometown committees representing various Sierra Norte villages intensified their cooperation at these weekend events, particularly brass bands and dance groups recruited from second-generation descendants. In addition, they involved their city district neighbors, who mainly came from Guatemala and El Salvador. Internet radio stations reported on these extended communities for a transnational audience. They promoted community concerns by consistently linking food sales, kermesses, and dance evenings of migrant associations in Los Angeles to the respective villages in Mexico. Their media practices also had a marketing dimension since they advertised ethnic cuisine, live music, and dances at the upcoming gatherings. The demand for food, as well as craftwork and clothing native to the Sierra Norte villages, and services like videotaping and live broadcasting constituted an Oaxacan fiesta economy that had captured an urban economic enclave in Los Angeles. Many migrants relied on activities in this niche for their livelihoods and engaged in its media space to increase their political agency.

Finally, I take a closer look at the digital practices used by internet radio stations and the extent to which these new media outlets helped to build the Zapotec community and shape its cultural knowledge. Although so-called ethnic media, particularly Latino media, are firmly established in Los Angeles, self-determined Indigenous mediamakers were cutting edge during this period: they were the first to recast Zapotec culture and politics transnationally by adopting digital technology and social media precisely to these ends (cf. Karim 2015/2016). Internet radio stations worked with minimal funding and a staff of volunteer reporters. On one hand, they imbued their media work with the communal resources and practices they had acquired in the course of their own eventful migrant careers. On the other hand, members of the 1.5 generation with scant knowledge of the Zapotec language, dances, and music gained new insights into their epistemologies through their involvement in the hybrid format of radio combined with Facebook.[5] Motivated by gender-specific experiences and needs, men and women took different paths when it came to shaping Zapotec cultural knowledge with customized digital tools. While on air with the networked publics that their radio station helped create, women reporters tested the possibility of new femininities; their popularity rose when they represented the wider community and acted as role models for their listeners and viewers. In the process, they brought more complex, previously invisible dimensions of their persona, citizenship, and community building into the media space of networked Facebook pages.

## COPING WITH DEATH VIA PARALLEL
## WAKES AND VIDEOTAPING

When Comitiva Proyecto Panteón Yalálag was launched in Los Angeles in 2016, its objective alone was a novelty: this hometown committee collected donations for the modernization of the cemetery in Yalálag, which proved to be controversial in the Mexican hometown. In response, the committee set up a live hookup to negotiate a solution. In this section I first present a review of early communal media strategies dealing with transnational death. They include the recording of innovative wakes by videographers in Los Angeles and their transnational circulation as a wake (velorio) DVD or *xhen ke benwat* in Zapotec, literally "video of a deceased."

In the face of their hampered mobility, Mexican migrants in the United States have long met the challenge of organizing death and ritually celebrating deceased members from afar. To cope, they have constantly forged new paths toward a "good death," that is, commemorating in a dignified manner a person who has passed away, while also drawing strength from the community in its transnational outreach despite adverse circumstances. Strategies for grappling with death have changed in response to altered U.S. policies and to the bonds that migrants have developed to multiple places and homes: for *braceros* and subsequent migrants settling in the United States, postmortem repatriation—returning the deceased to the village of origin as their primary home—was at first the preferred arrangement (Félix 2018, 101–135). Many hometown associations in the United States came into existence to raise the considerable funds required to transport a corpse to the family grave in their Mexican natal village (Lopez 2015, 171–173). But after starting their own families, first-generation migrants increasingly consider their bonds to multiple places: to the hometown, where their ancestors and the family grave are located, and to their place of residence in the United States, where their children are being raised. This is where they prefer to be buried since it is where they will be commemorated by their descendants (cf. Bada 2014, 76). The aggravated U.S. border regime prevents unauthorized migrants from accompanying family members in Mexico when they are seriously ill or on their deathbed.[6] Were they to return to their home village, they would run the risk of being stranded in Mexico if their next border crossing were to fail; thus, they would be involuntarily cut off from their families and workplace in the United States. For many, this dilemma is a heavy psychological strain (cf. Garcini et al. 2020). On the other hand, their income in the United States at least allows them to financially support relatives in Mexico who are ill or in need of care. To ease the emotional burden, transnational family members engage in long-distance communication to endure the hardship of a dying relative (cf. Bravo 2017).

A parallel wake in Pico Union, Los Angeles, for Enriqueta, who passed away in Yalálag, April 2016.

Since the turn of the millennium, the transnational Yalálag community has devised parallel wakes that are covered by self-determined media both in Yalálag and in Los Angeles, therefore involving mourners on both sides of the border.[7] Traditionally wakes in Yalálag are large events with scores of guests attesting to the deceased's rich relationships, generosity, and social status (De la Fuente [1949] 1977, 203–208).[8] One or more heads of cattle may be required to prepare a series of meals, including the traditional beef broth. The guests, for their part, are highly interested in attending since according to the ethics of reciprocity their support must be repaid at some point in the future. The monetary donations that guests deposit in a wooden box on an altar help to defray expenses. A large sum is interpreted as a sign of a successful wake. Since the 1990s it has been customary to videotape wakes. Similar to the early *tequio* videos, wake videos capture attendance at the ceremony as a form of keeping track of reciprocal assistance beyond the border. Wake videos are often financed and commissioned by relatives in the United States. Currently family members livestream wakes using their cell phones to document those who participated. By posting their video clips on social media they extend the mourning community in real time into a transnational media space.

Parallel wakes adapted to urban life have become the occasions where large numbers of Yalálag migrants most often meet in Los Angeles. Migrants from other communities describe parallel wakes as being unique to the Yalálag transnational community because of their spectacular size, frequency, and visibility on social media. Yalaltecs in Los Angeles make the point that "we are closely united in death." Although migrants often work two jobs, they take great pains at organizing the velorios held after work in the spacious backyards of private homes or at funeral homes; it is not unusual for up to three hundred guests to attend. Guests take part in an hourlong rosary for the deceased that takes place in front of an altar. In response to the high demand, three women have established themselves as rezadoras (prayer leaders) and consequently as religious experts, including Pam, my host. Guests are then served a simple but delicious meal of coffee, *champurrado* (a thick chocolate-based beverage), and tamales, prepared throughout the day with the help of communal volunteers. One reason for organizing a wake in Los Angeles is to raise funds to contribute toward hosting an even larger wake in Yalálag. Guests publicly testify to their *apoyo* (support) by attending the wake and depositing a donation in the box on the altar. Anyone present at a Yalaltec wake in Los Angeles can expect similar assistance when hosting a large celebration, such as a quinceañera (see chapter 6). Failing to attend a wake means running the risk that people "will hold a grudge against you," as a second-generation Yalalteco told me when explaining the pressure to assist. As a way of participating from afar, relatives now create digital death notices on social media using a cell phone photo of the deceased (often portrayed casually and cheerfully) and simply adding the name and crying face emoji. People who publish short messages or even just send an emoji from a distance communicate in a widely accepted way that they join in the mourning, offer their support, and identify with the transborder community (cf. Gutiérrez Nájera and Alonso Ortiz 2019, 95–96).

But in the case of transnational Yalálag, mediatized ceremonies do more than ease the pain of mourning: they help overcome the heightened vulnerability and emotional turmoil that occurs when a loved one dies and U.S. policies prevent unauthorized migrants from returning to Mexico. As an antidote, they engage in an alternative way of caring for a dying relative. An example is Amalia, a woman from Yalálag who lives in Los Angeles, whose eighty-four-year-old father passed away in Yalálag in February 2018. For many years her father lived in Los Angeles, but on becoming gravely ill he returned to Yalálag. Since she is undocumented, she saw no possibility of accompanying him and remained with her three children in Los Angeles. By coincidence, I was in Yalálag during his burial and worried about the pain she must have suffered because of her inability to attend to her father on-site. But when I returned to Los Angeles, she greeted me with a smile of satisfaction and immediately informed me, "We buried him with sheer *jarabe* dancing"—a key element of a "good death."[9] She had organized a parallel wake in Los Angeles and contributed to the Yalálag wake by financing the velorio DVD, which documented all the jarabe dancing. The DVD allowed her to vicariously experience the "cheerful" wake in Yalálag. She was also able to use it to show people like me how it had turned out: an event worthy of her father thanks to the financial support she provided as a migrant. Moreover, wake DVDs are a genre that not only shape the future memory of a particular death ceremony but also chronicle the wider history of mutual support across the U.S.-Mexican border.

At this point we can draw the initial conclusion that inhabitants of Yalálag and Los Angeles for decades have devised their own creative and communal ways of grappling with a family death and of celebrating this ritual collectively despite their impeded mobility in the transnational context. The mediatization of wakes hosted on both sides of the international border by circulating their sound and images has thus become a binder of transborder communality. In the next section, current digital innovations in the face of death and immobility, such as live transmissions, interactive comments, and audiovisual documentation, take center stage. These innovations allow practitioners and viewers to experience, identify with, and reconfigure community from a distance.

## THE "GRAVEYARDERS" CRISIS COMMUNICATION BETWEEN PICO UNION AND YALÁLAG

Exploring the working methods and media practices of Comitiva Proyecto Panteón Yalálag Los Ángeles is key to discerning the transborder media space it unfurled. This hometown association was set up in 2016 with the aim of renovating and extending the cemetery in Yalálag. It is not a coincidence that a versatile media expert took the initiative: Amado, a musician from Yalálag who has lived in Los Angeles for almost forty years. Hosting and organizing the musical programs for Yalálag and other migrant community events has been his main occupation for decades. In much demand as DJ Qdrin, he is active full-time in the Oaxacan fiesta economy of Los Angeles (see the next section). He recruited the first Comitiva members by promoting the idea on his popular Facebook business page, mobilizing "friends" for the unusual cemetery project in Yalálag. News had spread that older graves—and thus those of their ancestors—were to be made available for new burials due to overcrowding in the graveyard. This imminent danger struck a chord with a group of adults between the ages of thirty and sixty, most of whom had immigrated to Los Angeles in the 1990s.

Although Los Angeles migrant committees cooperate closely with the usos y costumbres governance of the hometown, their relationship has never been free of tension. The hometown officials are keen to limit the political influence that migrants might exert on their village of origin as a result of their financial strength. This translates to curtailing the membership rights of those who emigrated. Only people who reside in Yalálag on-site and have been registered as such are fully recognized as community members or citizens (*ciudadanos/as*). The community service that migrants perform on committees in faraway Los Angeles is considered "voluntary" and not recognized as genuine service in a political office or cargo.[10] Nonetheless, committees have been developed in Los Angeles in a way similar to

Meeting of the Graveyarders, a Yalálag migrant association, in a Pico Union backyard, Los Angeles, April 2016.

those in the hometown. They usually consist of five members: a president (*president/a*), a treasurer (*tesorero/a*), a secretary (*secretario/a*), and two spokespersons (*vocales*), all of whom are elected annually.[11] These volunteers require an official appointment by the authorities in Yalálag to qualify for collecting donations on behalf of their home village. Over the years, a division of labor has been agreed upon, whereby the migrant committee in Los Angeles provides funding and its partner committee in Yalálag organizes construction in the Mexican hometown on the basis of tequio communal labor.

Comitiva Proyecto Panteón Yalálag Los Ángeles, however, established new priorities for the transnational community. It made a unilateral decision to modernize and extend the Yalálag cemetery and negotiated directly with the Yalálag municipal president. As mentioned earlier, traditional migrant associations usually raise funds to remodel churches and chapels in the home village.[12] These "classic" building projects are linked to increased devotion to the patron saint, who now serves as a religious symbol and bond of unity between community members scattered across two countries as a result of displacement and migration.

At one of the first meetings of the Panteoneros, or Graveyarders, as they jokingly call themselves, in April 2016, I became familiar with the media strategies its members use to negotiate their cross-border project proposal: First, they install their own infrastructure for transnational communication on the ground. When I arrived at the spacious backyard in Pico Union, members were setting up patio chairs, while president Amado was arranging a tripod screen in front of the projector resting on a picnic table. While others were covering the backyard area with a huge tarp, Amado joked, "Here we are, spreading a canvas roof over the plaza right in front of the municipal palace." He alluded to how, through simple means, the backyard was being transformed into the U.S. equivalent of the main political building in Yalálag—and into a migrant community center. At the same time, the backyard is also firmly anchored in concerns relating to the Los Angeles neighborhood. Irma, who for the past twenty years has worked as a housekeeper in Los Angeles, had invested in buying a home. Service to the community is close to her heart and prompted her to make her backyard available on weekends for the Graveyarders. There she also hosts district gatherings that bring together urban residents from different countries, such as El Salvador and Guatemala. At the request of Gil Cedillo, the Los Angeles city council member in charge of Pico Union, hot-button social issues such as domestic violence, drug-related crime, public safety, and the "Keep It Clean Campaign" against street litter are discussed in her backyard.

Second, the Graveyarders are media-savvy when it comes to convincing others to become involved in a common cause. The sixty-year-old woman seated next to me shows me one of her selfie videos as an illustration of what motivates her to engage in the renovation of the hometown cemetery. In it she appeals to her Facebook followers by telling them that "it is a duty to commemorate the ancestors in the Yalálag cemetery and keep their graves in order." Later during our conversation, I found out that my interlocutor had reserved a space for herself at the prestigious Holy Cross Park Cemetery in Lynnwood.[13] (In fact, most Comitiva members have already invested in a grave in Los Angeles.) She complained about the hometown practice of using older graves after several decades for new burials, something customary in many of the Sierra Norte villages up to now. Migrants in favor of the Yalaltec graveyard project, however, are eager to export U.S. cemetery culture, which they see as modern and desirable, to their home village. The funds they collect are earmarked for building a wall around the graveyard and equipping it with sanitary facilities.

Third, the meeting is organized in accordance with the Yalaltec tradition of detailed public accounting for funds while using up-to-date technology to document and disseminate this information: President Amado reads the names of each individual, couple, or family that contributed between ten and a hundred dollars for the construction of three graveyard walls; each wall requires fifty tons of cement. Three men check two lists at the board table while the two spokeswomen transmit the proceedings with their cell phones. This method of bookkeeping for donations and services rendered remediatizes the Zapotec tradition of handwritten entries in gozona books (De la Fuente [1949] 1977, 147; Cook 2014, 100–101). There is genuine delight at the announcement that a total of $9,100 has been raised.

Finally, the climax of the meeting consists of a long-distance call between president Amado and Yalálag municipal president Constantino Mesinas, at precisely noon. For about ten minutes, Constantino delivers an address in Zapotec to the assembly in Los Angeles, which is amplified by the sound system. He then explains the necessary expenditure and the construction plan in Spanish. Completing the last wall by the beginning of November calls for an additional fifty tons of cement. The decision about whether to pay for masons or call on men in Yalálag to perform tequio has yet to be resolved. For decades, modernizing the home village has worked with this formula of transnational reciprocity. The municipal president declares emphatically, "Thank you indeed, thank you, paisanos, for all of your village support." Everyone in the backyard is listening and viewing carefully now. During the telephone conference, photos of construction at the Yalálag graveyard are sent from the hometown and projected onto the screen in Los Angeles. The images exchanged between the two countries conjure up a magnificent cemetery and a flourishing village; they are geared toward times to come. Hence, media practices shape the backyard meeting into a key site, where Yalaltec cultural knowledge and mutual support are negotiated and aligned across the border.

Two years later, in March 2018, Comitiva Proyecto Panteón devised its next media strategy when it faced a crisis in its relationship with the hometown. Just before hosting a particularly large dance evening, a *baile serrano*, it received breaking news: the village governance had denied confirmation of Comitiva's appointment. Thus, the organization was not entitled to collect funds in Los Angeles on behalf of the hometown. This jeopardized the entire dance event, which had taken months to prepare and had promised to raise substantial revenues, with a twenty-dollar entrance fee. The mood at Comitiva sank to an all-time low. This internal dispute shows us, on the one hand, the ways in which unevenness and division obstruct community building across the transnational terrain. At the same time, it allows for insights into how the migrant association allied itself with Radio Cantautor as a self-determined media outlet to tackle these obstacles. This internet radio station, along with a station in Yalálag, played a political role in resolving the conflict by setting up a remote hookup. In a live radio broadcast, the Comitiva Proyecto Panteón leadership made an effort to regain trust across the border in real time.

What were the reasons for the crisis? As mentioned above, the relationship between Los Angeles migrant associations and the usos y costumbres governance of the hometown has a history of both cooperation and conflict. In the case of the Yalálag transnational community, a general distrust of migrant associations has prevailed ever since the attempt to implement a Three-for-One program in 2004 failed.[14] When Antonino Acevez took over as the new municipal president in Yalálag in 2018, he did not grant official recognition to Comitiva Proyecto Panteón (whereas he did recognize the other Yalaltec committees in Los Angeles). His policy reversed the wholehearted welcoming of *migradólares* to their natal village and placed their administration on the U.S. side of the border under scrutiny. The failure to elect a new board every year may have subjected Comitiva to additional concerns. On a visit to Yalálag shortly before the crisis, I noticed that many villagers were suddenly skeptical of Comitiva's renovation work. They would rather have seen migrant money invested in a village-owned hospital. After a discussion at the General Assembly in Yalálag in February 2018, a consensus was reached that lack of local medical care was one of the village's biggest issues.[15] "We, the living, are more important [than the dead]," one Yalaltec woman commented, expressing doubts that Comitiva in Los Angeles was investing its vast donations wisely. Despite regular transnational communication people were not fully informed about the needs of *paisanos* and *paisanas* on the other side of the border.

When the Graveyarders learned that the governance in Yalálag had refused to authorize them to collect funds, they called an urgent meeting that turned into a live broadcast on the crisis. Radio Cantautor was to convey Comitiva's position on the dispute for listeners in Yalálag as well as for the audience in Los Angeles. Adrián Beltrán, a Zapotec musician from Zoogocho in the Sierra Juárez, had set up Radio Cantautor on a Facebook account in 2015, which has since been emulated by others (see also chapter 2). For the program about Comitiva, he shared his Facebook page with the La Voz de Yalálag radio station in Yalálag and broadcast live from the Los Angeles backyard. There I witnessed members venting backstage. Their impression was that hometown villagers failed to acknowledge what they as migrants had sacrificed up to now and ignored how much effort went into supporting their home village. Their fundraising activities had even made them neglect their own families in Los Angeles. It was rumored that an influential ex-migrant, of all people, had become their opponent in the hometown and rejected their project, albeit for reasons of intravillage antagonism between the factions of the Communitarian Group (Comunitarios) and PRI party followers (PRIistas).

In a half-hour program, producer Adrián asked the president (Amado), the treasurer (Walter), and a Comitiva member (Sebastián) informed questions in Zapotec and Spanish on the legitimacy and transparency of Los Angeles hometown associations. The use of both languages facilitated a discussion of several layers of the complex issue that concern transborder communal organization and crucial media practices. Listeners in the home village were able to hear the answers and send messages in real time. Adrián first wanted to know how they coordinated their decisions concerning the cemetery with the hometown. He also asked whether the construction involved a new graveyard or renovation of the old one, how tequio work was organized, and how records of the donations were kept. His interview partners replied at length, sometimes in Spanish and other times in Zapotec, repeatedly appealing directly to villagers in Yalálag. They argued that they were financing a project that the former municipal president had approved back in 2016. During the live broadcast, the treasurer explained the significance of this remote cemetery for migrants:

ADRIÁN BELTRÁN: You're telling me that you're engaging in completely new construction work, right?

WALTER: We are indeed. Remember, the decision taken in the village was to consider graves that dated back thirty years for removal—with the possibility of burying just one more relative there. No further burials were to be allowed for these graves. . . . But we would like to avoid the deceased being buried in just any old place or in a mass grave. We then took the decision to expand the cemetery, and based on that we began planning all the construction work that has been carried out there in the meantime. That cost us a great deal of money, and there is something else we want to make very clear: The municipal president supported us enormously in 2016 by contributing sand, gravel, and machinery to our work. And last year, we financed the construction work entirely on our own. Yes, at no time did we ask our paisanos in the village to help us. Neither did we ask local governance for what is commonly known as tequio in the village, a contribution of several days of communal labor, no, we did not! *We* are the ones who are financing everything.

ADRIÁN BELTRÁN: What you are saying right now is very important. But I'd also like to know: Is this all about completely new construction work or are you expanding the existing graveyard?

WALTER: It's an expansion.

ADRIÁN BELTRÁN: Okay, that has now been clarified. . . . Did the community authorize this project?

WALTER: The community did so via its president. Well, the president authorized it.

At this point it was revealed that only the municipal president had given his approval back in 2016; the issue had not been put before the General Assembly in Yalálag. Moreover, construction was not being carried out in the established manner in which migrants pay for the cost of materials and, in return, Yalálag residents perform tequio. Instead, a number of villagers had been hired and were paid for their labor. Due to their "gift" to the hometown, the distant migrants had largely determined what the cemetery would look like in the future—possibly more so than suited the villagers. President Amado, along with the treasurer and another Comitiva member, took advantage of the transmission to explain how the people involved in the project communicate in a transborder media space in which sounds, images, and text messages circulate. In sum, the broadcast gave insights into the respective communities in both countries and enabled transparency regarding the donations and their use. President Amado emphasized that the activities of the Los Angeles migrant community are open to scrutiny on the part of home villagers in the distant Sierra Norte:

ADRIÁN BELTRÁN: That's great! We'll follow up on this as soon as the cemetery project has been completed. Radio La Estrella de Oaxaca will be reporting on it as well. My congratulations to the project. I think this is a fine group of people. And you'll take whoever wants to support you, right?

AMADO: Certainly. Our door is always open. It's open because we are transparent. If you want to come over, if you have any doubts about our group, we keep records of the past three years. You can come and check the books, sit down, and take a look at them. We tried to do everything with clarity. And as he [Walter] said, enormous thanks to the other villages that are with us. We're not just people from Yalálag; this has simply expanded. Other villages are involved as well.

Sebastián pointed out how viewing videos of wakes and burials that are organized in the hometown contributed to Los Angeles migrants' engagement in the hometown cemetery. Although they may have left the hometown decades ago, unauthorized migrants from Yalálag living in Los Angeles remained informed and motivated to participate in the cemetery project, as Sebastián explained in Zapotec: "There's a lot of work to be done to help the people living in our hometown. Not only recently. For several years there have been urgent needs and we keep seeing that in the images from hometown videos (*rhao bxhenha*; literally: faces on video)."[16]

The treasurer gave glimpses of the enjoyment and advantage of building community by meeting both on-site in Los Angeles and in a transborder media space. Events organized by Comitiva are supported and attended not only by migrants from the hometown but also by those from "villages in its surroundings." Walter appealed to this extended community:

As members of Comitiva del Panteón we are infinitely grateful for such good work, and you too, many of our paisanos are connected via the Voz de Yalálag radio station. Many people will find out about this meeting through Facebook.... We'll carry on with this project and achieve the goals we set in 2016 to finish the cemetery renovation.... And it makes us really proud to have this group, it's so valuable. The truth is, really, that I'm very grateful to all my companions and all the villages, to Yalálag and the villages in its surroundings, because they have made cooperation with us possible in terms of food sales, dance events, simply everything.

In the last part of the radio program, Adrián performed some of the songs he had written in Zapotec. Finally, Rita, the Comitiva spokeswoman, promoted the sensorial and emotive aspects of the upcoming dance event as an expression of the bond between the hometowns and their satellites in the United States. She outlined the many dishes on offer, the live music (of Banda San Melchor Betaza and Banda Filarmónica Yalálag), and the opportunity for hours of jarabe dancing:

Good afternoon. We're grateful to all those who support us and even connect us to Yalálag. Hopefully we'll be supported by everyone. We're not just doing it for our own benefit, the cemetery renovation is for the whole village. When someone dies, that's where the body is taken. It's better to be laid to rest in the village you were born in, right? That's what it's for. We hope you'll accompany us on the 31st of this month, Easter Saturday, to Salón Oaxaca to coordinate everything and bring the project to a conclusion. It's a long-term project, it's implicit in our name: a "project" takes more than a year. Its length depends on the work done. And all of us paisanos living here, we have given up our time and our money, we've sometimes even failed to meet our workplace duties. But we are 100 percent committed and give our all. . . . My name is Rita. We'll offer *tlayudas*, hamburgers, *molotes, quesadillas, empanadas,* fruit beverages, beer, *cervezas, margaritas,* practically everything. . . . It's going to be a great party on Easter Saturday. We won't just drink water, right? We'll dance and sweat whatever our bodies can take!

These excerpts from the broadcast allow us to identify a number of efficacious new tasks, power shifts, and extensions that are negotiated in the transborder media space. The hometown association meeting is extended via livestreaming in a transnational scope—people engaged in conversation on the radio program reflect on and discuss these new circumstances. Radio Cantautor assumes a role of cross-border supervision with its investigative reporting on the controversy. As an independent media outlet, it does so from a Los Angeles backyard, teaming up with a Yalalág-based radio station and using media practices that are both grounded locally and simultaneously geared to the transborder context. Adrián has the legitimacy to intervene since he is versed in both the Zapotec language and cultural knowledge, as evidenced in the songs he composes and the finely tuned questions he puts to his program guests. It is clear from Walter's and Rita's words that Comitiva is thinking long term when it comes to maintaining the graves of the ancestors, an issue that for the moment seems to mean more to migrants than it does to local villagers. The hometown graves anchor the first generation's sense of belonging territorially to the distant natal village. Their preservation has the potential to resonate with the second generation as well. Amado, too, put his arguments on the table in order to dispel the generalized suspicion that all Los Angeles committees must deal with: that they are not genuine communal institutions but instead manipulated by a chosen few who avoid transparency where finances, that is, donations, are concerned. Hence Amado insists that anyone is welcome to come and check the Comitiva books. Similar to early tequio videos, internet radio enables viewers to witness and acknowledge cross-border commitment and community citizenship; it proposes a new form of audiovisual control with a transnational outreach.

The program was also published on YouTube and has become part of an archive on the digital platform, which already hosts a substantial number of video clips on Comitiva Proyecto Panteón Yalálag. The evening dance that took place Easter Saturday after the broadcast was a complete success. All four hundred admission tickets (at twenty dollars each) sold out beforehand. Several internet stations (Radio Cantautor, Radio Gobixha, Super Antequera Radio HD, and Enfoque Latino) reported from the dance on-site. In 2018, the renovations at the cemetery were called to a halt due to the disagreements. But in 2019 construction resumed when the newly elected Yalálag officials once again recognized and consequently legitimized Comitiva Proyecto Panteón. The cemetery project was finally completed in January 2022.

# FIESTA CYCLE ONLINE AND THE EXPANSION OF TRANSNATIONAL COMMUNITY

In the period of growing uncertainty after Trump administration executive orders spurred a wave of deportations, transnational Oaxacan villagers harnessed digital technology for several important concerns: cultivating cross-border sociality, circulating cultural knowledge, marketing ethnic products, negotiating internal conflicts, and warding off external attacks. In this situation Sierra Norte migrant associations increasingly organized fundraisers and advertised them using the full scope of digital media from committee Facebook pages to internet radio broadcasts. Oaxacan migrants relied on food fairs, rosaries, kermesses, evening dances, and wakes as an alternative to the political participation and public visibility denied them by the U.S. government. Between 2016 and 2021, new trends surfaced: while in the past festivities had been coordinated to raise funds for home villages in Oaxaca, now donations were also being directed toward the needs of migrant communities in Los Angeles.

For this purpose, migrants and home villagers established mutual support between Zapotec-speaking Sierra Norte hometown associations, uniting migrants from Yalálag, Zoogocho, Yatzachi El Alto, Yatzachi El Bajo, and Yaganiza in Los Angeles.[17] Internet radio programs now addressed this wider *comunidad serrana*, the Sierra community, and its dense cycle of fundraiser fiestas that developed into a social support system. Over and over again, I heard comments such as *"Feis* [Facebook] is an enormous help to us" and "digital technology is great" from members of migrant associations. Given the prospect of raising more revenues, they expressly welcomed additional visitors. Many new faces turned up at the events: in conversations with newcomers, who originally came from various parts of Mexico or from Central America, organizers learned that they had no direct link to their natal village. Facebook postings had incited them to visit the event and try Oaxacan food or to enjoy the cozy atmosphere of a backyard party in the company of people with similar migratory experiences.

Ever since the surge in migration in the 1980s, fundraising fiestas have been organized through fine-tuned transnational cooperation between the Sierra Norte hometowns of Oaxaca and their multiple satellite communities, the largest pockets of which are in Mexico City and Los Angeles. Media activities paved the way for their transnational liaison: the patron saint fiesta cycle in the Oaxacan Sierra Norte and the annual cycle of fundraisers in Los Angeles were dovetailed and their temporalities synchronized. In the Oaxacan Sierra Norte region, the sixty-eight municipalities host an even greater number of annual patron saint fiestas, since barrio communities and *agencias* (settlements within a municipality) dedicate celebrations to their particular saints. These "fiestas of all fiestas" (Martínez Luna 2010, 44) in the Sierra Norte are ritually prepared over a period of weeks and take place over several days, a temporality evoked by a series of ten or more fiesta DVDs that chronicle each celebration in epic length. Particular saints are considered powerful village or neighborhood icons that guarantee spiritual protection and ensure cohesion. A cluster of villages interacts closely at each festivity, with the host village inviting brass bands and dance groups from nearby villages in an effort to forge economic and political alliances. This dense cycle also creates a market system supplied by itinerant traders who travel from one patron saint fiesta to the next, offering a wide range of products and drawing customers from the surrounding area.

In Los Angeles, migrant communities from many Sierra Norte villages have reinvented a similar fiesta/market system to connect with each other in the metropolitan setting as well as with their respective Mexican hometowns. They draw on communal practices matching those of the Sierra Norte. Many migrant communities formed their own brass bands and dance groups as part of festive practices in urban neighborhoods and invite each other to their fundraisers. Today, these weekend events take place year-round in backyards or banquet halls. This cycle has been reconfigured in decisive ways. Food sales abound, a format invented in the Californian metropolis. They blend elements of a village celebration with a fundraiser, offering Oaxacan fast food, such as *tlayudas* (dubbed "the Oaxacan pizza"), and American hamburgers. Food sales are extremely popular since they provide a space and a time for Zapotec culture despite the excessive working hours imposed on the migrant labor force. Food sales offer flexibility, and people can visit whenever they have spare time. The analogy to fast-food restaurants is deliberate: The host community attracts guests by saying that instead of going out to a fast-food restaurant on the weekend, families should enjoy a meal at the food sale and invest in the community. To top it off, dishes are sold at fast-food prices, but prepared by first-rate chefs (i.e., Yalaltec men who work in the kitchens of exclusive steakhouses like the Grill in Los Angeles). Menus bridge the generation gap and take into account local preferences; in addition to traditional delicacies from Oaxaca, hamburgers with French fries are available for the youngsters. Besides beer, Margarita cocktails popular with women are served. Migrants not only reshape their culinary culture at food sales but to some extent also counteract demands to maximize productivity that are enforced on them by the urban restaurant sector. At food sales, the skills they have acquired within the capitalist labor system are reoriented toward the interests of their own communities.

The first *kermés* hosted by the Yojovi migrant community for their patron saint Santo Domingo de Guzmán in a South-Central backyard is an example of the way weekly fundraisers navigate several issues at once, ranging from political participation to marketing strategies. Yojovi migrants have long supported their Sierra Norte hometown with financial donations. But on Sunday, August 13, 2017, they hosted a kermés as a fundraiser for the first time, organizing it along the more inclusive lines of "clustering," that is, intensifying patterns of mutual support between migrant communities. Popular dance troupes, including Familia Zapoteca, and the brass bands Descendencia Yalalteca and Banda Juvenil Solaga USA offered their support. Their appearances drew crowds from the Yalálag and San Andrés Solaga migrant communities that managed these groups; both young and old flocked to the kermés. Many young people, who simply call them "parties" in English, came as a token of their friendship with the second-generation musicians of Banda Juvenil Solaga USA. South Central neighbors who hail from Central America were also eager to attend. Donations and proceeds from beverage sales were destined for Mayra, a young girl from the Yojovi community who was seriously ill with cancer. Numerous mediamakers promoted the kermés live throughout the event, so that people who logged into their Facebook page were motivated to attend. Since I was there from morning until late in the evening, I witnessed how livestream advertising galvanized the influx of visitors. A woman reporter from Radio Cantautor and a member of the Yojovi migrant association continuously posted highlights from the cultural program and interviewed visitors. To publicize the fundraiser's international character, they even taped my comments as a foreigner present at the fiesta.

The Yojovi festivity shows how migrant kermesses are frequently staged around the monoethnic cultural "village brand" of the hometown, that is, around certain dishes, a traditional costume, and/or a trademark dance performance. The Yojovi carnivalesque dance *recua con payaso* (pack animal train with clown) is one example of a trademark or signature dance. In Los Angeles this dance also parodied men and women, both young and old, and their fiesta habits, such as drinking liquor while dancing. But it also boasted a Donald Trump character, sporting the world-famous sneering face. As he walked around and distributed sweets, some attendees could not pass up the golden opportunity to give him a piece of their mind: "So you don't like us wetbacks? Beat the shit out of him!" At the same time, the event was enriched by cultural contributions typical of other villages. More recently, their live music and cultural repertoire have acted as a magnet for the second generation, who feel that they belong to a wider community of Oaxacalifornians (see chapter 6). They grew up in Los Angeles during a period when Oaxacan Indigeneity was emerging and increasingly inspiring a sense of pride. By practicing music and dance, cultural knowledge they often develop in Los Angeles in Oaxacan dance groups that no longer refer to a particular hometown (such as those of *folklórico*), they themselves have contributed substantially to this Indigenous revival.

Mediamakers at kermesses, food sales, and evening dance events also open up a media space for marketing: at each fundraiser they promote the ethnic cuisine that forms part of the Oaxacan fiesta economy in Los Angeles. DJ Qdrin, who anchored the Yojovi kermés, broadcast live on internet radio Super Antequera and recommended migrant-owned shops in the break between banda performances. He interviewed Alfonso "Poncho" Martínez, a Zapotec musician and owner of a new backyard restaurant called Poncho's Tlayudas. No one could have guessed that Poncho's outdoor kitchen would become one of the trendiest culinary addresses in Los Angeles in just a few months.[18] The promotional interview touched on the current political situation, the vulnerability attached to being ille-galized, and the Oaxacan fiesta culture as a source of pride:

DJ QDRIN: We are not easily bullied, we the Oaxacan race, and [in an ironic tone] even though we are now at the center of a certain political controversy here, no one bul-lies us. . . .

PONCHO: What we have, our communities, we have in our hearts. Just imagine, when we came here twenty years ago, we crossed the border barefoot. When we arrived, the comment on the shoes we had brought along was: "Throw them away. . . ." We began to work, working and working, making music, cooking food; after all we would never deny our culture. And here we are now, speaking Zapotec, enjoying our food, our music. That's a lot like—or at least a bit like—Oaxaca in Los Angeles, California.

Internet radio production is therefore ingrained in the fabric of market activi-ties carried out by Oaxacan migrant communities in Los Angeles, which center on the norms and values of communal life and its attendant needs. Requirements for the many kermesses and food sales organized by hometown associations are largely covered by what some specialists have termed an "immigrant" or "ethnic economic enclave" (Wilson and Portes 1980). Scholarship on the enclave concept emphasizes the benefits of spatial concentration and the retention of languages and customs for economic performance (as opposed to assimilation into the U.S. labor market). Often it fails to consider the political dimension of reciprocity, which is at the heart of economic networking, and simply ascribes characteristics such as mutual support to ethnicity (for a critique, see Valdez 2011). Instead, the Oaxacan economic sector in Los Angeles may be thought of as emerging from a diversity of entrepreneurs—from small shopkeepers to owners of a chain of stores—who do not rely exclusively on coethnic social networks. Their ethics of reciprocity attract a wider group of like-minded people. This sector encom-passes over a hundred businesses including *supermercados*, restaurants, butcheries, bakeries, ice cream parlors, florists, music schools, and parcel service shops. They supply, among other things, the necessary ingredients for the preparation of local village dishes served at migrant community events, which is why I refer to this business sector as the Oaxacan fiesta economy in Los Angeles. However, the fiesta economy offers more than just a range of products and a job market for Indige-nous migrants from Oaxaca. More important is the space of belonging it provides, which does not wholeheartedly embrace capitalism but instead carves out room for ideas and practices around the sense of Comunalidad that is imported from the Sierra Norte. YinEt, an internet radio station based in the Sierra, puts it this way: "Consume what your community produces and support what your people make." In the Sierra Norte, economic production is still closely linked—ideally at least—to agriculture and the desire of its inhabitants to continue growing their own crops, such as organic maize, and to a logic of reciprocity between nature and people, which together form a single unit.

Photographers, videographers, DJs, and banda musicians are also primarily active in this niche economy. Audiovisual documentation and live broadcasting of these festivities have become more professional, notably for the purpose of fundraising. Similar to shop owners and brass band musicians, videographers might support a community social event by offering their services free of charge, or they might be asked to do so by hometown associations. Self-employed Oaxacan migrants engage in the production of food and rental of party equipment such as tables and chairs, flower arrangements, handmade pottery and baskets, and village costumes. Although the fiesta economy is embedded within the capitalist market, its elements of reciprocity link these donations to cultural recognition, political leverage, and public recognition. On the whole, the patron saint market system of the Oaxacan Sierra Norte has been aligned to the urban setting of Los Angeles in a unique form. The creation of independent radio stations to advertise businesses in the Oaxacan community has a long tradition in Los Angeles. At the beginning of the millennium, the successful Oaxacan businessmen Zeferino García and Arturo Aguilar used their own radio station to promote their products and local brass bands that specialized in music from the Sierra Norte region and the Central Valley. Entrepreneurs organized in the Asociación Oaxaqueña de Negocios (AON) and the Indigenous-migrant umbrella organizations Frente Indígena de Organizaciones Binacionales (FIOB) and Organización Regional de Oaxaca (ORO) are the driving force behind the initiative to officially convert the neighborhood of Pico Boulevard between Crenshaw Boulevard and South Westmoreland Avenue into a city landmark called Oaxacatown.

In the course of migration, however, the festive events in both countries have been combined in a new transnational fiesta calendar and converted by self-determined media initiatives into an experience palpable from afar. Fundraisers in Los Angeles were dovetailed with the patron saint fiestas in the Sierra Norte and their time regimes combined, even though this was no easy task. Synchronization meant taking into account that celebrations in the Sierra Norte still align with the sacred time of the Mesoamerican ancestors, while adapting them to various mundane time regimes, such as the labor hours and holiday seasons of the United States. The integration of an increasing number of festivities on both sides of the international border generated a kind of "time-space expansion," similar to the way mobile phone use expanded exchange relations in Uganda, as Richard Vokes (2016) suggests. In our case Los Angeles food sales, dance evenings, kermesses, and Mexican hometown celebrations have been integrated into a joint fiesta calendar by arranging them according to slightly staggered dates. By adapting these events to logistic demands and cosmological requirements across borders, festive activities with their modes of reciprocity are expanded. This allows the committees and officials in charge of the celebrations to coordinate transnationally and transfer donations collected in Los Angeles to the hometowns in Oaxaca; meanwhile, transnational villagers can follow these events on-site or from afar, as they unfold. Cosmological beliefs embed the festivities in a calendar that has long

TABLE 4.1    Transnational fiesta calendar

| A few months before the patron saint fiesta | | | On the traditional saint's day | One week later |
|---|---|---|---|---|
| Food sale in Los Angeles | Dance event in Los Angeles | Food sale in Los Angeles | Patron saint fiesta in Yalálag | Kermés in Los Angeles |

combined Mesoamerican with Christian liturgical concepts, a traditional time regime now confronted with the rhythm of work and life in the United States. Hence fundraisers in Los Angeles and patron saint fiestas in Yalálag were organized as shown in table 4.1.

The schedule takes into account the geographic dispersion caused by international migration and its multiple temporalities. It reconfigures the two basic principles of communal living: communal work and mutual aid. The transnational division of labor in this context envisages funding from afar by those who live in Los Angeles, while inhabitants of the Sierra Norte village organize and carry out the work. All these social events also rest on digital communication to negotiate and sensorily experience coordination, reciprocity, and complementarity. The following section explores how media actors influence this arrangement and steer the transnational community in new directions.

## GENDERED ISSUES HIT THE AIRWAVES

From the outset the internet radio stations Radio Cantautor, Radio Gobixha, Radio La Estrella de Oaxaca, Super Antequera Radio HD, and La Voz de Yalálag Los Angeles provided new impulses for transborder community life. Zapotec men and women voluntarily invested their spare time in radiomaking after their work in restaurants, landscaping, hairdressing, or housecleaning. Their motivations diverged: some had a great deal of experience with volunteering and had helped establish Indigenous migrant organizations, while others were driven to produce radio by their ambitions in the music business. As women became involved as reporters, some also created their own stations and contributed their perspectives to radio broadcasting. Gradually—and discreetly at first—they began to address the daily problems that women face at work as well as issues dealing with education and raising children. They brought gendered issues to the fore by relating to their own experiences as mothers who belong to different migration generations and have diverse legal statuses, thereby positioning themselves as subjects at the intersection of race, class, work, and gender.

Such situated radiomaking meant that reporters focused on topics from different angles and contributed to a diversified program: Apart from fundraisers, internet radio stations reported live from major Los Angeles spectacles. I came across staff from Radio Cantautor at the Calenda, a parade leading up to the Guelaguetza

The Radio Cantautor Internet radio team at El Mercadito, Los Angeles, July 2019.

and organized by numerous hometown associations and folklórico dance groups. It also broadcast from the Central Los Angeles Library, where the Indigenous Literature Conference was taking place. At this event, which was hosted by the NGO CIELO, authors from Mexico, the United States, and Canada had been invited to read from texts they had written in their native languages. Furthermore, Radio Cantautor also informed its audience about current issues associated with U.S. migration policies. Against the backdrop of increasing raids and deportations, the station held a program with Lizbeth Mateo, who provided in-depth legal advice live in the studio in response to listeners' questions. In contrast, Radio Gobixha, headed by Maricela Morales, focused on second-generation Zapotec bandas, and the station broadcast from fundraisers to buy new instruments for young musicians in Los Angeles. Women reporters turned the spotlight on education, family life, and their rights as community members, as comuneras, overcoming the private-public divide. They created music radio programs to interest children in the Zapotec language and culture. In this process they rose to prominence as anchorwomen of radio transmissions. Throughout the history of Indigenous media, women have gradually carved out a space of their own, yet they are still underrepresented (Vásquez García 2018, 169–208).

I followed the work of Adrián, Leti, Verónica, and Maricela and later interviewed them to learn how they used digital technology and social media to shape communal Zapotec practices in the Los Angeles urban context. After several attempts, an extremely busy Adrián granted me an interview in his studio / living room in Koreatown, which to my surprise he arranged as a live broadcast. First, he asked me questions, and in the second half of the program it was my turn. My ethnographic discussion provided fruitful radio content for Adrián. Once the prerogative of the more affluent, the latest media technology has become increasingly accessible and is now used extensively because of its potential for empowerment. As an anthropologist, I was "simultaneously being observed and documented by [my] interlocutors on their phones, cameras, social media streams" (Gill 2019). For the Radio Cantautor listeners, I was first required to answer Adrián's questions about anthropology and its colonial past and to talk about my German-Cuban family background and my current research interests.

In return, Adrián told me about his origins in San Bartolomé Zoogocho and that in 1992 at the age of twenty-two he migrated to work as a musician in New York, New Jersey, and Connecticut.[19] In the midst of a music scene dominated by Salsa and Bachata, he and his band successfully offered Mexican regional melodies. In 2008, he moved to Los Angeles, attracted by its large Zapotec community. The commercial structure of established radio stations and recording studios that expected artists like him to first invest a substantial sum in their careers made him think about starting his own radio station. He began experimenting with the composition of Zapotec songs, envisioning that his many fellow countrymen and -women in Los Angeles were a potential audience. While telling this story, Adrián explained that Radio Cantautor's modus operandi combines social media expertise and Zapotec culture—with all its communal values and norms—in an inventive way:

> We're going on our fourth year now on December 22, we're getting there. We have a large worldwide audience, more than five million visits, WW radio, otraOaxaca .com, TuneIn, and above all Facebook, which is what we're using now. We're getting there, little by little. We're looking for even more support from people. Sometimes people are quiet and that's when you have to convince them to visit our page and click the little follow button. But that's our job, because everyone isn't going to say we "like" something if we don't really like it, right? There has to be something that convinces us to do it. . . . Other pages rely on funny posts and the kind of stuff that has millions of followers, but when you think about it, you wonder: What's that about? What does that teach you? We could choose to be rude, perhaps even funny with hilarious memes that make fun of people and things, because that's part of life too. But that's not our style. Our style is Zapotec, jarabe dancing, and serving the community. Radio Cantautor emerged because there was no medium where you could speak Zapotec without being ashamed, without being afraid. That's why we said, "We need an original formula." I can't do a format with current *corridos* [Mexican ballads] like the big radio stations because they're commercial outlets. Our radio station is not commercial and we're very clear about that. Here we don't go on air just to capture an audience and get rich. Because culture cannot be sold; our culture was given to us as a gift. . . . We really want to be "The Voice of Our Villages,"[20] and we want our audience to say "That radio knows

how to get our message out because they speak Zapotec on the air, they say *padiuxh* [greeting in Zapotec]." And to try to overcome that fear people have when they go out on the street and feel ashamed of speaking Zapotec. We ourselves, most of the presenters, we speak it.

On the one hand, Adrián demonstrates awareness of the affordances imposed by social media such as Facebook. He interprets the number of "likes," followers, and shares as social capital that is conducive to multiplying popularity ratings. Given that this social capital is publicly visible in the number of followers on the Facebook page and that users who navigate through networked pages perceive huge numbers as a hallmark of popularity, the social capital of this grid of online friends/fans lies at the core of internet radio (cf. Bonini 2014). This property of social media begs for consideration, given the pitfalls involved in the accumulation of followers on digital platforms whose data also benefit Facebook or surveillance capitalism (Couldry and Mejias 2019; Zuboff 2019). The corporation tracks and influences personal tastes and lifestyles to harvest user data for financial profit as part of a new or extended capitalism. Facebook encourages sociality for this specific purpose. Even though the mediamakers do not engage in a deep analysis of the structural constraints of data or surveillance capitalism, they manage to subvert them to some extent. Operating within the capitalist system, they place an emphasis on self-determined media practices and content that promote native values of reciprocity. In this way the radiomakers and users negotiate tension with the capitalist economy in which they participate. By investing effort in their own cultural values and orientation they question Facebook's ideological underpinnings and wield communication for decolonial aims.

Consequently, Adrián focuses on cultural content that he considers conducive to Zapotec values and to mobilizing an audience striving to uphold them. He developed his radio content in close contact with his brother Filemón Beltrán, a Zapotec writer and ethnolinguist who lives in Mexico City. Adrián's Zapotec songs are full of humor and clever word play. I saw how popular they were at Comitiva Proyecto Panteón meetings. In one love song, based on a Zapotec-style marriage proposal, he conjures up the Los Angeles job market: "Ask for anything you want, señorita. And I'll even get two jobs."[21] When I asked what made him write songs in Zapotec, he explained,

When I realized that my brother was composing songs, I said, "I'm going to try that too. . . ." I saw that he had created really beautiful songs and thought: How does he manage that? I began to try it myself and that's how "Two Jobs" ["Chop Llin"] came about. I had no idea people were going to like it that much, because sometimes I don't pay that much attention to my own songs. I mean I normally wouldn't have sung it over and over again. But it's the one hit song I have to perform all the time. It happened little by little, seeing the need to contribute, to sing, to see it as important, to say: Here we are in our own language. That's what the effort is for.

We're concerned about our mother tongues, which, unfortunately, overall, are sadly disappearing in the Sierra.

Apart from producer Adrián, as mentioned earlier, several reporters have put their stamp on the unique style developed by Radio Cantautor. Each staff member contributes to the fundraisers by playing music and dancing; often they even help with preparations. Radio Cantautor reporters come from different Sierra Zapotec villages, as their nicknames reveal: La Muñeca Yalalteca (Yalaltec Doll), Nolhe Yadao (Woman from the Hill), and La Princesa Tabeña (Princess from San Juan Tabaá). They provide information and conduct live interviews with committee members in Zapotec, Spanish, and English, so that the festivity concerned is advertised in advance and during the event itself. The methods of internet radio producers and their visions of the future diverge in accordance with their careers, migration experiences, cultural knowledge, and gender perspectives. Several women broadcasters at Radio Cantautor are well-known radio stars; Maricela Morales is one of two who left Radio Cantautor to set up their own internet radio stations along similar lines. These women radiomakers and reporters bring a different approach to radio production.

Leti, in her mid-forties, is one of the reporters who have added their own touch to Radio Cantautor, as exemplified by her program *Pleasant Nights with the Marquise*, in which listeners call in to request romantic ballads. In between playing music, she is La Marquesa, a reporter who addresses the daily problems women face at work and issues that come up when raising children. She offers her audience glimpses into her life as a mother with two grown-up children. As a migrant who now works at a fast-food restaurant and also does volunteer service, she supports her family as well as the Zapotec community. During our conversation she explained how as a member of the 1.5 generation, her life, community work, and recuperation of Zapotec culture intertwined. Born in the Sierra Juárez village of San Francisco Yatee in 1972, Leti, from the age of three, was raised by her grandmother in Oaxaca City while her parents toiled as farmworkers in California. Her grandmother wore a *huipil* (Indigenous women's attire of precolonial origin) and spoke Zapotec but avoided using her mother tongue in the state capital due to discrimination and the belief that speaking Spanish would help her granddaughter have a better life.

Leti sees her drive to volunteer and perform cultural work—including her commitment to Radio Cantautor—as a substitute for the parents she missed while growing up and as a way to repair her fragile relationship with the Zapotec village she never really got to know. When she turned seventeen, she also immigrated to Los Angeles. Unfortunately, because she had married shortly before entering the United States, she did not qualify for amnesty. During her initial years in Los Angeles, the Yalaltec kermesses became a space of belonging that allowed her to become more familiar with the culture of her parents' Sierra Norte hometown:

I remember how we lived in the city [of Oaxaca], we didn't have much contact with the village, we never went there. The city was my world. When I came to this city, to Los Angeles, I ran into a kermés by chance and that's where I saw for the first time la Danza de San José, which people from Yalálag perform, where one dancer holds a baby. I got goose bumps the minute they started singing because the lyrics began with: "Bread, bread, breadmaker." That was the song my grandmother used to sing to me as a lullaby! Because in the villages, grandmothers don't know lullabies. If they want to sing something to their grandchildren, they sing a song from a danza. That's when I realized: Oh, she used to sing me the words to this dance.[22]

As La Marquesa she regularly broadcast from kermesses, acquiring much of her knowledge of Zapotec culture while reporting. To increase her expertise, Leti began taking weekly Zapotec-language classes in the Westlake district of Los Angeles. She pointed out,

What I most appreciate about working at Cantautor is being able to help some community raise funds, money needed to repair a church, or offering my service in some other way. And I made a lot of friends, loads. I try to give my best every day. In the past I wouldn't have accomplished what I have right now. For example, now I read a lot and do research. Because sometimes I want to explain something and I know I'm making mistakes. But I'm aware that there are many people out there who are well versed in Oaxacan cultures and I can't afford to make those mistakes. So now I don't talk about certain things unless I've done the research.

When Leti anchors from a kermés, she does so with great enthusiasm. She boosts the event by presenting a radio show that delights fundraiser attendees as well as her audience on the air. In her presentation she dedicates time to explain and translate what Zapotec lifeways are all about: certain types of food, music, and dance, resources with which the community of listeners identifies. Leti mentioned in the interview that current food fairs have been enriched by the integration of dishes from other villages and cities and ethnic cuisines. The expansion of the traditional menu to include hamburgers has much to do with the second generation. At fundraisers, Leti especially enjoys interviewing children and teenagers from migrant communities who are becoming more involved in performing with bandas and dance troupes:

I think that the generation after us—I'm talking about the ones who are eighteen or twenty years old—they are pretty much in love with Oaxaca. Parents just have to make sure they don't lose this feeling. They have to get them to become even more involved. . . . Not all young people [have that attitude]. There are American kids who have turned away [from Oaxacan culture], but all the same this generation is highly committed. There are folkloric groups, they wear the garb of the Oaxacan regions and they already know a lot about Oaxaca. On the other hand, we—I'm talking about people my age, around forty, fifty, and sixty—we weren't that involved in our traditions. . . . I know lots of people who were into dance groups in Oaxaca City or in their villages. When they arrived in this country, some set up dance groups here too. They're sharing the knowledge they have. And that's a good thing, knowledge has to be shared. If you don't share it, it stops right there.

In contrast, Verónica, nicknamed the Yalaltec Doll, capitalizes on her own controversial position as an "unconventional" woman in the Yalaltec transnational community. This lively reporter in her early forties earns her living by working in a restaurant kitchen and cleaning houses. I happened to catch her career launch with Radio Cantautor in July 2017, when she chatted openly about how some paisanos and paisanas had treated her badly. But she also announced her mission "to help compatriots who own stores, so they can make progress." In the Yalaltec migrant community Verónica's radio debut was met with much disapproval and scorn. She was mocked for every slip of the tongue, the criticism underpinned by inside gossip from the village. Probably no one was as surprised as Verónica when her program's popularity began to rise; however, she confidently moderated in three languages. Eventually she would primarily present in Zapotec, which greatly pleased her audience. I managed to interview a very busy Verónica at a migrant association meeting. Straightaway she told me about the social pressure she had endured from childhood. She began by explaining that she had acquired her nickname Muñeca (Doll) in Yalálag because of the fancy clothes her siblings would send her from the United States:

> Basically, I didn't need anything in my village [Yalálag], because my brothers and sisters used to send me everything. That's why they called me "doll" in the village. When I went to a fiesta, I wore one dress in the morning, another one in the afternoon, and for the dance in the evening I used to change clothes again. I kept changing my clothes because I could afford it, I was very, very slim. And I had to put up with a lot of bullying there, it was all too much. When I came home, I used to cry to my mother and tell her, "Mom, they stepped on my shoes, they poured water all over them, they called me this name." . . . That's how I lived with people bullying me. And even today, shall we say, various fellow countrymen have different nicknames for me, which is fine for them, of course.[23]

In the course of our conversation Verónica described the derogatory comments she still receives from the transnational community. She had married in Los Angeles, but by the time she was pregnant with her second daughter she had divorced. Confronted with insinuations that her ex-husband was not the biological father of her daughter, Verónica shot back with humor. "Now when they say that she [my daughter] looks a lot like him, I reply: 'Really? But he isn't her father. Do they really look alike?' That's how I deal with them." From early on she had worked out the strategy of being direct with others and ready with quick-witted replies to challenge the norms imposed on her as a woman. One reason for her self-confidence is the fact that she has built up financial reserves and invested them in buying her own home in Los Angeles. Her radio breakthrough came when she began presenting in Zapotec:

> I said to myself: This is what I feel inside and I speak Zapotec, so what could be better than that? When I began to talk in Zapotec, that's when a lot of people started tuning in. One way or another they liked it. A lot of people still follow me, but now there are no negative comments. I get a lot of messages on my phone, about [she whistles]—no exaggeration—a hundred messages a day. . . . I try to stay in touch with my listeners and encourage them to say what they think.

She looks at issues in women's everyday lives:

> There are numerous concerns right now. For example, we women don't appreciate ourselves enough. Many women endure abuse because they're afraid to be on their own, they put up with infidelity, heartbreak, just about everything. And there are those who don't appreciate mothers, mothers who work at home. We mothers have a lot on our plate, we do a lot. It's just that we don't get paid for it. We work more than men. Men can't put up with it. . . . If they have the flu, they won't go to work, they'll stay in bed. A woman with the flu, with a temperature, will look after her children, she'll work.

As public figures, role models, and radio stars, women reporters like Leti and Verónica set new standards for performing femininity in networked publics. I experienced how many people would talk to them at migrant association events and were happy to be interviewed. Their approachable manner and the topics they address made it easy for interviewees to express an opinion. These qualities also helped to break the ice with listeners and users who had previously adopted a somewhat passive role in the networked publics.

Maricela is an activist with family roots in the tiny Zapotec village of San Juan Tabaá. After starting a family and teaming up with her husband, a musician from San Andrés Solaga, she reoriented radiomaking. First volunteering at Radio Cantautor as La Chaparrita de la Sierra (Shorty from the Sierra), Maricela branched out on her own in early 2018. In a specially equipped attic room above her hairdresser salon in Koreatown, she launched her own station, Radio Gobixha, with eight volunteers. I later met the staff reporters at many fundraisers, including the Big Food Sale (Gran Venta de Comida) in April 2018, the proceeds of which were earmarked for the purchase of new instruments for young recruits of the Banda Juvenil Solaga USA. This backyard party was packed during the day; the food sale a resounding success. Growing up, Maricela spent most of her time in Oaxaca City before moving to the United States. She belongs to the 1.5 generation and considers herself lucky because despite the prevailing disdain for the Zapotec language and discrimination in Mexican public schools, she learned to speak and write Zapotec as a child. Before engaging in internet radio, she worked as a coordinator at Frente Indígena de Organizaciones Binacionales in Los Angeles. Now she continues her political work by using the new resources of an entertainment medium:

> The idea behind this project [Radio Gobixha] is that it's for everybody. In fact, our slogan is "The Radio That Lights Up Your Day," in other words the sun shines for everyone. I didn't advertise the station as mine, even though I created the project, because I wanted everyone to get involved with it, little by little. Because there's so much culture, so many traditions and customs, there's a lot to teach the community. So that was when we said, "We'll launch it and see how far we get with the communities." Fortunately, right now we've been on the air for a month and ten days, and people are responding very well. At the moment we can't even accept all the invitations we're getting. People ask us to go a lot of their activities, because that's what happens, a lot of folks are watching us in the [Oaxacan] villages and see them through the videoclips we post. They want to see their fellow countrymen and -women, even if it's just for a while. "Ayyy, that's where my daughter is, that's were my son hangs out," and people get excited when they see them. We try to record the brass bands, the musicians, as best we can, because people keep it as a souvenir. Many of those living on their own in the village, without their parents, get excited when they see them playing in a banda. There's a lot of emotions involved with something like our project.[24]

Maricela emphasizes that the cultural production of music in conjunction with self-determined media lends a sense of cross-border belonging, while offering support in the face of political adversity. Broadcasting live banda music helps to preserve fleeting moments of social harmony, making them memorable. These gender-specific paths of digital radio exemplify how air time is designed and media space created for a range of voices and cultural expressions according to age, occupation, migrant generation, and gender.

To summarize, I would like to highlight that internet radio has created new communicative spaces for people involved as producers and interactive users on both sides of the international border. They met various challenges with regard to the digital inequalities and gaps in coverage across the transnational terrain. One such negotiation traced in this chapter was the alliance between the hybrid radio format and the migrant association Comitiva Proyecto Panteón to carry out its cemetery renovation project. Through close collaboration, Zapotec migrant associations representing Yalálag and a cluster of Sierra Norte villages and internet stations such as Radio Cantautor, Radio Gobixha, Radio La Estrella de Oaxaca, Super Antequera Radio HD, and La Voz de Yalálag contributed to the heightened cycle of fundraiser fiestas hosted by the Oaxacan migrant community in Los Angeles and coordinated transnationally with Mexican hometowns. The fiesta cycle constituted a social support system and its media coverage offered unauthorized migrants a comforting media space in Los Angeles during the Trump administration. The Comitiva Proyecto Panteón focused on the modernization of the hometown graveyard in light of recurrent crises. It engaged in working out a truly visionary project; tragically, more hometown graves would soon be needed because of the pandemic. Internet radio allowed stakeholders at various localities to witness the many-layered aspects of death in the context of transnationalization, even when participation was limited to posting comments and transmitting short interviews. However, several elements facilitated meaningful communication and emotional involvement, such as the use of three languages (Zapotec, Spanish, and English) with their respective conceptual worlds. Issues of common interest were raised from different vantage points and gender perspectives via a digital format appealing to the auditory and visual senses. As a result, traditional ideas and rituals that revolve around life and death were refreshed to counteract the large uncertainties of the Trump years. Through its media initiatives, the extended Zapotec collective managed to spur transnational communality as a worthwhile way to live.

# 5 · AYUUJK BASKETBALL TOURNAMENT BROADCASTS

Expanding Transborder
Community Interactively

Lately Oaxaca basketball has received some long overdue attention. Although Indigenous peoples of the Sierra Norte, as well as their migrant communities in the United States, have been hosting huge tournaments with gripping, high-quality games for decades, the fact that they have built up impressive, self-managed sports structures has been widely ignored. To date, scholarship has focused mainly on the baseball and soccer leagues and tournaments of Latin American migrants (Iber et al. 2011; Meneses and Escala 2015; Alamillo 2020). Some attention has been directed to migrants in the United States from the Sierra Norte, including the Sierra Juárez region, and their basketball leagues (Quinones and Mittelstaedt 2000; Quinones 2001; Ramírez Ríos 2019). It is this context that made the March 2019 visit of President Andrés Manuel López Obrador to the forty-second edition of the Copa Benito Juárez in the Zapotec village of Guelatao such a novelty—it was the first visit of any Mexican president to the huge tournament.[1]

This chapter embarks on a journey, both historically as well as geographically, across transnational terrain in pursuit of the transformations and outreach of a tournament older than the Copa Juárez: the Copa Mixe or Copa Ayuujk. Today it is a key identity symbol that unites the Ayuujk ethnic group—it may even be considered its main ethnic event and representation. The Copa Ayuujk has its roots in the Campeonato Regional Mixe, conceived in the late 1960s as a kind of mini Olympic Games. Media practices have been and remain crucial for organizing and disseminating the games. Live transmissions via communal radio and TV stations were initiated at the beginning of the 1990s (see my documentary *The Very First Fiesta Film*). Nevertheless, this self-determined media coverage is another aspect of the games that has failed to attract attention, perhaps because Oaxaca basketball has been racially stereotyped in newspapers and magazines as an "Indigenous game." Accordingly, aspects such as the dexterity of Oaxacan Triqui children who play basketball barefoot and the short stature of Oaxacan basketball players in comparison to NBA professional players are highlighted by the sensationalist press.

All this hints at the unique history and sociocultural dynamics that these games and tournaments originating in the Sierra Norte possess. Meanwhile, the legendary ethnic basketball tournament hosted by the Ayuujk ja'ay or Mixe in Tamazulapam in their Oaxacan rural homeland has been exported to migrant destinations such as Celaya in Central Mexico and to Los Angeles, where teams consisting exclusively of Ayuujk players regularly compete. These tournaments are interconnected, with self-determined media practices playing a pivotal role for this emerging transnational sport.

I propose that looking into sports and media practices at these three tournaments is a further useful approach for investigating how and why actors engage in forming translocal and transnational communities, that is, for investigating how these communities are actually "made." Adopting an actor-centered approach, I am particularly interested in those persons who create and modify tournaments as initiators, organizers, sponsors, and mediamakers. In the Ayuujk villages of the Oaxacan Sierra Norte people have combined athletic and media practices and embedded them in their communal lifeway called Comunalidad—which concerns everyday citizenship practices of cooperating in administration, organization, labor, and sociability. A closer look at the way they remodel, shed, or perhaps even intensify their communal orientation when exporting their sport and media activities to new places and countries of residence promises insights into the scope and limitations of their cross-border community building. The tournaments take place in localities which offer very diverse and often adverse living conditions for Ayuujk people. In turn these local settings influence their social position, ethnic identification, legal residence status, and employment structure. Participating in sports and covering basketball in the media are conceptualized as forms of asserting citizenship in different places of residence. Ayuujk notions of citizenship are grounded in communal lifeways but in the course of migration are renegotiated at new places of residence when engaging in businesses and employment governed by market economy. Citizenship practices in sports and media therefore serve as decolonizing strategies in the face of marginalization and oppression in urban settings.

Tournaments or competitions have been studied as sites where colonial powers introduced their sport, which their former subjects "indigenized" during the postcolonial period, like cricket in the case of India after its independence from the British Empire. Media such as radio sports commentary played a decisive role in India's adoption of cricket, where it was used as an instrument for mobilizing national sentiment before the country's independence (Appadurai 1995, 31). In other cases, subordinated ethnic groups have devised tournaments in order to redefine their relation to the state from the bottom up (Vang 2016; Besnier, Brownell, and Carter 2018, 115). For example, the Mien hold a sports competition

Tamix Multimedios covering the Copa Ayuujk, Tamazulapam, Mexico, August 2019.

at their panethnic festival to enforce their ethnicity in a novel manner that aligns them with the Thai nation, even though this display is mainly watched by a local audience (Jonsson 2003, 318).

In the present chapter I pick up the thread of the postcolonial "indigenization" of sports (in this case the "Ayuujkisization" of basketball) and shed light on the way Ayuujk people have adapted the sport to their changing communal lifeways in the context of international migration and displacement and the unevenness of the transnational terrain. I am certainly not the first to suggest considering sport and media as a powerful combination for expressing citizenship and forging nation-hood (see, for example, Scherer and Rowe 2014; Fernández L'Hoeste, McKee, and Poblete 2015), but research on Indigenous self-determined media and sports is still missing. Therefore, I explore a striking characteristic of the Ayuujk basketball tournaments: they are broadcast by media managed by the Ayuujk people them-selves. Small communal and commercial media outlets have emerged that prefer-entially cover village events by recording or transmitting them live in Ayuujk and Spanish. To what extent and in what way are sports and media practices combined to assert recognition and produce a sense of community anchored in multiple places?

In the next sections I look into how Ayuujk people who developed their own radio, television, and digital multimedia facilities in the course of international migration and the Indigenous movement for autonomy have used them in ways adapted to their communal basketball tournaments. Their respective citizenship practices negotiate gender relations, criteria for Ayuujk ethnicity, and migrant rights in various localities. They also engage in redefining the relationship between the hometown and satellite communities. To a large extent, Ayuujk migrants rely on digital means of communication to uphold citizenship practices and social relationships with hometown residents from a distance, while promoting affective ties to their new place of residence at the same time. The community mediamakers' use of novel digital outlets to cover basketball has added significance because of the way that communal senses of belonging are experienced by actors in diverse places and exchanged by an extended audience.

## BASKETBALL'S RISE TO AN AYUUJK (TRANS)NATIONAL SPORT

The specific ways in which basketball has historically been shaped into an Ayuujk sport—as it is perceived today—are briefly outlined.[2] In 1891, Canadian educator and coach James Naismith invented basketball in Springfield, Massachusetts, as a lower-risk alternative to American football. In contrast, in the agrarian villages of the Sierra Norte region, basketball took root in the context of postrevolutionary struggles for political power in the 1930s. Strongman Luis Rodríguez from the village of Zacatepec popularized the sport to advance his idea of a territorial and political centralization of the divided Ayuujk villages and to gain political power as well as a larger degree of independence from the state of Oaxaca (Smith 2008). He implemented basketball inspired by Lázaro Cárdenas's socialist education and its notion of the cultural autonomy of Indigenous groups in Mexico.[3] In 1938 Rodríguez succeeded in incorporating the majority of the Ayuujk villages or municipalities into the Distrito Mixe, a new administrative unit within the state of Oaxaca, which endowed the ethnic group with recognition and visibility.

To this end Rodríguez resorted to violent political repression to subdue villages, but he simultaneously engaged in forging alliances with the growing social group of Ayuujk public schoolteachers. He forced people throughout the region to invest *tequio* communal labor in building basketball courts (Smith 2008, 225). Tournaments in this new sport were regularly hosted as an attraction when teachers congregated in Zacatepec for their union meetings and at larger ethnopolitical events. This prompted basketball's institutionalization in the Mixe region since tournaments involve a subset of competitors, a set of rules recorded in a charter, and a division of labor between sport actors (Guttman 2004). Rodríguez hired external experts from Oaxaca City to professionalize the new practices. Other Ayuujk villages also contributed to popularizing the sport by holding basketball "flash championships" at their patron saint celebrations.[4] On the whole, between the 1940s and 1950s the Ayuujk people naturalized basketball as "their" supreme discipline.

When they created the Campeonato Regional Mixe as a new ambitious sports event in 1967, public schoolteachers in Tamazulapam built on this regional model. As part of a rising group of power, together with teachers from other villages, they

organized Club Deportivo and assumed the role of unifying all Ayuujk municipalities via sports competition. The novel championship was devised as a mini
Olympic Games, with the Olympic Games to be contested in Mexico City in 1968
serving as a further blueprint. Over the years, track and field as well as cultural
competitions were also included. The venue of these games rotated between the
Ayuujk villages. The host village resorted to its usos y costumbres governance and
contributions of tequio to board and lodge teams from up to twenty villages participating in diverse sports comprising more than a thousand athletes. This self-
organization of the games became part and parcel of grassroots administration as
practiced in the villages of the broader Sierra Norte region, of Comunalidad, the
term later coined by the Ayuujk intellectual Floriberto Díaz and Zapotec scholar
Jaime Martínez Luna for this form of citizenship practices.

Village membership and ethnicity were reconsidered at these games and in
early local writing reflecting on this Indigenous sports movement. As explained
by Marciano Rojas, a teacher from Tamazulapam and one of the championship's
founders, the tournament was specifically conceived to foster the ethnic unity of
the "great Mixe family" (Rojas García 1975). At the time, inhabitants of the Mixe
region primarily identified with their respective village and its land (recognized by
the state as an administrative unit or municipality). Meanwhile, Ayuujk political
organizations in the 1970s were raising claims based on ethnicity for the first time.
They explicitly addressed demands of autonomy over control of their ethnic territory and its natural resources to the state,[5] whereas members of Club Deportivo
like Rojas García were keen on promoting unity from within the ethnic group.
Therefore, they promoted sports competition mainly as a political instrument to
counteract ongoing land disputes between many Ayuujk villages, in which Tamazulapam was also involved. The expectation was that the sport discourses and
practices at the championship would mobilize an ethnic sentiment of belonging
to the Ayuujk ja'ay. People who participated in the championship perceived their
villages as equal units, peacefully competing within a larger ethnic community,
similar to countries meeting at the Olympic Games. In this context, ethnic commonalities were increasingly expressed in "national" symbols like an Ayuujk flag
and hymn (Barabas and Bartolomé 1984). Later on, the term nación Ayuujk
became popular, in tune with the claim that "we are a people with our own
history, religion, culture, education, and further intrinsic elements of nations,
nationalities, and peoples," as Floriberto Díaz ([1995] 2007, 152; my translation)
formulated it.

From the 1960s on, Club Deportivo became influential in defining rules gov-
erning player eligibility in ethnic terms and recording this provision in a charter,
which formalized ethnic ascription. Basketball players had to provide a birth
certificate and prove that both parents came from the same Ayuujk village or
choose one village of origin to deter outstanding athletes from participating on
two teams. They also had to prove their command of the Ayuujk language to show
that they were "pure Ayuujk ja'ay" (puros mixes). Eventually—due to the decrease

of village endogamy and the advance of the Spanish language—these criteria became more flexible. Players were required only to prove one parent came from an Ayuujk village; command of the Ayuujk language was no longer obligatory. Starting in 1976, women were included as active players in all sport competitions—a comparatively early example of gender equality in athletics. As former athletes pointed out to me, the basketball practices themselves became a form of ethnic self-identification: participating on-site in the basketball tournaments in rotating venues contributed to a growing sense of belonging to the larger Ayuujk community among people from different villages. It became fashionable to sponsor prizes. Those who donated a bull as the grand prize in the basketball tournament began feeling comfortable with the idea that those other villagers might reap the benefit of their sponsorship since they now perceived them as coethnics worthy of such a prize.[6]

In this era prior to the use of radio stations for diffusion, the "postal service" of the village governance system was key. Once the General Assembly had accepted hosting the Campeonato Regional, it took on the task of writing invitations to the participating villages. These letters were delivered by the *topiles*, the lowest-ranking officials, who at that time essentially acted as messengers of official letters, a system of convoking villagers. The games were not reported in the newspapers in Oaxaca; their impact was directed exclusively toward the regional level and the villages themselves as a means of fostering social cohesion.

Due to economic problems, the games were discontinued in 1985. It was not until 2005 that they were revived in a new format as the Copa Mixe, which was now influenced by the Copa Benito Juárez, launched in 1977 in the Zapotec village of Guelatao, birthplace of Mexico's famous Indigenous president Benito Juárez.[7] By the new millennium Tamazulapam had prospered by engaging in the coffee trade, transportation services, and construction. Moreover, the migrant diasporas that had settled in Mexico City, the Bajío, and the United States began triggering a visible upswing in the hometown economy through remittances. Once again agrarian strife, this time between Tamazulapam and the neighboring village Ayutla over a water source, motivated a resumption of the games as an antidote to conflict. Tamazulapam village officials reinvented the tournament as the Copa Mixe (later renamed Copa Ayuujk) in this context. They conceptualized the competition as an Ayuujk counterpart to the Copa Benito Juárez; this tournament organized by the Sierra Zapotecs admits teams from all three Indigenous groups of the Oaxacan Sierra Norte and is the largest basketball tournament in Oaxaca (Ramírez Ríos 2019, 87–97). Tamazulapam became the permanent base for this new Ayuujk basketball championship. A further innovation was influenced by the Copa Benito Juárez and consisted in awarding the winning teams expensive silver trophies—a symbol of modernity and market orientation. From the beginning, well-off villagers financed trophies—often migrants, both women and men, signaling gender equality in their earnings and expanding their village membership rights on par with men's rights. In the context of increasing educational and work displacements, village governance recognized this investment as the equivalent of a community member's obligation to serve as a village official on-site (see the next section).

Having concluded this trip to the Ayuujk tournament's history, we will now take a leap in time and examine the way that media and sports are currently harnessed to create communities that adhere to their own principles of citizenship and Comunalidad. The stakeholders seeking to define Ayuujk ethnicity in order to wield political power in the region and the notion of ethnicity itself have changed over the years. The following sections examine how Ayuujk basketball, along with its elements of Comunalidad, has been adapted to new migration destinations, thereby transforming the original championship in the Sierra Norte homeland.

## FIRST STOP: THE COPA AYUUJK IN THE MIXE HOMELAND

The Copa Ayuujk tournament in Tamazulapam del Espíritu Santo is the central attraction of patron saint fiesta in honor of Santa Rosa de Lima. The basketball tournament is organized as part and parcel of the village's governance system. As usual every year, at the end of August 2019, the competition was held over a three-day period in this village of some seven thousand inhabitants. More than one hundred male and female teams from twenty-seven Ayuujk villages and *agencias* competed in thirteen categories. On the one hand, the tournament attracted visitors from all over the Mixe region due to its matches between numerous first-class teams, its professional organization, and its hospitality in lodging and boarding the teams. Villagers cater to the approximately one thousand athletes during the celebration as a form of communal labor service, paying the costs entailed out of their own pockets. On the other hand, the audience following the games transcends the village and its on-site visitors: since the tournament's revival in 2005, community-based media outlets have been a vital element in popularizing the championship. Radio Jënpoj from the Ayuujk village of Tlahuitoltepec regularly broadcasts it throughout the Mixe region. Starting in 2013, the local internet provider Tuuk Nëëm and internet station Yin Et Radio have been covering the games live, with commentators narrating the action vividly in Spanish or Ayuujk. Currently interactive community media such as Tamix Multimedios and AR TV have triggered a new boost and sparked dynamics of centering an expanding community on Ayuujk basketball. The multimedia platforms livestream the playoffs on its Facebook page for a cross-border audience. Broadcasting the tournament for a transnational viewership has therefore become an integral component of this sports competition.

The village official in charge, the *regidor de educación, cultura y deporte*, and the local sports committee have deliberately designed the tournament's inauguration ceremony in a way to express ethnic collectivity in a modern, globally legible version. The ceremony combines original Ayuujk culture with elements of the Olympic Games. For example, cosmological notions and local religious ceremonies have been transformed into symbols of an "Ayuujk nation." A few years ago, the

Basketball player carrying the "Olympic Flame" at the Copa Ayuujk in Tamazulapam, Mexico, August 2019.

tournament was renamed Copa Nación Ayuujk. As Joaquín Ortiz Aguirre, a teacher who was the regidor in charge the time, explained to me, "We use the term 'nation' in the sense of resistance [to the state] and insist on preserving our own language, culture, identity, education, health, environment, land and rituality—all that defines us as a people and frame our essence as a nation."[8]

The tournament is initiated with the *tamtä'äky* ceremony, presided over by a traditional religious specialist, a *xëmääpy* or diviner, at which female officials and the wives of male village officials offer *päknë*, a sacred beverage of agave nectar, to Mother Earth. In daily life this is an intimate Ayuujk religious ceremony, part of the ritual sacrifices carried out at home, in the church, and at sacred natural sites. At the tournament the offering of päknë is transformed into a public act of "national" Ayuujk symbolism.[9] When the basketball teams solemnly line up at the venue, they use local identity symbols in a style similar to national flags at international competitions. In most cases, one or two girls or young women represent the team of their municipality or of an agencia by dressing in the respective garb as an identity marker. The accompanying brass band music program includes singing the Ayuujk "national" anthem in honor of Konk ëy. This mythical founder of the Ayuujk people is a symbol of resistance in the face of the precolonial Zapotecs— and in a figurative sense any oppression. Then the "Olympic" flame is ignited on the roof of the municipal palace; in 2019 a female player carried the torch for the first time. For the hundreds of visitors attending this ceremony on-site as well as those watching online, this combination of music, religious ceremonialism, sport, and politics is emotive, as they express in comments during live transmission. It is presided over by village officials and sponsors of the silver cups for the winning teams.

The sponsors of team prizes and sport infrastructure are key actors in issues concerning transborder citizenship.[10] Membership in the Mexican hometown has been merged with sport sponsorship, which in turn coincides with fiesta sponsorship. Sponsors—whether women, men, or couples—have a say in the combination of sports and media coverage for the transnationalized community. Their donation of silver trophies for winning teams has been adjusted to—and at the same time alters—village governance and the practice of citizenship in the hometown. In Tamazulapam recognition as a community member normally requires serving on the spot as an official during a one-year-period every six years without remuneration. Since the 1990s migrants from Tamazulapam can compensate for their lack of on-site political participation if they donate to village celebrations. They are then accepted as full members/citizens (called *comuneros/as* or *ciudadanos/as*) of their hometown. This has encouraged certain migrants in the Bajío, Los Angeles, and Milwaukee areas to sponsor one of the trophies. To assert themselves as full-fledged comuneras women often invest the earnings they obtain through migratory work in a prize (Kummels 2018, 47). In general, transnational families divide tasks: members in the United States finance celebrations and the relatives in the hometown do the work and represent the family locally. The donation of a cup along with the home party (see below) might cost up to five thousand dollars, an investment that qualifies as communal service for a year.[11] Self-determined digital media outlets allow distant sponsors to manifest belonging to the home village before a wider audience that transcends the Mixe homeland, as shown by this scene from the awards ceremony, which I recorded in my field notes:

> The 500 spectators who fill the seats in the middle of the main plaza are not the only people watching the climax of the tournament: the final in the men's freestyle category. Tamix Multimedios is transmitting the endgame live via mobile phone on its Facebook page. More than 17,000 viewers from the Mexican states of Oaxaca, Estado de México, and Guanajuato as well as the U.S. states of California, Washington, and Wisconsin watch the match on livestream.[12] From a distance, viewers also follow the transmission of the award ceremony, when the winning teams in thirteen categories are honored with silver trophies. Some of these cups were sponsored by migrants living in the United States, such as the trophy presented by 23-year-old Dina filling in for the donor—her uncle, the manager of a thriving taco truck in Milwaukee. The final match was interrupted by applause as she entered the playing field with the silver cup to complete a lap of honor, accompanied by a brass band of more than 50 musicians. An undocumented migrant, her uncle avoided the risk of returning to his hometown for the tournament. Nevertheless, due to his contribution he was "present" as a community member as local mediamakers broadcasting the event spread news of his donation beyond the Mexican border.

In the case of the final basketball matches, digital broadcasting in the hometown has become de rigueur. But other aspects of Ayuujk basketball are omitted from the online sphere due to the belief that particular sacred natural forces and their energies can be experienced fully only when physically present in the village of origin. Participation in required sacrifices on-site exerts a strong pull on Bajío migrants who are able to visit their hometown (Jiménez Díaz 2020, 194–201). In contrast, those living without legal authorization in Los Angeles rely on the following arrangement: when sponsors donate a trophy, they ensure that their relatives will consult a xëmääpy or diviner and carry out ritual sacrifices (*costumbres*) that guarantee well-being at natural sites. Donors who live undocumented in the United States also depend on hometown relatives to host lavish private parties that take place afterward—feeding hundreds of guests as they enjoy the music of the brass bands invited to the fiesta. Sponsors abroad in 2019 commissioned village videographers to document their home parties. Any villager can join in and dance to brass band music while showing off the silver trophy—a relatively new custom in an effort to integrate the cup into "original" Ayuujk fiesta culture. Afterward sponsors or their substitutes make their dramatic public appearance as described above. As they arrive at the tournament venue, any final match is immediately interrupted. A hierarchy is expressed in this manner: having proven himself or herself as a worthy comunero/a, the sponsor takes priority over the game, which normally imposes its spatial order and time regime on the audience (Huizinga [1938] 1980).

New Ayuujk media facilities such as Tamix Multimedios now cover the tournament by continuously broadcasting the event live. The operators of this multimedia platform hosted on Facebook have in mind an audience of Ayuujk people who work and live at a distance and yearn to experience the highlights of hometown life, such as the basketball tournament playoffs. In 2019, viewers from major migration centers like Mexico City, the Bajío, as well as California and Wisconsin followed the livestream of the final match between the Juquila Mixes and Totontepec teams in men's freestyle.[13] Because of their roots in community media the operators of Tamix Multimedios give a lot of thought to the way their audience has changed: it now extends beyond those with family origins in the village. Eliel Cruz, one of the operators who lives in Tamazulapam, commented on the fluidity of this audience and its networked characteristic, due to the endless interconnections enabled by social media (cf. boyd 2010). The Tamix Multimedios audience currently includes people who are not rooted in the village but now find cultural events in Tamazulapam attractive because they become acquainted with it as "friends" that villagers have accumulated via their individual Facebook pages. When livestreaming from the games this mediamaker is mindful that most of the seven thousand followers he caters to live dispersed throughout Oaxaca, Northern Mexico, or the United States. Many users will send greetings or short affirmative comments indicating their distant location: "Greetings from Mexicali—I'm dancing virtually," "Hi there from Gilroy, California," "Greetings from San Luis Potosí, Taco Restaurant La Flamita,"

"Sending all of my love from Milwaukee, Wisconsin." By adding these comments, users testify to the infinite number of places where people from Tamazulapam have settled. Affluent migrants recently have begun to use Tamix Multimedios as a showcase by financing a livestream of the sports event they have sponsored.[14] Having a say in what is transmitted is a means to climb the social ladder within the context of a transnational audience interested in sports.

That is, users also have an active influence on how community is imagined via the basketball tournament. They take advantage of the possibilities that Facebook offers as an interactive platform designed for socializing by commenting and participating in ways that the mediamakers administering the page did not foresee. In 2019 users of Tamix Multimedios heatedly debated the designs of the silver trophies. Several donors had for the first time commissioned Ayuujk silversmiths to craft trophies with symbols of Ayuujk culture, such as the goddess and the frog.[15] In contrast one donor chose a different innovative source: she had ordered a "classic" silver cup from England via online shopping. Followers commented extensively on these new trends some days before the tournament, since Tamix Multimedios had published photos of the new trophies with a brief mention of the respective sponsor. They either supported the "Ayuujk-style trophies" and frowned on the English cup as "cultural betrayal" or defended the latter as an equally legitimate choice to enhance Ayuujk culture. Thus, the online debate on Tamix Multimedios contributed to and alters how Ayuujk ethnicity is expressed at the tournament.

Meanwhile, certain aspects like the tournament's capacity to unite the Ayuujk ethnic group were mostly discussed on the ground and less on interactive media. Tamix Multimedia broadcasts of the tournament convey the image of a close-knit ethnic community by disseminating the games and highlights of Ayuujk basketball beyond the Mixe homeland. In contrast, year after year people in the home village talk about the Copa Ayuujk's capacity to bring together teams from all twenty-one Ayuujk municipalities in Oaxaca. Since the basketball event has been expressly designed to overcome intervillage conflicts in the region, there its success is measured in terms of the number of villages and teams that participate. Every year some are absent. In 2019, the neighboring municipality of Ayutla did not participate (for the third year in a row) due to an ongoing agrarian conflict with Tamazulapam (see Kummels 2020). The tournament's capacity to promote social cohesion within the regionally based ethnic community reached its limit with this dispute over land and water in which village interests and a more parochial sense of belonging prevailed.[16] The self-determined digital coverage omits these regional fissures.

## SECOND STOP: AYUUJKNESS AND THE TACO BUSINESS AT THE COPA MIXE BAJÍO

For over a decade, migrants from Tamazulapam have exported their "Ayuujki-sized" basketball to the Bajío region of North-Central Mexico. Since 2009 the Copa Mixe Bajío has been held in the city of Celaya, Guanajuato. In contrast to the original tournament, it is not hosted at a patron saint fiesta but instead takes place during a regular Tuesday in March. This is a first indication of how the tournament has been adapted to the daily routine of most Ayuujk migrants in the wider area, who predominantly work in the taco restaurant business. Tuesdays after the weekend rush are the days when they can best afford to take time off.

Ayuujk basketball in the Bajío has evolved in a tight intertwining with the specific working environment and the conditions imposed on Indigenous ethnicity in this diaspora. By way of background, in the 1970s inhabitants of Tamazulapam began migrating to Mexico City in large numbers. Men often worked as employees in taco restaurants and women as housekeepers; in both cases they were extremely exploited. In the 1980s many of these migrants moved to the Bajío when this industrial zone was experiencing an economic upswing, particularly the cities of Celaya, Guanajuato, Irapuato, and Salamanca.[17] Migrants originating from villages such as Ayutla, Tamazulapam, Tlahuitoltepec, Tepantlali, and Tepuxtepec for the first time opened their own *taquerías*. These hardworking pioneers built up small-, medium-, and even large-scale enterprises by employing coethnics from their own and neighboring villages, giving rise to an ethnic economic enclave (Wilson and Portes 1980). My interviewees coincide in that initially the disperse taco restaurants did not constitute a community in the Bajío region. One reason for this is the pronounced racialized hierarchy that privileges solely mestizo identity and invisibilizes Indigenous ethnicity; the Indigenous population in the Bajío is less than 2 percent of the total population. Ayuujk people at first chose not to emphasize ethnic solidarity in public spaces.

However, in the taco restaurants themselves ethnicity traverses cultural, social, and economic relations. Insiders recognize Ayuujk businesses since they tend to use names with the innocuous suffix "mix," which stands for "Mixe." Moreover, owners and employees speak in Ayuujk as they work; they often share religious beliefs called costumbres.[18] Entrepreneurs depend on ethnic commonalities when building up a business. Next to family members, they prefer to recruit *paisanos* or *paisanas* from the hometown who are willing to work up to twelve hours daily. Many employees are attracted by the possibility of copying this model and becoming entrepreneurs themselves. At the same time, the business model relies on a hierarchy according to which an employee often begins as a dishwasher and ascends to a *pastorero*, cutting the meat towered on the skewer; meanwhile, owners and close family members manage the business. The entrepreneurs decide whether to promote workers and support them based on personal criteria when they are ill or need credit to open their own restaurant. The working conditions vary: owners may impose exploitative conditions similar to those they once faced or may treat their staff fairly in an effort to retain hardworking laborers.

The Copa Mixe Bajío has grown considerably in recent years particularly due to Ayuujk migrants' specific use of Facebook for networking, for both labor and leisure. Restaurant owner Eliseo Martínez initiated the Copa Mixe Bajío in 2009 in a period of relative prosperity for the Ayuujk economic enclave as a tournament of

The team of taco restaurant Brasimix at the inauguration ceremony of the Copa Mixe Bajío in Celaya, Mexico, March 2019.

"pure taco workers." His vision was that it would enable "a unique community with its own culture, language, and religion to unite" in the face of the disrupting forces of discrimination and migration in Bajío society.[19] Splits also had to do with the harsh rivalry between Ayuujk taquerías. Martínez managed to convene eight teams on his private property for a competition that combined elements of culture and sports. This first tournament followed the model of the Copa Ayuujk in the hometown, although with a decisive difference: in compliance with the hierarchy of a taco business the entrepreneur introduced this spin-off "from above." At first owners recruited team players from their predominantly male staff. In general, they gave time off for exercising and financed player jerseys and the trip to Celaya. More recently they have even financed professional training to prepare players for the games. Since a second generation of Oaxaqueños had grown up (the Ayuujk ja'ay are generally categorized as Oaxaqueños in the Bajío), parents relied on basketball as a way of familiarizing them with Ayuujk culture and strengthening family ties (cf. Ramírez Ríos 2019, 57). Moreover, this sport connects them with the mestizo society of the Bajío.

Currently, dozens of owners sponsor the games; laborers from different restaurants also team up on their own initiative, bolstering the tournament "from below." Most teams adopt the name of their restaurant, like Los Guerreros de la Salsa (Salsa Warriors) and La Flamita (Little Flame), or their new place of residence, such as Alacranes de Villagrán (Scorpions of Villagrán) and Combinados de Salamanca (Commingled from Salamanca). In 2014, public visibility of the Ayuujk ja'ay as an Indigenous people with their own sports tradition increased considerably when the competition relocated to public space at the Miguel Alemán Stadium. Celaya's leading daily newspaper, *El Sol del Bajío*, began reporting on the tournament. However, this new prominence was above all a result of the digital networking upon which the diaspora of taco workers relies to connect since they are dispersed far beyond the Bajío. In recent years, Ayuujk taco entrepreneurs have increasingly opted for the economic strategy of opening restaurants in towns that have not yet been tapped economically by fellow countrymen. Ayuujk taquerías currently extend from Chiapas in Southern Mexico to the state of Washington. Facebook pages have become popular to network, such as the one created by an entrepreneur to advertise jobs in the taco enclave economy in Mexico and the United States.

In 2015, Leónides "Nido" Calderón, a restaurant owner in Querétaro who had initially studied computer science, launched the Facebook page Tamix Del Bajío Ayuuk Jääy to organize the tournament and to involve "pure Ayuujk ja'ay who can be added as friends and can get to know each other."[20] On the website, he describes the purpose of the diaspora tournament: "It serves to continue to keep alive our identity which has characterized us since ancestral times. The intention is to continue our practice of exchange [*trueque*] since this was one of our ways of obtaining a product without the necessity of resorting to money. . . . This sports event is a way to try to recreate the participation of all the Ayuujk brothers and sisters [*hermanos mixes*] living in different cities with the aim of continuing this practice of respect among each other and strengthening our cultural identity as Ayuujk ja'ay [*mixes*]." Nido reinterpreted the guiding principles of Comunalidad, addressing the division caused by the monetary economy and emphasizing the need for communal conviviality via sports in order to unite what he perceives as members of an ethnic group dispersed throughout various towns and cities. Further announcements mainly concerning the Copa Mixe Bajío are made from an impressive virtual location: Nido created a studio for the Facebook page with Open Broadcaster Software that bears a striking resemblance to a "real" sports studio on television. Several restaurant owners living in distant towns who had already formed a sports committee also began using the Tamix Del Bajio Ayuuk Jääy platform to manage the games. On the one hand, this media showcase serves as an instrument to disseminate the committee's authority. On the other hand, users also intervene with their commentaries. This was the case at the Tamix Del Bajio Ayuuk Jääy live broadcast of the lottery to draw the specific order of the matches three days before the 2019 tournament. The expectations of this broadcast were high since the committee would define the lineup of teams and the number of matches they would play. The Bajío tournament is organized as a "flash tournament," which allows for flexibility in determining the duration of the game in which all-male teams compete in the freestyle category. At the Facebook transmission some restaurant owners and workers from faraway locales sent messages arguing that each team had to participate in at least four matches for the long trip to Celaya to be worthwhile. The committee members finally agreed.

The day of the tournament itself demonstrated how Bajío migrants build community by combining logics hitherto considered incompatible: both through the communal practices of Comunalidad as well as the mercantile rationale of individual entrepreneurship. The tournament, however, took place at a time when Celaya as well as the entire state of Guanajuato was severely affected by a massive raid that the state government had initiated on March 4 against the reigning drug lord, El Marro, whose cartel ironically is called Santa Rosa de Lima. The raid was followed by daily shootings, massacres at crowded urban premises, and the burning of cars to mark territory; several leading Ayuujk taco restaurants were extorted to pay "protection money."[21] Nevertheless, on March 12, 2019, twenty-six basketball teams (and ten *fútbol 7* teams)[22] from nine states of Central and Northern Mexico and from restaurants as far as Veracruz and Mexico City competed against each other.[23] Some five hundred fifty men and women from these nine states convened in Celaya. A striking difference of the Copa Mixe Bajío is that only men play. Women are not banned from playing, but neither are they encouraged to play. Nevertheless, just as many women participated: most as fan groups cheering their teams, while some acted as trainers and referees, that is, exercising authority over sports matters too. In addition, women engaged in catering. This gendering of communal practices in Bajío basketball mirrors the hierarchy of the ethnic enclave economy where men dominate as taco entrepreneurs. Some women, like the female trainer of one team at the tournament, openly expressed criticism of *machismo* on the part of Ayuujk men, which they consider more pronounced in the Bajío than in the hometown.

The intertwining of the tournament with the Bajío work environment also shapes its version and display of Ayuujkness. Although the inauguration and sponsorship partially imitated practices at the hometown tournament, they were also markedly less ethnic, more urban, and accordingly globally legible. The basketball teams that lined up in the stadium displayed not the names of their villages of origin on their jerseys but those of a taco restaurant and global brand names like "Fly Emirates" in the way professional teams refer to their sponsors. Nevertheless, this was combined with an ethnic display since two young girls dressed in Tamazulapam garb led the teams, while typical Ayuujk brass band music played on a YouTube recording. Those who sponsored prizes aimed above all to cover the relatively high costs of logistics in the city, including the rental fee for the impressive Miguel Alemán Stadium. One restaurant owner financed its live transmission through the communal outlet Tamix Multimedios and the cost for a village mediamaker from Oaxaca to travel to Celaya. No silver trophies were donated; instead, the winning teams were honored with prize money derived from the total amount of their participation fee.[24]

Still another difference concerned how the ethnic criterion for player eligibility interacts with the Bajío's world of employment: as in the hometown, organizers allow only Ayuujk people to participate, but in addition they must comply with the criterion of being taco workers. In sum, players should be "authentic Mixe *taqueros.*" According to organizers, enforcing both criteria guarantees a competition on equal terms, since taco restaurant employees lack opportunities to train in basketball. This provision is supposed to prevent teams from smuggling in "reinforcements," that is, outstanding Ayuujk players from the homeland. Organizers exercise leadership precisely by redefining ethnicity in a translocal setting where homeland Ayuujkness is blurred. I experienced how organizers personally "checked" the physical appearance of players during the preliminary matches and singled out mestizo players because of their light skin and eye color and excluded them. Ayuujk players on the affected teams were very upset about the ban on their mestizo work pals. This prompted the organizers to consider including some mestizo taco workers for next year's tournament. Village affiliation is also manifested in ways that deviate from what happens in the homeland. Because they work together, most participants play in teams whose members come from several Ayuujk villages, even villages that have been involved in an agrarian dispute in the Mixe region. Since migrants from hometowns "at war" depend economically on one another in the supply chains of restaurants, they explicitly choose to circumvent the quarrel in the diaspora.

The coverage by Tamix Multimedios of the Copa Mixe Bajío created a communicative bridge between Ayuujk people dispersed throughout the Bajío and elsewhere in Mexico, their home villages and satellite communities in the United States. The media outlet's livestream forcibly put an emphasis on the matches themselves (rather than ceremonial elements), starting with the elimination matches taking place in the stadium through the finals between Brasimix and La Tablita de Cortazar. While part of the audience that joined in live on Facebook originated from the hometown and the state of Oaxaca, a majority were migrants who have settled in a larger region that extends from Chiapas in the south, into the Bajío, and north to the U.S. state of Tennessee, the taco business being one of their commonalities.[25] The composition of this audience points to the mutual interest that Ayuujk satellite communities have in each other. It also mirrors how migratory flows related to a (former) hometown now originate from many places and the extent to which the dispersion of the Ayuujk diaspora has increased. Migrants who commented on the Tamix Multimedios livestream from the Bajío identified with fellow migrants and how they meet the challenge of holding a basketball tournament in a new place of residence. Through their specific use of media and their viewing of sports, they related to this networked public that coproduces a transnational community.

The games concluded with a hasty awards ceremony since all present were keen on attending the evening dance, a further key element of sociability. The two main tournament organizers used the evening dance as a strategy to attract teams from far away. In 2019 a popular band from Tamazulapam (Los Kiwas) was contracted: while approximately five hundred fifty persons attended the tournament, six hundred tickets were sold at the dance hall. These numbers reveal another important layer of community building on the spot via the Copa Mixe Bajío. The tournament serves as a rare physical place of encounter for a diasporic group of people who work hard and compete with one another in their everyday business life, with little time to get together. The majority of my interview partners commented in a positive vein on how the combination of tournament and dance party allows for taking a break from work, chilling on-site with kindred spirits, looking for romance or a spouse, introducing second-generation youth to a larger Ayuujk community that speaks their Indigenous language, watching Ayuujk basketball, and enjoying music and dance originating from the "hometown."

These sports-related forms of sociability intensify migrants' sense of belonging to the "Ayuujk ja'ay of the Bajío" and of constituting an independent ethnic community. Bajío migrants accordingly adopt a reserved attitude toward Tamazulapam's politics of centralization, including requests for sponsorship in the hometown. Given the affluence of Bajío entrepreneurs in 2015, a delegation of village officials traveled to Celaya and appointed three restaurant owners to the sports committee of the diaspora tournament. In return for the recognition, the officials hoped the entrepreneurs would financially support the hometown celebrations. However, the formal integration of the Bajío basketball tournament into hometown governance did not persist very long. The taco restaurant owners insisted on retaining financial independence, even though they also sought to uphold membership in the hometown and the possibility of resettling there in the face of high levels of insecurity in the cartel-infested Bajío. In 2019 the economic upswing was threatened. For the first time, organized crime under cartel leader El Marro was severely affecting the Ayuujk enclave economy. Nevertheless, habituated to crisis, Leónides "Nido" Calderón chose to express rootedness in the Bajío in an interview he gave to the newspaper El Sol del Bajío that year. As one of the tournament organizers he emphasized that basketball is "a link that we [the Ayuujk people] have for the purpose of gathering and maintaining our customs, our roots and our language," while at the same time he stressed that having teams come to Celaya from the surrounding area was key.[26]

## THIRD STOP: THE AYUUJK TOURNAMENT IN LOS ANGELES AND A MILWAUKEE OFFSHOOT

The Ayuujk Basketball Tournament of Los Angeles is the final stop of this journey involving promotion by successful taco entrepreneur Rolando, who created the competition in 2016. In other respects, the parameters that define this event are quite different from those of the Mexican Bajío. Migrants from Tamazulapam and other Ayuujk villages in Los Angeles form part of a vibrant community re-creating Oaxaca in this multicultural city. As has already been mentioned in the introduction, the current situation of Indigenous migrants from Oaxaca varies considerably, depending on the time period when they arrived and U.S. migration policies at that time. Zapotecs from the Central Valleys and Sierra Norte pioneered Indigenous migration and were able to profit from the Immigration Reform and Con-

Ayuujk taco truck in Mid City, Los Angeles, April 2015.

trol Act of 1986 and regularize their status. They introduced early Oaxacan-style basketball tournaments to Los Angeles (Ramírez Ríos 2019, 51–53). In contrast to the Sierra Zapotecs, most Ayuujk migrants are latecomers to Los Angeles who immigrated in significant numbers at the end of the 1990s, an era with diminished opportunities to legalize their residency. They suffered disadvantages in building a community, and for a long time most did not envision settling in the United States permanently. People from Tamazulapam remained keen on upholding membership in their hometown by sponsoring a prize to its Copa Ayuujk tournament.

The Trump era was characterized by an increasingly anti-immigrant policy that fueled uncertainty through aggressive rhetoric and deportation crackdowns. Nevertheless, the Tamazulapam community, with approximately five hundred members, was beginning to establish itself with a second generation of U.S.-born children. An indicator of their urban integration in Los Angeles is the economic success of two owners of taco truck chains, both so well-known throughout the city that their brands were in demand for cameo appearances in Netflix series. Ayuujk migrants still organized loosely and not as a formal hometown association, supporting community members via mutual aid and congregating on special occasions like the day of the hometown's patron saint fiesta and on Thanksgiving for their new Los Angeles basketball tournament.

Rolando is one of these two particularly successful entrepreneurs. He did not limit himself to following the hometown model when he launched the tournament;

his initiative was also in line with the tradition-steeped basketball leagues created in Los Angeles from the 1970s on, among others by Zeus García from the Zapotec Central Valleys (Quinones 2001). In the meantime, a variety of more than forty Oaxacan basketball tournaments are held yearly in Los Angeles; each is associated with a particular migrant community and often supported by a hometown association. At larger tournaments teams identifying with certain Oaxacan regions like the Valles Centrales or the Sierra Norte build a sports cluster and meet for competition. The organizers and winning teams strengthen their position within the Los Angeles urban ethnic hierarchy. These tournaments have become key events supported by Los Angeles city policies. The city's migrant media, which report on them, have their own history rooted in binational political organization and the Oaxacan enclave economy in Los Angeles; they form part of a counterpublic there that advances organizing transnationally (Mercado 2019). In the 1990s Ayuujk migrants participated in existing tournaments but later discontinued them because of disagreements with the pioneer Zapotec organizers over the outcome of final matches.

When Rolando initiated the Ayuujk basketball competition in 2016, coethnics were already eager to control a tournament of their own.[27] The ethnic tournament provided new possibilities for getting together, educating U.S.-born children and participating in a larger Los Angeles tournament from a position of strength. An excellent performance in basketball makes a particularly positive impact because it is the city's supreme sport as home to two professional teams, the Clippers and Lakers. When Ayuujk people play basketball in Los Angeles they often trigger admiration, according to Rolando, since many excel ("they carry the game in their blood") despite their short stature. As a defining element of "being Ayuujk" basketball is therefore conducive to connecting children from the Ayuujk diaspora both to Los Angeles as well as to their parents' homeland. When Rolando sent his son on vacation to his home village, an agencia of Tamazulapam, he sponsored a children's basketball competition to celebrate his son's birthday. At the same time, participation in an ethnic-based tournament taps into a dense network of Oaxacan migrant basketball leagues in Los Angeles and fosters links to the larger Oaxacan migrant community in the megacity.

The Ayuujk tournament of 2018 was held on Thanksgiving, the holiday on which most people can take a day off. Ayuujk men mainly work in the construction industry or in taco trucks, the women as housekeepers. On November 22, they formed men's and women's teams and named them after one of Tamazulapam's agencias, a Los Angeles taco truck chain, or the Los Angeles district where team players resided, such as Mid City. Rolando sponsored the cost of the venue, a gym at Toberman Park, a referee, and plastic trophies. Player eligibility was dealt with flexibly: team captains were responsible for ensuring that only Ayuujk people were recruited. At first only individual Facebook pages reported on this modest tournament. Nevertheless, the best players of Rolando's league competed at the Copa Oaxaca Basketball on December 20, in a final covered by Los Angeles migrant media and Tamix Multimedios. There the veteran men's team from Tierra Blanca (an agencia of Tamazulapam) defeated the Chinantec migrant community of Comaltepec. Moreover, this win took place at the Staples Center, the home venue of the Clippers and Lakers and a transnational mecca of basketball. As a result, the Ayuujk basketball players made an impact within the Oaxacan migrant community. On the other hand, they visibly contributed to this major tournament that César Bravo, who is Zapotec and has family ties to the Sierra Norte, revitalized in 2017. The tournament has become a source of prestige and pride for Indigenous migrants from Oaxaca, who are often discriminated against in Los Angeles based on their skin color and short stature.[28]

On the whole, the explicit transborder character of Oaxaca or Oaxacalifornia basketball derives from organizers like Rolando, who advance networking between migrant communities via basketball. Defining the tournament in ethnic terms serves this goal and simultaneously reinforces community bonds within Los Angeles. Like in the Bajío, the Los Angeles tournament is embedded in and at the same time negotiates the particular terms of Indigenous ethnicity and urban ethnic hierarchy in which Ayuujk people situationally either compete against or ally with Zapotec, Mixtec, and Chinantec migrants in the California metropolis.

Migrant sponsorship fueled by business success stories such as Rolando's intensifies the nexus between sports, coverage by self-determined media, and transnational community building. In the process, migrant initiatives such as the following Milwaukee Offshoot are currently influencing the hometown's long-established tournament organization. A migrant who manages a thriving taco truck chain in Milwaukee sponsored a *baby fút* soccer competition for Tamazulapam in 2019.[29] Funding the organization of an entire hometown tournament was a novelty; officials in Tamazulapam incorporated it into the traditional Copa Ayuujk championship during a long weekend. However, the migrant sponsor placed an emphasis on soccer, a team sport now rivaling basketball as a result of the global popularity that European and Latin American soccer leagues enjoy. Relatives of the Milwaukee migrant organized this smaller tournament on-site in Tamazulapam and integrated elements of the larger Copa Ayuujk, such as the *tamtä'äky* ceremony. In addition, the tournament donor commissioned Tamix Multimedios to livestream the playoff games; he did not attend because of his undocumented status in the United States. Instead, he watched the broadcast at home in Milwaukee in front of a widescreen television and FaceTimed himself viewing the broadcast. People in Tamazulapam commented on these images a lot since they conveyed the impression of a successful migrant who enjoyed donating to his hometown; although he was physically alone watching the tournament at a distance, he was indeed connected with a cross-border online community. Two-thirds of the audience who followed the final match between the baby fút teams of Tierra Blanca and Tlahuitoltepec on social media included the migrant destinations California, Wisconsin, Mexico City, and Guanajuato; only one-third was from the state of Oaxaca. In sum, migrants now substantially reshape the sporting event environment in their hometown. By introducing their own tournament and overseeing its broadcast, they shift the balance between the hometown and the satellites, boosting their position within the transnational community.

## THE IMPACT OF SPORTS AND MEDIA ON TRANSNATIONALISM

The three tournaments reveal hands-on sports and media activities that are crucial for translocal and transnational community building. This chapter showed how initiators, organizers, sponsors, and mediamakers in particular have developed and exported "Ayuujkisized" basketball to various settings. These settings differ significantly with regard to the position attributed to Indigenous ethnicity and Indigenous migrants within the respective city, state, and country as well as the actors' access to legal residence and their insertion into the labor market. These elements factor in their capacity to build a community on-site and across the international border. Stakeholders relied on an Ayuujk version of basketball and citizenship practices (Comunalidad) when they adapted to the new setting, renegotiating its respective ethnic hierarchy. In each context of tension between a communal way of life and market orientation self-managed sports and media have been combined, thereby paving distinctive ways of being Ayuujk. The Ayuujkness conferred to each tournament varies considerably with regard to the form and salience of ethnicity, gender relations, urbanity, and global legibility. The Copa Ayuujk in Tamazulapam constructs an Ayuujk "nation" as based on villages located in the Mexican Sierra Norte with their unique culture, a center of gravity with a translocal and transborder outreach. The Copa Mixe Bajío defines Ayuujkness in the Bajío as also grounded in the hierarchy of the taco business and its gender division. It manifests a dual orientation that seeks to connect to the Bajío as well as to the Ayuujk homeland through basketball. This also applies to the tournament in Los Angeles, which taps into larger migrant leagues and championships that bolster the position of the multiethnic Oaxacan community within the sanctuary city. By organizing their own tournament, the first migrant generation establishes itself in Los Angeles and enables the second generation to connect to the parents' Mexican hometown and its Indigenous culture.

By following persons who engage in tournaments as initiators, organizers, sponsors, and mediamakers, my research revealed common motivations for creating these ethnic basketball tournaments. In each case the tournaments aimed to redefine the relations of power to the respective state and dominant society by countering their specific forms of oppression, exploitation, and discrimination. For this reason, the hometown version, according to which basketball is "an Ayuujk sport"—understood as a sport based on communal administration, organization, labor, and sociability (Comunalidad)—has been exported; migrants have not integrated into other existing basketball leagues. The people shaping the tournaments such as public schoolteachers and mediamakers in the hometown, as well

as taco entrepreneurs and working people in the satellite communities, are culturally versatile and media-savvy. They invested their ideas, creative work, and intellectual endeavors in the promotion of the event via self-managed media, choice of
venue, design of inauguration ceremonies, criteria for player eligibility, sequence
of games, professional supervision, presentation of prizes, educational aspects,
elements of sociability, and transnational media infrastructure. Thus, these initiators, organizers, sponsors, and mediamakers have remodeled the citizenship practices of the respective basketball tournaments in the context of economic and
sociopolitical disparities among different localities. They essentially enabled
translocal and transnational community building, even when defining and limiting membership in that community according to criteria of player eligibility.

The respective tournament versions are disseminated via Ayuujk media outlets
like Tamix Multimedios and Tamix Del Bajio Ayuuk Jääy to a wider community.
The outlets inform an audience dispersed across two countries on the outcome of
games and the activities of sponsors and therefore on the ways that communal
practices have been combined with the mercantile rationale of taco entrepreneurship in the case of the Bajío and Los Angeles. Community media showcase the
diversity of Ayuujk basketball tournaments, communicating the cultural differences between the hometown tournaments and the diaspora spin-offs as well as
the imbalances of the uneven terrain of transnationalism. In particular, self-
managed media coverage mobilized sentiments attached to the emotiveness of
athletic activity, competition, and sociability conveyed in one's own language and
culture, thereby making it possible to relate to a sport-based Ayuujk ethnicity
from different localities. At the same time those who view and use these outlets
also engaged as media actors. During livestreams, they seized the opportunity to
actively influence how community is imagined by commenting on subjects not
limited to the tournament itself. Through greetings that indicate the distant places
from where they are posting, they evoke the imaginary of the infinite number of
dispersed locations where Ayuujk people now play their own basketball games.
Through interactive user participation, self-determined media show how an
increasing number of satellite communities relate to Tamazulapam as an original
source of Ayuujk basketball. Emerging centers such as Celaya and Los Angeles,
which now codefine Ayuujk collective identity, are also prominent in these broadcasts. Interactive community media and their engaged audiences proved to be key
to the process of centering an expanding transborder community on Ayuujk basketball as an antidote to marginalization and oppression in urban settings.

# 6 · TURNING FIFTEEN TRANSNATIONALLY
## The Politics of Family Movies and Digital Kinning

In Salon Oaxaca, an elegant banquet hall in downtown Los Angeles, over four hundred guests watch mesmerized as a fifteen-year-old girl named Francis is balanced in an impressive lift by seven male dance partners to the sound of waltz music. A videographer from Yalálag, where her parents come from, records the event called a quinceañera in minute detail with his camcorder mounted on a rolling tripod. After changing from her red ball gown into a *huipil*, original Yalaltec attire, Francis takes to the floor to perform the couple dance with her father as the Nueva Imagen brass band plays live *jarabe* music. The dance is an icon of the Mexican hometown. A number of guests are both watching the show and checking their cell phones to follow postings of the event cascading via Facebook Live. The livestreams are commented on in short messages, and inundated with heart emojis, particularly from people watching the party in Yalálag. It's a big day, not just for college student Francis, who was born in Los Angeles, but also for her parents who came here from Yalálag twenty years ago—her father has a job in a fast-food restaurant, her mother works as a housekeeper. In addition to cell phone snaps, more formal portraits are also taken. Her mother's employers and their daughter and son-in-law are special guests. Francis's parents and their two daughters take time to pose with them in the banquet hall to visually capture the close relationship between these two families.

—Field notes, April 14, 2018

Taking pictures, video recording, and livestreaming are not just another aspect of the celebration: in the transnational context they *are* inherently kin work or, in other words, mediatized ways of cultivating family ties both locally in Los Angeles and across the border in Mexico. This chapter explores how professional community videographers, volunteers, and guests, as well as members of the quinceañera family, engage in this combination of kinship and media practices in order to capture and disseminate images of their multilayered relationships and defy the threat of social disintegration. In the case of Francis, the celebration took place under the particularly harsh conditions to which Mexican migrants and their families were exposed during the Trump administration. By celebrating a coming-of-age party and performing family life in the public limelight of video and social media, they gave it a cross-border communal and political dimension.

For decades, global economic inequalities have forced or motivated family members to migrate in search of better paid work. These relatives nonetheless often maintain close links across international borders due to their sense of belonging to a family and as a means of caring for each other in multiple ways (Goulbourne et al. 2011; Bryceson 2019). Scholars have also emphasized that ever since cell phone calls became affordable and social media offered free communication, these new opportunities have been seized for transnational networking (Vertovec 2004; Nedelcu 2019). At the same time, transnational family members have adapted digital devices and media formats to their cultural needs for care and sociality (Madianou and Miller 2012; Miller et al. 2016). In their study of the social support that relatives extend via digital communication tools to elderly family members living far away, Loretta Baldassar and Raelene Wilding (2020) coined the term "digital kinning." In my opinion this concept is also well-suited for the self-determined media activities involved in the coming-of-age rituals designed for cross-border sociality. Indigenous transnational family members face unique challenges in performing and imagi(ni)ng kin between Mexico and the United States. Digital connectivity and technology are not seamlessly accessible across the transnational terrain, and the media environment is marked by the digital divide. Relatives and friends in Yalálag participate to a lesser degree in the networked publics since the Mexican hometown lacks digital infrastructure due to structural marginalization. In addition, there are generational differences when it comes to expertise with digital tools and social media. Moreover, members of mixed-status families in the United States differ in terms of mobility and the capacity to take care of relatives in Mexico; therefore, they rely on various media strategies when building and extending family ties between Los Angeles and Yalálag.

In this context, many Yalaltec parents and their children in Los Angeles make a point of celebrating a daughter's fifteenth birthday on a grand scale. In Latin America and among Latinas/os living in the United States and Canada, quinceañeras are classic coming-of-age rituals for daughters on the cusp of womanhood (Davalos 1996; Cantú 2002; Rodriguez 2013). Their origin is somewhat vague, but parties for fifteen-year-old girls are rooted in the mestizo milieus of Latin America and were previously not a common practice in Indigenous villages of the Oaxacan Sierra Norte. Quinceañeras celebrated by Indigenous migrants and their satellite communities are thus a comparatively recent phenomenon. When Yalaltecs in the United States began hosting these festivities around the turn of the millennium,

Francis's quinceañera celebrations at Salon Oaxaca, Los Angeles, April 2018.

they also exported them to the Mexican hometown. Sweet sixteen parties (popular coming-of-age parties in the United States), surprise parties (celebrated at round birthdays), and baby showers are further examples of transnationally adopted festive events.

The exhaustive audiovisual documentation of the ritual of passing from childhood to womanhood has become the norm. Professional and semiprofessional photographers and videographers are commissioned to produce the infinite number of photos and videos now seen as obligatory for a quinceañera gala. As a former quinceañera explained, "[The video] stays as something physical, like a memory."[1] Yalaltecs in Los Angeles usually commission a mediamaker from their own community to produce a *xhen ke chinhoiz* (Zapotec for video of fifteen) or a Yalálag-style movie (*video estilo de Yalálag*). Even if its audiovisual narrative on the coming of age resembles many of those within the wider U.S. Latinx community, it has distinguishing elements such as a particular lengthy duration and portrays the village brand, including the fifteen-year-old wearing the hometown *huipil*.

Scholarship on transnationalism has so far paid little attention to the crossborder dissemination of medial narratives of the quinceañera party. I draw attention to how video and cell phone recordings focus on and simultaneously construct celebration highlights with their deeper messages. They allow viewers who cannot be physically present to more fully participate in the ritual and to experience its narratives and sociality through visual and auditory perception (cf. Härkönen 2011; Savage 2012). In addition, viewers abroad comment on the live transmissions of quinceañera performances in real time on social media. These media aspects are analyzed for a better understanding of how family and collectives are digitally imag(in)ed, that is, conveyed, apprehended, disseminated, and shaped interactively between Los Angeles and Yalálag.

In her study on Latinx quinceañeras, Evelyn Ibatan Rodriguez (2013, 109) pointed out that "the quinceañeras are political . . . they are resourceful and strategically deployed by immigrants to gain and use power within their families, their communities, and the larger U.S. society." During my ethnographic research I experienced how, on the one hand, the anti-immigration policy pursued by the Trump administration forced mixed-status families to withdraw from a number of public spaces since the separation of parents from their children through deportation was an imminent danger. On the other hand, Yalaltec migrants and their descendants hosted a growing number of big celebrations, each of them time-consuming, some incurring considerable financial expense.[2] Taking the quinceañera party as an example, I show how it developed a unique political dimension during this period of growing uncertainty. It was precisely through quinceañera movies, smartphone photos, video clips, and social media content that the exchange with and care of family members was intensified across the restrictive border between the United States and Mexico. Moreover, family solidarity and the support it provides in difficult times was made publicly visible to a large online community via social media. This chapter traces how the actors involved—community mediamakers, mothers/ *comuneras*, and a politicized second generation—experienced and shaped kinship, collectivity, and Indigeneity in various places when imag(in)ing kin. Quinceañera celebrations found creative ways to overcome borders, such as those between Mexico and the United States, and those that course through the everyday lives of transnational families in terms of ethnicity, race, social class, gender, and generation (cf. Goulbourne et al. 2011, 3).

I participated as a guest at several quinceañera celebrations in Los Angeles and Yalálag but focus here on the media practices and the making of kinship at Francis's celebration. I was present from preparation to post-celebration (the *recalentada*, the warmed-up meal) as both a volunteer and a guest. My initial insights into media and kinship practices were later expanded by the perspectives of key actors, including community videographer Salvador, two quinceañeras, their parents, other immediate relatives, and volunteers invited to the party. This approach serves to elucidate the mediatization of the party in a transnational setting and the political significance it acquired during the Trump era as seen by those engaging in cross-border kin and media work.

## SCRIPTWRITING A YALÁLAG-STYLE QUINCEAÑERA VIDEO

A video is a core element of almost every quinceañera, not least because it portrays and disseminates how gender and collective identities are performed at festivities that are otherwise not discussed or are even ignored in U.S. public life (cf. Davalos 1996; Rodriguez 2013, 27). This also holds true for the videos of coming-of-age parties hosted by members of the Yalaltec migrant community, which follow a particular script. The population that is categorized as Latinas/os in the United States and often constructed as a uniform cultural identity is in fact very diverse. The Yalaltec migrant community performs and disseminates a version of Zapotec Indigeneity that contradicts this alleged Latino homogeneity. In general, hosts of future celebrations can avail themselves of a wide range of services offered online by firms and shops that set the tone for the "ideal" quinceañera party (González-Martin 2016). Migrants from Yalálag, on the other hand, turn to videographers in their own community because their cultural knowledge ensures that they will capture the family's preferences. Hence, I show how the community videographer and the mother of a fifteen-year-old essentially negotiate the script of a celebration at a sales meeting. In the movie industry "scriptwriting" refers to the process of telling a story visually, that is, expressing where it takes place, its main characters, and their actions with striking locations, catchy clothes, and bodily movements that do not require much textual explanation or lengthy dialogues. I first introduce the videographer, Salvador, who caters to the demands of documenting family and community celebrations as part of the Oaxacan fiesta economy in Los Angeles. Then I delve into a sales talk at his home studio, which goes a long way in shaping the screenplay as a blueprint for the on-site celebration, facilitating the exhaustive video portrayal that is primarily intended for relatives in Mexico.

Community videographers distinguish themselves through life experience and cultural knowledge resembling that of their customers. This allows them to respond appropriately to the specific needs and preferences of their paisanos/as. During my stays, Salvador, who photographed, filmed, and livestreamed at Francis's party, was one of three extremely busy videographers in the Los Angeles Yalaltec community. When I asked him about his life story, he responded that he had spent only a few years of his childhood in Yalálag; his subsequent migrant trajectory ran through Veracruz, Mexico City, El Paso, Miami, and Los Angeles. While working as a carpenter he began to teach himself the ins and outs of filming. In 2000, a Yalaltec committee member spotted him filming as an amateur at a children's birthday party and gave him his first assignment—recording a Los Angeles kermés free of charge. Since filming was his passion, he spent much of his free time editing. With time, Salvador became more and more professional and today earns a good living from the video business.[3]

His current focus is on producing quinceañera movies on DVD or Blu-ray, as he told me in his studio apartment in Koreatown. He has always kept up with the times in terms of video equipment and the latest Adobe Premiere Pro editing software. Once the festive season takes off in April, he is booked every weekend until September.[4] To document his belonging to the Yalaltec migrant community, he occasionally records his own cameo appearances while filming on assignment. His movies are therefore evidence that he is not just a videographer observing from the outside but also an invited guest. That said, his clientele extends beyond his fellow countrymen and includes members of Indigenous migrant communities from the wider Sierra Juárez, the so-called *pueblitos*, and the Valles Centrales, about which he also has the requisite cultural knowledge.

In August 2017, I witnessed a two-hour sales meeting in Salvador's apartment and learned how preparations for the video launch those for the actual celebration.[5] Both the videographer and his clients took time to negotiate the visual storytelling that would result in a stunning quinceañera movie in "Yalaltec style." The clients, a couple (he from Yalálag, she from a satellite community in Veracruz), came with their daughter. For the most part it was the mother who expressed concrete ideas about what should be captured in the movie. As mentioned in chapter 3, mothers/comuneras shape family ties and values by assuming the essential task of collecting visual memories and assembling them in family photo albums, scrapbooks, and the emergent "mini-archives" on social media. Women's kin work and the creativity invested in family photo albums and scrapbooks are seen as essential aspects of motherhood in most European, North American, and Latin American societies (Hof 2006, 368; Rose 2010; Gómez Cruz 2012, 20). But in the case of mothers/comuneras, family is depicted by linking it closely to migrant community lifeways.

Salvador offered his clients a choice of three package deals (priced at $1,000, $1,800 and $2,400, respectively) for three 1.5-hour DVDs. He does so as a favor to Yalaltecs; other clients are content with one or two DVDs. While the mother wanted him to film "the whole event" and features like the mass in real time, he repeatedly told her that he would have to limit their duration to capture everything important on three DVDs. It was only when he added that a film longer than four and a half hours would increase production costs that she finally agreed to cuts. Apart from the length of the movie, Yalaltec music, dances, and costumes are indispensable components of *estilo de Yalálag*. Its audiovisual narrative has altered the popular storyline in which the "court" of young men (*chambelanes*) pays their respects to the quinceañera as a princess; instead, the princess is turned into the likeness of the ideal Yalaltec woman.

Village branding also concerns the items that take center stage in community-style quinceañera videos. The celebration and its audiovisual portrayal are meant to convey its magnitude and opulence to guests on-site and to distant viewers in order to impress and to "shock" them. Camera close-ups capture the many luxurious aspects of the party, which materialize living the American Dream the Zapotec way. With the quinceañera and her nuclear family as protagonists, trendy locations, gowns, decorations, prestige vehicles, and buffets with American food play "supporting roles" in the movie. Meanwhile, it has become standard for quinceañeras from the Yalaltec community to present not only conventional adornments such as a tiara and a Bible for close-ups but also iconic Yalaltec attire such as a huipil and *rebozo*.[6] In the evening, a community banda based in Los Angeles usually plays the Yalaltec rhythms of *jarabes y sones* in addition to the cotillions performed by the court. The quinceañera celebration thus testifies to the way in which members of the second generation, born and raised in Los Angeles and most comfortable speaking English, produce "authentic" Yalaltec culture on U.S. soil. A year before this sales talk Salvador had explained to me what his clients want to see in a quinceañera video:

> Well, it's true that my Yalaltec paisanos are somewhat demanding . . . they want me to record everything from head to tail. They don't want to miss a thing and fear that other videographers might edit out something important. They spend months rehearsing dances for a quinceañera. And as a videographer, imagine if you cut out part of the waltz—it loses its flavor. . . . Other videographers will only capture the guests in the banquet hall hastily. Not me, I film them all, panning slowly so you can see them. . . . Normally all the videos recorded here go the village of Yalálag and those filmed in the village are sent here. The family sending the video bears in mind that the members living over there want to see everyone who was present at the celebration here. Some videographers only point their camera at the dances and forget about the details, but it's the details my clients insist on. For example, if the mariachi musicians start playing . . . the point is to start recording before they play to get a good video. Blending in from the very beginning is necessary to edit well too. If you edit too much, you lose the flavor, so what's the point of doing that? I believe that's what my people want.[7]

During the sales talk, the clients repeatedly sought Salvador's expertise in balancing Los Angeles opulence and Yalaltec reciprocity. The couple asked for advice on the venue, banda, luxury vehicle, and photo shoot location, all of which would take center stage in the movie. Nothing is too good for the party on-site, given that the props facilitate the creation of great photographic images and video content. The lavish visuals and cultural meanings help to shape messages and eventually become enduring memories. But at the same time, the host family and the videographer keep in mind the viewership in the Mexican village. For them, the quinceañera movie is "the real party," since it is the one they can experience visually and aurally even from a distance. Salvador has his eye on the migrant community in Los Angeles, on their purchasing power and inclination for extravagance, and on the hometown's insistence on communal work and reciprocity. He takes care to record moments he knows have a special meaning, such as giving each guest an embroidered napkin (servilleta) from Yalálag as a memento of Francis's fifteenth birthday. As he edits, he deliberately highlights such token scenes of transnational reciprocity.

In the case of kermés movies, the videographer films the community festival as choreographed and structured in advance by the committee in charge and by the dance groups. In a manner of speaking, the committee writes the screenplay. With the quinceañera movie, on the other hand, the videographer directs most of the time, giving explicit instructions. As Salvador says, "You have to tell them what they're supposed to do. They won't do anything on their own initiative, I have to direct

*Preparativos* at El Mercadito, Los Angeles, July 2019.

them." He seeks to convey both the protagonism of the quinceañera and her nuclear family as well as the ethos and communal collaboration so typical of the hometown, as we examine in the following sections.

## THE COMMUNITY TOOLKIT: THE BACKSTAGE PARTY FOR VOLUNTEERS

Early on a Friday morning (April 13, 2018) I accompanied Pam from the Los Angeles Yalaltec community to what she referred to as *preparativos* (preparations) for Francis's quinceañera. She reassured me that as a volunteer I would be welcome, even though the host family did not know me. By the time we reached the spacious backyard in Mid City, a group of volunteers were already absorbed in extensive food preparations.[8] Most were members of the first immigrant generation, between thirty and sixty years of age.[9] The volunteers and the host couple knew each other well from other gatherings such as committees and kermesses; they were friends, familiar with community work such as cooking traditional Yalálag dishes, and had lived in the city for years; some were undocumented. Most of the women worked as housekeepers or cleaners in private households and tried to take one or two days off work to be part of the celebrations as volunteers and as guests.

I was in the middle of experiencing how a private gala becomes "communalized." Preparativos incorporate the logics of reciprocity; volunteers are generously hosted and fed throughout the day, which is why approximately sixty people work in shifts. Those arriving at seven in the morning are served a delicious breakfast of sweet bread, Oaxacan spiced coffee (*café de la olla*), and a thick chocolate-based beverage (*champurrado*). They then begin their shift, making several kinds of tamales that will be served for breakfast on the main day of the festivities. Most performed these tasks with impressive speed, much skill, and obvious pleasure. This informal party relies on a once-rural community toolkit that has been adapted to the Los Angeles asphalt jungle. Through mutual help and sociability, the back-yard is transformed into a crucial site for the production of Yalaltec cultural knowl-edge. Several members of the first generation have earned the title of experts in the village brand—for instance, as cooks, tailors, dance teachers, or prayer leaders. They acquired their expertise not in the village of origin, however, but in the course of community life in Los Angeles. Newcomers (like Marta, described below) are carefully monitored while learning to contribute in the proper manner.

The preparativos are key places for the acquisition of cultural knowledge iden-tified with Yalálag, but the conversations mainly centered on Los Angeles and on the political issues that preoccupy the migrants who have made their lives there. While kneading the dough, I joined in the conversations of mothers discussing their children's education. Ana and Marta are keen to raise their children in the U.S. educational system as well as with Zapotec cultural wisdom transmitted at banda music academies and dance schools so that the second generation will always "remember where their roots are." They were worried about the having to choose between a charter (public) and a private school and were trying to strike a balance, given their household economy, public safety in the respective neighbor-hoods, and the cultural orientation offered at the schools. A third mother defended the charter schools, using her adult son as an example. He spoke Zapotec and upheld Yalaltec culture "despite" his (more affordable) charter school education. Marta was also anxious to raise her son in Yalaltec culture, although she herself had spent most of her life in Ciudad Juárez and had only recently joined the migrant community in Los Angeles after marrying her Yalaltec husband. Although barely acquainted with the Sierra Norte in Mexico, she now immersed herself in Los Angeles backyard parties to help construct a Yalálag village brand. Her cul-tural advocacy was inspired by her six-year-old son. To her surprise, he had become a fan of Yalaltec dances and now took part in *folklórico* performances at the Los Angeles Guelaguetza.

The work of chopping, cooking, serving, and clearing tables, that is, the prac-tice of collaborating that demonstrates community belonging, is usually filmed as a record for the hosts. They can later check the video to see who was behind all the work that went into the feast at the main event. In this case, the backyard prepara-tions were not part of the quinceañera video, but the volunteers were systematically recorded as guests. The preparations took place backstage (Goffman 1959), while the "real" celebration played out front stage in the ballroom.

A year later when I interviewed Francis, her older sister Matilde and their mother Eustolia voiced their opinions on the preparations. Francis was keen to emphasize that the collective activity was an intimate expression of the Yalaltec sense of community in Los Angeles: "We like to take it a step further. And make everything even bigger than it is! . . . We didn't have to have [the volunteers] eat three times at our house and the day before. And the day after. It's just something we do as a community. Because we're really close. It's pretty small. And we just like making sure everyone liked that."[10] Twenty-one-year-old Matilde explained that the preparation was itself a party within the actual party: "In Yalálag everyone is so used to starting preparativos the day before, you do everything. You cook everything. I don't know if it's a cultural tradition, even if you don't want to do it, it just ends up happening, right? And you invite everyone, like close family and friends, to help you prepare all that."[11]

Relatives in Yalálag and Oaxaca City also played a major part in the preparations despite the physical distance. Both sisters stressed that their contributions were vital: small souvenirs and identity icons from Oaxaca made specially for the party, such as the hand-embroidered servilletas, napkins used to store tortillas and keep them hot, stitched by her mother's relatives. Embroidery, especially the floral motifs stitched on her huipil, transmit cosmological knowledge. Materialized in the napkins and the huipil, this knowledge—like the DVDs—regularly crosses the border thanks to transnational infrastructure established by migrant entrepreneurs: the *paquetería*, which Matilde compared to the U.S. Postal Service. The fellow countryman who offers the Yalálag–Los Angeles route flies on a regular basis to personally deliver parcels. Items sent by post or parcel services constitute a key form of communication and care that reworks kinship and allows participants to exchange cultural ideas on family from afar (cf. Soch 2018). Relatives in Oaxaca were also invited to the party, although it was clear to everyone that they would not be financially able to travel to the United States as tourists.[12]

Eustolia explained how reciprocity is both a moral compass as well as a way of accumulating social capital based on the support a person regularly gives to other community members (cf. Cruz-Manjarrez 2013, 53). Those who help at the party of a relative or a friend do so in expectation of receiving a similar contribution to their own festivities. This tradition of mutual support in the Mexican Sierra Norte is known as *gozona* and called *gwzun* in the Sierra Zapotec language. Eustolia told me that she had begun preparing for her daughter's party five or six years prior to the event by volunteering at her friends' celebrations. In the Sierra hometown gwzun is at the core of Comunalidad, but when transferred to Los Angeles it conveys a specific political message as an antidote to individualism. In the wake of their insertion in the capitalist labor market, members of the migrant community readily avail themselves of this form of communal support with its balance of give and take. Despite time-consuming jobs, Eustolia and her husband, Francisco, regularly serve as volunteers on migrant committees to raise money for infrastructure and construction projects in their hometown. In 2019, Eustolia even took over as president of the Santiago *barrio* committee, which is responsible for fundraising and celebrations in honor of the patron saint. Francisco also lends community support as a part-time musician with the Banda Nueva Imagen, which was founded in Los Angeles in 2003 by migrants from Yalálag. As a rule, the band plays for free at events such as kermesses, wakes, and quinceañeras and therefore can expect a return performance by the band of the migrant community sponsoring the event.

Hence the mother/*comunera* and the father/*comunero* were able to draw on this intensive communitarian investment for their "private party." The people involved in the lengthy food preparations resemble those volunteering at a community food sale or kermés, except now their work benefited the "private party" of a nuclear family. The many volunteers who prepared the food over the course of two days contributed substantially to the impressive feast. Nevertheless, this group takes a back seat on the main day of the party and in video recordings, which place the spotlight on the quinceañera and her immediate family.

## NEW COUSINS AND U.S. BOSSES: LAYERS OF FAMILY FRONT STAGE

Among the popular features of a quinceañera video are the events that evolve on the main day of the party: the entrance of guests into the banquet hall, the show that takes place after the dinner buffet (with seemingly endless music and dance performances, such as the waltz with family members, *padrinos*, and *madrinas*), the toasts, and, above all, the presentation of the cotillions that the quinceañera and her court have been rehearsing for months. Each feature must appear as a chapter in the video.[13] How were nuclear family and cultural identities manifested and simultaneously extended in these chapters? How were they designed and performed for video circulation in a transborder outreach?

The main celebration took place at the luxurious ballroom of Salon Oaxaca with a diverse group of four hundred fifty guests: in addition to the volunteers, they included padrinos and madrinas, the quinceañera's classmates, and her parents' employers. The show began with a tribute to reciprocity: Francisco, the quinceañera's father, presented the Banda Amapola, a ten-piece commercial band specializing in Northern Mexican Tamborazo music, whose members had emigrated from various states in Mexico. From the stage, he described his special connection to the band: he used to be a part-time trumpet player, but "precisely fifteen years ago when my daughter was born I gave up the job. I gave up music because my princess arrived!" Now his fellow musicians were giving him a one-hour concert as gozona dedicated to his daughter, for which Francisco expressed gratitude: "Thanks are due to my buddies of Banda Amapola for giving me an hour of music." Added Francis, "We won't pay them, but we'll load them up with applause." Thus, one of several layers of mutual gozona had now been performed, while Francis situated her roots in a Mexican American music scene that transcended her parents' Oaxacan hometown.

This was only the prelude to cotillions, the focal point of the celebration. Nueva Imagen, a brass band of first- and second-generation Yalaltecs, played the traditional first waltz, which the quinceañera danced with relatives and then with ritual kin (the padrinos and madrinas who give presents, such as clothes, jewelry, the cake, beverages). The banda then provided musical accompaniment to choreography that the quinceañera and her seven chamberlains had been rehearsing with a renowned dance teacher for months. The male dance partners, ideally the quinceañera's cousins, charm and court her in a performance that conveys the impression of a large extended family. But since most cousins in fact live in Yalálag, "new cousins" in Los Angeles had to be recruited. Dance teacher Aldo Cruz immediately came up with a solution: he recommended several young men who were good dancers. After contacting them, the quinceañera's mother asked these young men pointed genealogical questions and was able to find out that two were indeed distant relatives. Such inquiries are a common form of establishing (or limiting) kin relationships in the Mexican hometown. Eustolia, who is still well informed about lines of descent in Yalálag, activated this kind of traditional knowledge to trace distant family ties on the basis of a classificatory system in Los Angeles. During rehearsals, Francis and her "new cousins" indeed grew closer, and this additional "family layer" was captured on a sneak-peek video by videographer Salvador. His recordings transformed seemingly irrelevant distant kin into meaningful protagonists by "solemniz[ing] and materializ[ing] the image that the group intends to present of itself" (Bourdieu and Bourdieu [1965] 2004, 601). But as highlighted in chapter 3, these "sociogram"-style images can alternatively be conceptualized as "futurograms" since they link an important family memento with the future vision of a wider transnational community, selectively tying it to elements of the past. Each corner of the Salon Oaxaca was equipped with a large screen so the guests could follow the video starring the quinceañera and the entourage of seven "cousins" on a trip to the Santa Monica beach. Each chamberlain introduced himself courteously by name, some explicitly as a cousin of the honoree.

The cotillions enacted this image of extensive kinship as well as contrasting versions of womanhood. In the first choreography, where the quinceañera and her court made their entry, the seven chamberlains took turns dancing with the quinceañera, spinning her around, and balancing her in the air, prompting guests to remark, "Francis looks like a perfect doll!" According to Rodriguez (2013, 100), "Women's ability to successfully train their bodies to move as . . . señoritas" is assessed at the coming-of-age dance show since kin work essentially relies on women's bodies. Later Francis performed the "surprise dance"—a cumbia—in a tight, silvery bodysuit, embodying sexuality via auto-eroticization as a decisive point of entry into womanhood. Her attire was a radical contrast to that of the traditional Yalaltec woman, which calls for wearing a wide huipil tunic over a long, wrap-around skirt covering the entire body. As the quinceañera receives her last doll and symbolically becomes a woman, her coronation takes place to the theme song of *Beauty and the Beast*. Next is a feature that Yalálag migrants have added to the celebrations: the quinceañera dances to *jarabe* music dressed in the attire of the village of origin. "Yalaltec style" was a challenge for Francis, who was brought

The *jarabe* couple dance in Yalaltec attire at Francis's quinceañera, Los Angeles, April 2018.

up in the United States. Putting on the wrap-around skirt and fixing the voluminous black wool *rodete* headdress is not an easy task. As Matilde later explained, experts in Yalaltec culture are there to help; they participate in the quinceañera's movie set as costume assistants, tailors, and dance choreographers—a first-class consulting team that ensures the cultural authenticity of the smallest detail. The family engaged Aldo Cruz, the director of a renowned folklórico dance group, as choreographer for the cotillions and as master of ceremonies at the quinceañera itself.[14]

As master of ceremonies he expressed the political dimension of turning fifteen transnationally. Addressing the quinceañera in Spanish during the toast, he spoke of the importance of higher education and of pursuing a career to overcome the obstacles that Mexican migrant communities were forced to endure under Trump: "Francis, remember that the most delightful thing an intelligent and enthusiastic girl like you can give her parents is a degree, since we are living in a difficult era, where education is one of the barriers in coping with our current problems."

Yet another feature/chapter highlighted the Yalaltec village brand: La Danza de los Ratones (the Mice Dance), which commemorates a historical watershed, albeit a painful one evoking village dissension. Practically all the guests with ties to Yalálag joined hands and formed a circle for this upbeat, highly energetic dance that goes on for thirty minutes while the quinceañera swaps partners as she dances in the middle. The quinceañera video dedicated seventeen minutes to its performance.

For the host nuclear family this particular dance recalls unsettling memories of Yalálag in 1986, when a number of musicians left the Banda Municipal and formed a second band by the name of Banda Autóctona. This led to a severe crisis in the village since the municipal brass band is conceived as an expression of unity and political power. Village officials tried to squash the second band; they imposed a performance ban on its members and even sent them to prison. To discredit the renegade band, it was vilified as the Mice Band, a name that has stuck to the present day. As a young trumpeter in the Autóctona/Ratones band, Francisco witnessed the excesses of this bitter dispute that went on for years and became a factor in his decision to migrate to the United States. Today Eustolia's two brothers in Yalálag are band members. As Francisco told me the story of the conflict, he explained that the dance is a way to express solidarity and symbolically become a member of the Autóctona or Mice Family: "When one of the guys belonging to the Autóctonos marries a girl belonging to the other faction they would talk about baptizing her and say: 'How are we going to baptize her? She'll have to dance in the middle of the circle, that's where we'll baptize her, because she has to become part of our people.' They said: 'She'll be a Mouse, she'll be one of us.' But many people don't know about that. They join in the circle and they enjoy dancing, but they don't know what it means."[15] Francis herself later broached the issue of how much it meant to her that La Danza de los Ratones was performed at her quinceañera. For her, as a member of the second generation, it triggers feelings of belonging to a transnational community despite its turbulences. It is particularly interesting to see the extent to which Los Angeles–born Francis was socialized in the village conflict. Hence, at the quinceañera and through its recorded memory on video, antagonistic affiliations are passed on between generations and redefined in the Yalaltec community of Los Angeles.

Still another feature/chapter in the screenplay of the transnationalized party referred to the social ties that Eustolia formed with her U.S. employers, for whom she had worked as a nanny and a housekeeper for many years. By including them at her daughter's quinceañera, Eustolia both strengthened this close relationship and redefined existing social boundaries. At the evening meal, she seated the employer's family prominently in the ballroom. Not only were they the only White family present (accentuated by their nonparticipation in the dancing), they held a position of honor. She asked them to pose for formal portraits, thus placing them in a family-like category. I later was told that the host family see their life as closely linked to the U.S. employers. As Eustolia explained, when she migrated to the United States at the age of sixteen, her first bosses in Los Angeles callously exploited her inexperience and paid her well below the norm. Her application for the job with her current employers was a turning point: they paid her above-average wages and she felt appreciated. Nevertheless, employment in so-called care chains (e.g., Hochschild 2000) is a challenge for Mexican nannies. Their own children are obliged to cope with the "hidden costs" of having to share their mother's affective attention with the employers' children (cf. Romero 2012). When Eustolia was raising her employers' three-year-old daughter, her sister was caring for Matilde. Still, she emphasized how close she was to the employers' daughter, who never left her side: "Thanks to the little girl I got that job."[16] Today the little girl is grown up and Eustolia works in *her* household and looks after her offspring. Over the years, she has been invited to her employers' major festivities, such as a wedding attended by two hundred people. With pride, she recounted that these well-to-do Americans had commented on the size of the quinceañera party, telling her, "Our parties are not that huge!" They were amazed by her ability to mobilize so many guests and organize countless volunteers without having to pay them. In short, the festivities and their record on video propel a vision of reciprocity that outweighs financial wealth and overcomes ethnic and social class boundaries in Los Angeles.

In sum, a wide variety of close family and family-like social relationships is performed at each stage of the quinceañera, documented in video chapters, and made publicly visible. Dance and other experts in Yalálag culture who take on the role of movie set assistants are also vital to digital kinning and the broadening of social ties in this media space. The party itself is sustained by the cultural, social, economic, and media resources that migrants accumulate throughout their lives. This forms the perfect backdrop for the dissemination of new ideas about family to an extended audience. Self-determined media practices convey a multilayered image of family and cultural belonging and project this fluid combination of kin and solidarity into the future.

## FAMILY LIFE (AND RIFTS) IN REAL TIME
## BETWEEN LOS ANGELES AND YALÁLAG

Francis's quinceañera has so far shown the extraordinary degree to which the nuclear family established kin and friendship with the approximately four hundred fifty guests physically present at the party venue. But in fact many more people participated in real time because both the videographer and guests livestreamed from the Salon Oaxaca ballroom. Communicating via social media while physically present at a social event has become common practice. Without intending to do so, the guests extended the number of visitors present. While interacting with guests on-site they also communicated online by taking snapshots, filming video clips, and publishing them on social media. Meanwhile, they checked to see who else was streaming the party on Facebook Live. Online "guests" participated interactively by posting emojis and short comments. Moreover, community influencers intensified digital communication since they were keen to update their Facebook pages, "feeding" them regularly to maintain their followers and attract new ones.[17] Persuaded by this growing demand for immediate online images, videographer Salvador has broadened his film services and now attaches a cell phone to his tripod to broadcast from parties. His wife, Yolanda, an invited guest, also livestreamed with her phone. Although her Facebook page was only a few months old, she already had hundreds of followers as a result of her frequent live coverage of Yalaltec celebrations. As Salvador commented appreciatively, "She's famous now!"

Recording and posting at the party from one's own perspective testifies to "networked publics" (boyd 2010) that one is among the select group of people who are in fact experiencing it physically on the ground. Who exactly are the people behind this extended viewership following the party, and who does not or cannot access it? As shown in chapter 2 (see "Indigeneity in Real Time: Multimedia Platforms, Internet Radio, and Ethnic Influencers") the origins of Yalaltec's online community lie in Los Angeles and a natural disaster that befell the hometown in 2010, a massive landslide caused by heavy rainfall. Yalaltecs from several satellite communities in Oaxaca and Mexico City, as well as Los Angeles, began to network on Facebook to stay informed and appeal for donations (Gutiérrez Nájera 2012, 9). That is, the migrant community in Los Angeles first used social media to complement established face-to-face communication with screen-to-screen interlocution (cf. Hepp 2015, 209). Social media users in small communities (of several thousand residents) display common characteristics, according to the results a comparative study of Trinidad, Italy, and China. These users "conform to norms, expectations and values that they share with others" and are cautious when expressing deviant individual opinions online, because their "social relationships are relatively more intense and confined" (McDonald, Nicolescu, and Sinanan 2017, 89; see also Haynes 2016). To a large extent, they reproduce and intensify on social media the values and social control they share with others in the offline community.

I gained insight into the Yalaltec Facebook community and its normativity when I attended the morning mass for the quinceañera on the main day of the party. To my surprise several guests greeted me with a mischievous smile and the question "How bad is your hangover?" I then realized that this group of volunteers—first-generation migrants between thirty and sixty years old—and the cluster of users who had viewed a particular livestream from the night before had overlapped. Many do not separate communication about their personal lives from transmission of community and cultural activities. The night before one of those volunteers had invited Pam and me to a small, improvised birthday party at a Mexican-style locale, half restaurant, half disco, and livestreamed us dancing to a mix of American R & B and Mexican pop music, enjoying several margaritas. Well versed in the use of social media, the birthday girl (in her early forties) posted evocative pictures of the three of us in high spirits, making a big impression on a group of viewers that coincided with the on-site quinceañera volunteers. Interestingly, in this way she was also disseminating an image of herself as an independent woman having a good time with her girlfriends and without her husband (who had to work that evening but congratulated her via Facebook, addressing the same networked publics). The image departed from the "conservative" ideal of wives who are submissive to their husbands and adhere to "proper" behavior in public. That said, it is precisely first-generation women in their forties and fifties who circulate images of themselves having fun on their own as a means of renegotiating the tacit norms imposed on women.[18]

The online viewership attracted by the quinceañera opens a media space that has both a geographic and a practice-related dimension and serves as a platform for imagining community with a view to the future (Kummels 2012; Kummels 2017a, 13–22). The concept of media space, on the one hand, allows us to take into account the diversity of media actors situated in this process of affective community building. People are motivated for varying reasons, depending on their gender, age, education, and other differentiating categories, to overcome uneven access (such as the digital divide) and socialize within the transnational space. Second-generation youth, for example, mostly preferred Instagram and Twitter for connecting exclusively within their age group (see the last section). This has the added advantage of being an escape from the social control their parents exercise via Facebook. Mirca Madianou and Daniel Miller (2012, 124–139) use the term "polymedia" ("poly" means much, many) to describe a plethora of media, technologies, and platforms, each forming a niche in relation to the others while mediating a specific layer of social relationships. This concept is useful in contemplating the range of apps, platforms, media devices, and technologies that converge in a communicative environment. Yet the plurality and proliferation of digital media within the transborder community of Yalálag is fraught with a digital divide. Relatives and friends in Yalálag resort to a narrower range of options and have limited access to certain media options only occasionally since the Mexican hometown lacks digital infrastructure due to structural marginalization.[19] In addition, the above-mentioned generational differences affect the use of digital media. In other words, access to the array of polymedia is limited because the transnational media space is riddled with disjunctures. In the quinceañera case, the combined use of media could be more accurately described as *allomedia* (*allo* means different, opposite), using communication technologies selectively to bridge incompatibility due to location and position in the cross-border media space. In Yalálag, landline telephones remained a dominant medium, although cell phone use was growing. Only a minority could go online for a limited time in a public cyber room; a privileged few had private connections. Thus, it was impossible to fully combine the wider range of media, given the scarcity of internet connections, scant opportunities to develop skills, and prohibitive costs of being online.

Overcoming communication disjunctures through inventive use of allomedia therefore has a special significance for enabling family based on common values and a sense of belonging that motivate people to take care for each other, even from afar. The members of the quinceañera's nuclear family emphasized that apart from the latest digital technology, the quinceañera DVDs and their specific materiality were vital for networking across borders. Since the beginning of the millennium, DVDs made by self-determined mediamakers, encased in carefully designed sleeves, have been sent by parcel service to Yalálag or delivered in person. DVDs remain popular in the hometown because of limited access to internet services. Major providers are not interested in furnishing the relevant infrastructure to less densely populated, rural regions, and the state has been negligent in enforcing their obligation to do so. Moreover, these DVDs are cherished because they have become a transnational archiving tradition: these epic mementos, played on a DVD player, are dear to many in Yalálag. As tangible keepsakes guarded in private repositories, they satisfy needs that cannot be met by short text messages, snapshots, and videoclips posted in real time.

A few months after her quinceañera, Francis traveled to Yalálag to personally deliver copies of her DVDs. She felt the need for a post-quinceañera celebration with the Mexican part of her family, especially her cousins. To overcome immobility across the transnational terrain, mixed-status families have adopted a division of work according to the legal immigration status of its members. The second generation born in the United States assumed the responsibility of cultivating holiday visits to Yalálag. In Francis's case, such visits have contributed to her sense of belonging to her parents' hometown, and she is accustomed to acting as a key figure in maintaining transnational family relations. During her three stays in Yalálag she forged a close relationship with maternal cousins of the same age. She admires the way her extended family in Yalálag gets together, as they did to watch the DVDs.

> I wanted to go celebrate [the quince años] with [my cousins], because I know it's very difficult at a distance. I didn't just want it to be [a party here in Los Angeles]. . . .

I wanted to spend it with them, too. So, I went to Yalálag, and we kind of celebrated it. We also brought copies of the movie and gave it to them. They asked about it, to see pictures. I showed them and we talked about it. . . . They thought it was beautiful. Because in Yalálag it's different. Obviously, there are no banquet halls. . . . It was pretty fancy, I have to say about [my quinceañera]. They asked how long the rehearsals took and how long it was, because only one of them had celebrated a quinceañera.

Francis talked about how the post-quinceañera celebration allowed her relatives to be involved, but at the same time raised the issue of the gap in income between her family in Los Angeles and her cousins in Yalálag. Those who live in Los Angeles have a positive opinion of the enormous cost of the celebration and its display of purchasing power. They see themselves as the vanguard of the transnational community. Recently there have also been extravagant quinceañeras in Yalálag, but unlike in Los Angeles, they tend to be the exception. Eustolia mentioned that before she migrated to the United States (1989), events of that kind were highly unusual: "No, they never used to celebrate it because they simply didn't have the money. Later when more migrants were living over here, they used to send money for celebrations back there. Now they're more common [in Yalálag]." For her, the party in Los Angeles meant that her daughters and the nuclear family were now living the American Dream: "They will have . . . they already have a better future." She perceives her daughters' education at recognized high schools and universities as the guarantee of this better future, although one that involves considerable expense.

Those who live in Yalálag, on the other hand, tend to view the flamboyance of their paisanos/as in Los Angeles with a critical eye. Higher incomes lead to parties that deviate from the ideals of the home village, according to which festivities should be based primarily on communal reciprocal support. In addition, many home villagers disapprove of the idea of their fellow villagers in the United States shaping their own version of Zapotec culture and promoting it with large sums of money. Criticism of this kind is also voiced in Yalálag during the family viewing of quinceañera movies. I was present at one such viewing (not of Francis's party) when a nephew who was visiting relatives brought with him the party DVD of a girlfriend from the Yalaltec community in Los Angeles. His aunt was happy to recognize old acquaintances but was astonished at the ostentatiousness of the event. She chided her people in the United States for their decadence and criticized the "Yalaltec gringos" (a term of disapproval) for their many "distortions" of genuine Yalaltec culture. Thus, quinceañera videos are received differently depending on the location within the transnational media space where they are viewed. At the same time, their circulation opens this shared space and allows for an opportunity to discuss an important issue for transnational families: how to prevent social disintegration and the loss of communal values.

## THE POLITICIZED SECOND GENERATION:
## BELONGING TO OAXACALIFORNIA

The quinceañera opens media spaces for notions of community geared to the future that are manifested in dance and music and remediated by videographers and social media users. When I interviewed the sisters Francis and Matilde a year after the party, they both raised the following issues: How does the second generation define its senses of belonging in the transnational context when celebrating a quinceañera? How does it position itself in relation to Yalálag, the parents' hometown, and to the United States with respect to specific identity issues? In recent years, Latinx activists have increasingly highlighted the diversity of this panethnic group in order to counteract the invisibility imposed on many Indigenous and African American communities of Latin American origin through exclusion and discrimination (Blackwell 2017; Chávez 2020). Francis and Matilde were keen to clarify how their commitment to their mixed-status family was part of their broader political engagement and ideas of transborder community and Indigeneity. They explained that their civic activities evolved as they began to identify with the transnationalized Oaxacan culture of Los Angeles and became critical of the cultural homogenization that results from globalization, as it has in Yalálag. As twenty-one-year-old Matilde told me,

> [Yalaltec culture is practiced] especially here in Los Angeles, or rather Oaxacalifornia, as it's known all over California. I did research while majoring in sociology at [UC] Davis, and focused on migration studies to understand how we adapt culture transnationally. I'm thrilled to learn more about my culture, especially learning Zapotec and trying to speak it. It was a difficult situation because when I was young, I learned to speak Zapotec first, but when I went to school everything was in English and I couldn't practice Zapotec or Spanish there, so then it got harder to preserve those language skills. When I travel to Yalálag, it's sad to see my cousins are not fluent in their mother tongue. Even when I'm staying with them, I still don't get to learn more Zapotec. They prefer to ask me: "How do you say that in English?" They don't care much about preserving their mother tongue or learning more about their own culture. They do dance *jarabes* and all that, but that's not the same.

Matilde advocates for Yalaltec culture because of her sense of belonging to Oaxacalifornia. Coined by anthropologist Michael Kearney (1995) with a view to the transnationalism of Oaxacan communities and their ethnic politicization, Oaxacalifornia has long since become part of colloquial language, notably among the second generation in Los Angeles. The two sisters are skeptical of their peers in Yalálag, as far as their knowledge of Zapotec language and culture is concerned, since they may understand their mother tongue but do not speak it. Matilde disapproves of their preference for English as the presumably more prestigious language, adding, "Due to globalization, they put more effort into that mindset and no longer care or reflect on their *own* culture." The sisters emphasize that because they are from Los Angeles, they have grown up with a heightened sense of cultural awareness and, in a way, are the true guardians of the culture. In this instance, their long-standing participation in folklórico dance groups is key. From an early age, they both took an active part in public events that serve the Oaxacan community's identity politics of promoting greater visibility and recognition in Los Angeles, such as the Oaxacan Heritage Month and the Guelaguetza Festival. They were trained by cultural experts like Isaí Pazos, who is himself a member of the 1.5 generation and was the president of ORO from 2014 to 2019. Francis recalled how he would repeatedly lecture them at Guelaguetza rehearsals:

> Isaí is really good at keeping people knowledgeable, knowing their roots and stuff. Because not everyone who dances is in a folklórico troupe and learns about their traditions. "What does the *huarache* [leather sandals] mean? Why does the *huarache* have velvet in it?"—"The reason why your *huaraches* have velvet is because it symbolizes *La Conquista*. Because velvet wasn't made in *México*. That came from *los españoles*." He knows a lot, he really does. So, he goes: "What's the point of you guys dancing if you don't know your own traditions? When someone comes up to you and interviews you asking: 'What does your outfit mean?' And then you guys say: 'Oh, I don't know!'" . . . So, he goes over this a lot with us when we have to dance.

The decolonization of knowledge—which includes instruction on how colonial dominance and Indigenous resistance was inscribed in attire and dance—is communicated and applied in folklórico groups. Francis was nine when she started her training. Her fellow dancers reflected the diversity of Latinx youth living in Los Angeles: some were the children of long-established residents, others of recent immigrants; some were youth in the DACA program.[20] Young dancers become aware of immigrant rights issues when socializing with one another, and today Matilde and Francis show political solidarity with a wide spectrum of immigrants in Los Angeles. Matilde describes how folklórico activities intersect: FOCOICA (Federación de Comunidades Oaxaqueñas y Organizaciones Indígenas de California) is an umbrella organization that represents numerous Indigenous migrant communities in Los Angeles.[21] FOCOICA's president Gerardo Vázquez, their *padrino*, encouraged the sisters to perform in public and further contributed to their politicization.

Today both Francis and Matilde aspire to be immigration lawyers and plan to open their own law firm in the future. Their career choice is part of a wider trend among members of the second generation in Indigenous Mexican communities who recognize the crucial impact of current U.S. legislation on the "social production of illegality" (De Genova 2005) and want to get to the root of systemic injustice. Meanwhile, a core element of Francis's kin work is her desire to honor her parents for having immigrated. In a school poetry competition, she thanked her mother publicly:

I recently wrote about my mom's story about how she migrated to the U.S. . . . . I was really thankful for my parents coming here. I know they struggled a lot, and I know that there are people out there who are still struggling and are undocumented. It affects me, because I understand what it's like to live in a mixed-status household. So, I want to try to help as much as I can, to help people who fear for their lives and fear ICE and being deported. Because if you turn on the news it's horrible. . . . People like to assume the worst of our country, Mexico. But it's not like that, honestly. We're a country full of traditions and culture and it's a really beautiful place.

Francis and Matilde are therefore U.S. citizens who strongly identify with Mexico as "our country." They translate this outlook into concrete actions in support of immigrants that are not limited to the Latinx community. When we spoke, sixteen-year-old Francis had just become a volunteer with the Koreatown Immigrant Workers Alliance (KIWA), which supports both Korean and Latinx workers in the city's low-income sector. Having completed internships with law firms and migrant legal aid organizations in the United States, Matilde was about to take part in a program called Leadership in Social Justice and Public Policy. The political activities of both sisters should also be seen against the backdrop of the critical stance they adopt toward cultural loss and factionalism in their parents' hometown, one whose horizon they are eager to broaden and reform with an eye to the future.

At this juncture, we can draw a preliminary conclusion about the political dimension of a mediatized quinceañera. As pretentious, extravagant, and frivolous as they may be, these parties nonetheless negotiate and communicate notions of identity politics that have much in common with those of the umbrella organizations that advocate on behalf of the Oaxacan community in Los Angeles. Performing Oaxacan dances in the United States is part of a larger strategy to enhance the visibility of migrant communities and claim citizenship rights. As we have seen, politicization was designed to counteract the anti-immigrant policies of the Trump administration. The Yalaltec first and second generations were motivated to intensify sociality, along with communal lifeways, as an antidote to restrictions on their personal rights. Family ties were strengthened and extended via quinceañeras and their coverage with video cameras and cell phones. Seemingly banal communication via smartphone snapshots contributed to interaction within and between the many layers of family. Postings to the networked publics of a cluster of Facebook pages are used to declare forms of citizenship in ordinary ways (Haynes 2016); voicing opinions in the public spaces of social media is a digital means of civic agency (Beltrán 2015). In the quinceañera case this communication made members of families with diverse immigration statuses equally visible, persons affected by what Deborah Boehm (2013) calls "intimate migrations." These are "flows that both shape and are structured by gendered and familial actions and interactions, but are always defined by the presence of the U.S. state." In the case of Francis and Matilde, the quinceañera celebration and its video portrayal are strategically deployed for imag(in)ing the United States as a country with a genuine multicultural model of society—and used as an audiovisual blueprint for designing the future.

## FROM SHAME AT THE QUINCEAÑERA
## TO PRIDE ON #NATIVETWITTER

Sandra, the daughter of videographer Salvador and his wife Yolanda celebrated her quinceañera eight years ago. Talking with her about her party in retrospect allowed for further insights into the second generation's politicization in Los Angeles: Sandra grew up with the genre of community videos and periodically works as her father's assistant. Although she plans to carry on his business, she is also pursuing her own path as a creative artist. She studied art and has portrayed the Oaxacan migrant community at several exhibitions, making it visible in public spaces such as galleries and social institutions. I met her for the first time at one of these exhibitions in Los Angeles, where her artwork voiced a critique of gentrification in Koreatown and the displacement of Yalaltec residents. She had created a miniature model of a typical Los Angeles apartment building decorated with a mural of a Yalaltec woman wearing the hometown huipil. In the summer of 2019, one of her works caused a sensation in the Yalaltec migrant community, a zine in Zapotec language.[22] People rushed to tell me: "Sandra brought out a book about Yalálag in Zapotec! It was launched in Santa Monica." She had chosen a medium typical of the alternative scene to convey her mother's migrant life in an inventive manner. The zine, titled No'l Yara'rj (Yalaltec Woman), was displayed at a Santa Monica art exhibition; it was also available online through a QR code that provided access to Spanish and English versions. When we met for the interview, she gave me a copy. The ten-page zine mirrors the layers of family and close social ties that Francis's quinceañera had orchestrated with dance, video, and social media postings. It also addresses the multilayered and uneven family relationships produced by care chains. The zine will therefore be discussed here in detail.

What does No'l Yara'rj say about family and social ties? Collages and photos with short passages in Zapotec, English, and Spanish are combined with text to chronicle her mother's life from the moment she migrated to the United States. The title page shows an ID card indicating that her mother is a "resident alien." This is the green card she acquired following the 1986 "amnesty." An aerial photo of Yalálag forms the background and above the card is a necklace with the triple Yalálag cross (Krus Yonn), an iconic piece of hometown jewelry. Sandra's text in Zapotec explains, "I made this zine so that we do not forget our language. Thanks, mom, for coming to this country to work and sacrifice for me so that I can do well." On the opposite page are two more IDs; one is a citizenship card from the Mexican consulate in Los Angeles. In Yolanda's own words, "I left my pueblo and arrived here in the land of the gringos." The next two pages testify to her cross-border ties. The left-hand page shows a picture of her at a young age in front of the

Santo Domingo Church in Oaxaca City with her parents. The opposite page depicts an envelope addressed to Yolanda in Los Angeles from her sister in Oaxaca—a reminders of what was once a common transnational communication tool. Yolanda's comment reads, "Four years later I went back across the border to visit my parents."

The next two pages combine four pictures of Yolanda looking after a baby, Gustavo, and a toddler, his brother Luke. The text provides Yolanda's perspective: "Thank God when I arrived in this country, I found a job taking care of children." The opposite page shows a picture of these two boys as adults. Attached is a hand-written message to Sandra from the now adult Gustavo: "Hi Sandra!! Tell your mom I love her very much!!! Without your mom there, my mom wouldn't have been able to make it. . . . I love you guys!!" The collage evokes the harmony and happy times of an unusual "family" providing mutual support: Yolanda's employer Nancy, her two sons, and Sandra. Yolanda comments, "My employer was like my second mother. She was good to me." Nowhere in the zine is there a "classic" sociogram showing Sandra exclusively with her mother or her biological nuclear family. As we leafed through the pages of the zine together, she explained how this family constellation emerged: Nancy, a TV film editor, had just been divorced when she began looking for a housekeeper to take care of her two sons. Yolanda looked after Gustavo as if he were her own child, with the loving care that Sandra interprets as characteristic of Yalaltec nannies. She often brought Sandra to her employer's house, where she became friends with Nancy's children from an early age. It was Nancy who encouraged her to study art.

The zine explores the many layers of a family defying social boundaries in Los Angeles; coping with this challenge is a key component of the migrant life of *No'l Yara'rj*. Yolanda's life was painful at times but also rich in affective relationships, those she forged as a housekeeper as well as those shaped by her employer. The close ties that she established as a nanny are reminiscent of Eustolia's family con-stellation. The children they raised as nannies consider the Yalaltec women their second mothers. In turn, Sandra developed a close relationship with the family of her mother's employer. For her Gustavo and Luke are like brothers, and of course she invited them to her quinceañera. By interweaving heterogenous layers of transnational "family," the zine makes both an artistic and a political statement: here, the non-Indigenous U.S. employer is family, along with Indigenous relatives living in Oaxaca. This extended family is rooted in differences in ethnicities, racial ascription, social status, and location; it is sustained by the Yalaltec community in Los Angeles and villagers in faraway Yalálag. The zine's cover itself is an aerial photograph of the mother's hometown, a distant panorama, and reflects the layers of close ties—not unlike what Francis's quinceañera conveyed through dance, video, and social media.

When I asked Sandra to comment on her own quinceañera, both parallels and important differences emerged when compared to Francis's experience. Both par-ties featured an enormous guest list (six hundred for her party), relatives in Yalálag who participated from a distance, and several hours of cherished mementos in the form of quinceañera DVDs. But one aspect differed: at the time of her coming of age, Sandra had no political commitment to the Yalaltec and Oaxacan migrant community, nor was she particularly proud of Zapotec culture. In line with the concept of "intimate migrations," her residence status in the United States had a bearing on these differences. Since she was born in Mexico, she was still undocumented when her quinceañera took place.

When she was fifteen years old, Sandra was bullied at school by her classmates in Culver City. But she also felt like an outsider in the Yalálag migrant community. Her passion for Rockabilly and the music of punk rock bands was publicly mocked at a kermés as part of a traditional parody known as *burla*.[23] She suddenly said this when I innocently asked what it was like to wear Yalaltec traditional dress for the iconic dance with her father at her quinceañera. She admitted it took her a while to overcome her reluctance to put on the huipil, but she refused to wear the rodete:

> I feel like at that age I didn't understand. And I was kind of rebellious: "I don't want to do this. I don't want a banda . . ." And also, you're not necessarily aware of how lucky you are to have such a vibrant culture. So, I told my mom: "I don't want to wear it! But if I wear it [the huipil], I'm not going to wear the rodete." I feel it's because I was bullied when I was growing up; it was a constant thing. If you say you're from Oaxaca, people make fun of you. And I really took that in and kind of hated that part of me. . . . Now I'm so proud of where I come from. I'm so proud of everything and want to preserve everything, you know. . . . I learned to accept and love myself, being brown and being from an Indigenous community. It's hard, because if you look at society . . . what's "beautiful" is light skin, blue eyes—and not really our strong features like our noses and our faces that are very different. A lot of people told me: "You know, you look weird." And: "Oh, you're from Oaxaca." . . . Once I got older, I met more people who were aware of themselves. They were kind of, I feel, a very good influence. And so now—Wow! I appreciate my skin color, my family, and everything.

The quinceañera did not coincide with a period in her life when she had a defined sense of pride in her Oaxacan roots and culture. Today, in contrast, Sandra's work as an artist revolves around Yalálag and Oaxaca but not the traditional formats, such as migrant association kermesses popular with the first generation. She has forged new paths and has brought Yalaltec and Oaxacan perspectives to various issues, shaping Zapotec culture in the process. This has influenced her work as a member of Art Division, a nonprofit organization that focuses on underprivileged young people between eighteen and twenty-six years of age. Since 2010, it has been active in Westlake, a neighborhood with a high percentage of migrants from El Salvador, Guatemala, and Mexico. Sandra regularly gives courses to disadvantaged young people in Los Angeles and occasionally in Mexico City and Oaxaca.

Sandra also engages in advocacy and shares her ideas about Indigeneity and communality on Instagram and Twitter, notably #NativeTwitter, a digital forum of Native American artists and activists. It is no coincidence that an array of young Indigenous activists articulates their demands—or speak up as she terms it—via Twitter. This format is conducive to fast-paced rhetorical exchanges, "instantly turn[ing] events into stories" (Papacharissi 2015, 44) that cascade on threads and mobilize followers via hashtags with the potential of becoming trending topics. In this digital space Sandra positions herself by posting photos she took of Yalaltec dancers at the Calenda parade prior to the Los Angeles Guelaguetza, for example, as well as skaters of any ethnicity at Santa Monica beach. She prefers #NativeTwitter to communicate with like-minded Indigenous artists in her peer group about political issues that both encompass and transcend the Yalaltec transnational community. In her words, "I feel Facebook is more about family."

According to Chelsea Vowel, a Métis influencer, #NativeTwitter was founded as a "social space where we can focus on our issues and concerns . . . because those things are not represented in mainstream media."[24] The majority of those who participate are Native Americans, First Nations, Métis, and Inuit artists, writers, and intellectuals. The space is also frequented by Mexican Indigenous communities in the United States and Canada. Based on the contents and interactions that Sandra follows on this platform, she endorses the notions of Indigeneity that #NativeTwitter and its users propose, particularly their criticism of Canada and the United States as nation-states with an ongoing settler-colonial structure that continues to influence social relations and forms of oppression. Although the term "settler colonialism" was coined to refer to Anglophone imperialism based on territorial dispossession and the elimination of native populations, #NativeTwitter influencers advocate thinking of Latin American nation-states in similar terms. They argue that historically state power relations in Latin America also evolved via displacement and extermination—not only by control of Indigenous labor—and that today Indigenous peoples throughout the Americas suffer exclusion due to the persistence of colonial ethnoracial hierarchies (cf. Speed 2017; Schiwy 2019, 18).

In line with this analysis, the piracy of Indigenous cultural knowledge on the part of global capitalist enterprises is a hot-button issue on #NativeTwitter. In these controversies Indigenous epistemologies take center stage. They are conceptualized as a common good, whose cosmological dimension must be safeguarded in the name of Indigenous communities while unauthorized commercialization must be legally sanctioned. Sandra identifies with Indigenous artists such as @chinantecpower, who have family roots in Oaxaca and now effectively campaign against the University of California, Davis and its involvement in the biopiracy of an Indigenous corn variety from the Sierra Norte.[25] In turn, she recently ignited debate on a case of cultural piracy concerning the Yalaltec huipil into which sacred knowledge is inscribed. She discovered that a fashion designer from Mexico City was selling a collection that incorporated an element of the huipil known as the *trenza* (decorative tassels) as part of his current collection. A similar charge against French fashion designer Isabel Marant triggered a major uproar in 2015, when it was discovered that she had commercialized the cosmological motifs and typical style of blouses from the Ayuuk village Tlahuitoltepec without authorization.[26]

This last section has revealed how Sandra as a member of the second generation shapes community in a dialogue with a collective of radically critical artists from North America, who ardently defend Indigenous cultural rights and whose lingua franca is English. Her example shows how diverse media formats such as artwork in Los Angeles galleries and the quick rhetorical exchanges on #NativeTwitter are used by the second generation to redefine Indigeneity and for specific political purposes. Their socialization in self-determined media—in Sandra's case clearly influenced by both her biological parents and the American employer family—has allowed them to quickly explore new horizons. Their media practices and spaces extend and remodel transnational family and cross-border community as well as Indigeneity.

# 7 · EPILOGUE

## Reloading Comunalidad—Indigeneity on the Ground and on the Air

This book began with the characterization of Zapotec and Ayuujk media actors as experts in the eradication of distance long before the whole world was forced to tackle the issue because of the COVID-19 pandemic. After having been forced into a long period of immobility myself in 2020, the following year I was able to reassess the impact that the initiatives dealt with here had on Comunalidad and transnational community building during the health crisis. Once again, digital communication strategies that mediamakers such as internet radio reporters, multimedia platform teams, and community influencers had developed in culture- and gender-specific ways became a key factor in upholding increasingly complex, multisited Indigenous lifeworlds. Nevertheless, the pandemic entailed an unprecedented challenge. While on lockdown in Lima, I began reading news on the web that scapegoated patron saint fiestas and kermesses as super spreader events; Oaxacan online newspapers highlighted the alleged failure of Indigenous villages to comply with sanitary measures. The newspapers did not mention the distinctive features of these villages whose usos y costumbres governance had been officially recognized by the state government in the mid-1990s. This allowed them to take autonomous decisions about coronavirus policies in the spirit of Comunalidad; the General Assembly, where all comuneros and comuneras convene and vote, is the village's highest political body.

In August 2021, when I was finally able to get back to Los Angeles and Tamazulapam on-site, I discovered that Yalálag was still maintaining the "communal fence" (cerco comunitario) that its General Assembly had voted to install in March 2020. Even its migrant population was permitted only limited village access in special cases; those who entered were required to observe a two-week quarantine period. As a result, the village had not experienced a single case of COVID-19 as of that date and was celebrated by the Mexican Ministry of Health as one of the "municipalities of hope" (municipios de la esperanza). Meanwhile, Tamazulapam's General Assembly had opted against controls over who entered or left the townlet, and cases of coronavirus occurred. As explained throughout this book, the case of Tamazulapam tends to be different due to multiple factors. Unlike Yalálag, which can be closed to traffic without impairing the surrounding region, it is located at a major road axis. Among the rationales that I heard when I asked about its coronavirus policies were "We live from trade" and "We have long been part of globalization." Nevertheless, in online newspapers the headlines read, "Officials in Tamazulapam Disobey Quarantine and Host Popular Dance Event."[1] These accounts reproduced the old colonial narrative according to which Indigenous peoples were "immature" and in need of paternal guidance. To my surprise, despite hostile public opinion from outside the village, the Santa Rosa de Lima festival and its huge basketball tournament were indeed hosted in Tamazulapam during my stay in 2021. They took place under protocols decided upon by the General Assembly, in which everyone had to follow strict sanitary guidelines. The fiesta preparations were even more elaborate than usual, and soon hundreds of disciplined festivalgoers appeared, wearing face masks and maintaining their distance.

I accompanied Tamix Multimedios during the five-day celebrations, which allowed me to see how performing the patron saint fiesta on the spot and involving a transnational audience digitally were entwined. As mentioned in chapter 2, Eliel from Tamix Multimedios uses his cell phone to report from festivities in the guise of a "regular" visitor. Many of his livestreamed encounters therefore emerge as casually as they would for other guests on-site: he experiences, captures, and transmits magic moments as the outcome of serendipity, as he did when he followed the municipal brass band and the Los Negritos dance troupe as they were leaving the village plaza for lunch. Some fifty persons walked into a building under construction, where food was being prepared in an improvised kitchen. There we heard about the young, undocumented couple with a profitable taco truck business in Los Angeles who had sponsored a basketball trophy; in their absence their parents had prepared the event taking place in the hometown.

Noé Aguilar, the leader of the municipal brass band and a multifaceted media creative himself, delivered an impromptu speech that was transmitted by Eliel. More than ten thousand viewers in Mexico (in Oaxaca, Distrito Federal, and the Bajío) and the United States (mainly in California, Washington, Tennessee, and Wisconsin) either watched live or viewed the archived file on the Tamix Multimedios Facebook page, where they listened to Noé admonish the young dancers and musicians to never lose sight of the meaning of Comunalidad. He first praised the sponsors in faraway Los Angeles who had not forgotten to pay tribute to their hometown; then he linked migrant aspirations with ongoing communal responsibilities:

Right now, this [sponsor] couple is working in the United States. Fortunately, and unfortunately, we're going through this part of life when we're trying to get ahead. To have something for tomorrow, have a way to make a living, which is something that they want to show the community, how they've been working. Today they're sharing a trophy, and not only with those who are participating in the sports event. They're

Communicating with her son in Los Angeles: mother of a basketball trophy sponsor during the Santa Rosa de Lima fiesta in Tamazulapam, August 2021.

also sharing this trophy to honor Santa Rosa de Lima. Those young people who went to the United States to seek their fortune and new opportunities. . . . May God bless them. They became an overnight success with their taco restaurants. Because Mother Earth and Mother Nature gave to them, they reciprocate in this manner. May God and Mother Nature protect them so that they can continue to share.

While the party guests recorded him with their cell phones and Eliel kept on transmitting, Noé defined communality as anchored in indispensable teamwork—even when performed from afar: "This is Comunalidad! No matter where we live, where we are, but when our heart tells us, our mind tells us, I want to support the community, that's what I do. Even if I'm not there in person. That's Comunalidad. I'm inviting you, musicians, basketball players and dancers let's invest our time. . . . Let's contribute our grain of sand to work together, as a team. The dancers can't perform without the musicians. And the musicians can't play dances without the dancers."

The performance of La Danza de los Negritos to the melody played by Tamazulapam's municipal brass band was then livestreamed. This constellation—oratory, dance and live music, food preparation in the background—struck a nerve with those who were viewing from afar, as well as those in the village. The band leader had been able to capture the spirit of communality in his speech, while dance, music, and the collective meal conveyed this same spirit throughout an expanded media space and made it possible for everyone to witness and enjoy the same special moment, an *exta'n*, no matter where they were.

This glimpse into media activities in Tamazulapam during the pandemic allows me to briefly review some of the findings of this book with regard to Zapotec and Ayuujk digital communication during the Trump era. First, I would like to delve into the way mediamakers closely entwined elements of autonomous online media work with the existing communal toolkit: radio reporters and multimedia platform curators would often create teams and engage as voluntary workers or operate digital means of communication in coordination with the hometown officials and representatives of migrant committees. This was also the case with the individuals I characterized as ethnic or community influencers, those who used their narrative skills to guide followers in terms of the cultural forms and ideals that they considered expressions of the Zapotec way of life or Ayuujkness; they were also involved as comuneros and comuneras in the events they documented. Videographers often teamed up in family businesses.

These media experts generally installed a transnational infrastructure: they often did their own engineering as a first step to communicate digitally, mobilize networked publics, and share knowledges. Untapped spaces were equipped at sites where small groups or large collectivities could meet, prepare food, and celebrate the act of eating together. They also operated from their homes, grocery store cyber rooms, village plazas, Los Angeles backyards, and ballrooms. In addition, they invested their time and cultural knowhow in presenting and exchanging arguments in Zapotec, Ayuujk, and other languages. The communal toolkit also included artisanal activities rooted in the long tradition of Sierra Norte villages, such as storytelling, singing, playing an instrument, dancing. Mediamakers captured these activities and transferred them to the digital realm, remediatizing them. Moreover, they built upon their village history of mass media like photography, video, analog radio, and television, as well as genres such as tequio, fiesta, and mayordomo videos. These established genres frequently served as a blueprint when curating and designing content on social media and crafting text, sound, and images into digital artifacts.

Reconfiguring communal lifeways by multimedia means and adapting them to the needs and desires that emerged in the course of international migration and transnationalization can be dubbed as "reloading" Comunalidad, to resort to jargon from information technology. The term "reload" normally refers to adding data to a computer's memory—a process that implies extending the documentation and archiving upon which strategies of imag(in)ing community are based.

Second, the itineraries covered by this book revealed that self-determined media outlets created novel forms of cross-border sociality premised on communal values. Mediamakers and users had different perspectives depending on gender, education, occupation, age, legal status, migrant generation, and other factors. And yet they exchanged these perspectives when harnessing digital tools and formats to communicate across the international border between Mexico and the United States. They also challenged other "borders" within the community caused by inequalities in terms of gender, social class, ethnicity, and generation that result from the structural deprivation and marginalization that trigger displacement and migration. In contrast, self-determined media mobilized audiences to discuss community concerns about passing on age-old cosmological knowledge inscribed in Zapotec dances and practicing them in a transborder setting; coping with death by organizing the rituals and maintaining graves in a way that strengthens the transnational community; exporting and rooting Ayuujk basketball in multiple towns and cities to sustain the cohesion of people dispersed by the taco restaurant business; and "doing" family, making it visible in light of multiple homes and politicizing the multiple layers of family cultivated to counteract illegalization and immobility in the United States. In a twofold movement, mediamakers and users combined the communal issues with demands for visibility and recognition of transborder Indigenous lifeways in multiple places—in the state of Oaxaca, in the Mexican Bajío, in California, and beyond.

Third, I would like to expand on the role of real time for generating a collective sense of belonging, that is, imagi(ni)ng and boosting community digitally. The mediamakers and users featured in this book devised novel ways of experiencing time as if it were the present. They were able to produce the experience of live—or timely—communication despite adverse conditions and create "Indigeneity in real time." An example of this is the use of allomedia, synchronizing time regimes, dovetailing fiesta cycles, and "piecing our story together" to place Indigeneity transnationally on the public agenda. These media strategies concerned vital dimensions of Indigenous lifeworlds: individual life cycles, kin work, major sports tournaments, religious festivities, and fundraisers as well as refurbishing and construction work—they anchored them both in the villages of origin and in the urban jungles. Indigenous-managed high technology, formats, and outlets have become an integral part of these settings. Allomedia—resorting to disparate analog and digital media technology (such as physically handing over fiesta DVDs to supplement online sociality practiced during livestreams)—was applied to remedy sporadic connectivity across the transnational terrain. To "piece our story together," diverse time regimes were synchronized with cell phones and social media in order to mobilize efficiently and affectively across the restrictive border (cf. Eriksen 2021). Investigative radio journalism became an integral part of conducting meetings and discussing community affairs in a transnational setting, exerting social control from afar. Essentially, all these activities served to manifest Zapotec and Ayuujk people's coevalness, which was projected into the future in multiple ways. Digital technology for processing data, which allows an electronic image to appear almost instantaneously, therefore does not predetermine real-time experience (cf. Ernst 2013, 87).

Theories of present-day societies, postmodernity, and digital globalization claim that capitalist interests in the economization of time inevitably impose speed and acceleration in all fields of human existence (Virilio 2006; Ernst 2013; Rosa 2015). In line with this argument, digital instantaneity would seem only a further step increasing velocity in social life, economics, and politics, which leads to alienation from place and makes social relations volatile, fluid, and fleeting. However, Zapotec and Ayuujk media actors set their own priorities. Self-determined mediamakers stretched the experience of real time by combining livestreaming with the prolonged duration and pleasure of communal activities. They reported from the heart of cultural production, mutual support, and political reunions, and by doing so intensified communal lifeways both on the ground and on the air, dimensions otherwise suppressed in the dominant public spheres of the United States and Mexico. As early as the 1980s, when mass media like photography, video, analog radio, and television were first adapted to communal needs, Sierra Norte videographers devised genres such as the tequio and fiesta videos. These genres were a first step in transforming local forms of mutual support (like gozona bookkeeping) into structural elements of transnational reciprocity. One feature of these genres is their emphasis on rendering an event in its entirety. Here real time is understood as "the actual time during which something takes place" (*Merriam-Webster*). Creatives were key in exporting and rooting communal values such as gozona, tequio, and guelaguetza to urban, capitalist settings in the course of international migration. Radio reporters, multimedia platform operators, and community influencers connected digital communication with communal temporality in their immediate surroundings where they coordinated ideas and took action on-site with kindred spirits. As volunteers, these mediamakers worked at other jobs to earn a living. Like their audience, they made time—and expanded time—for communality. To dovetail new fundraising formats and community meetings on both sides of the international border, they coordinated various mundane and religious time regimes, which included the sacred time of the Mesoamerican ancestors and school and national holidays in both countries; all of these were integrated into one transnational festive calendar. This allowed for broad participation and the cultivation of sociality by people in different life situations, resulting in a kind of "time-space expansion" (cf. Vokes 2016; in contrast to Harvey 1989). On the whole, the Zapotec and Ayuujk peoples have devised strategies to make spare time pleasurable and therefore "longer," even under the adverse conditions.

Fourth, reloading Comunalidad in no way took place in spaces and time regimes free of conflict. Instead, the pitfalls of digital media—due to their insertion in capitalist economic structures—have been highlighted: data mining, corporate monetarization strategies, as well as acceleration of everyday life induced by social media affordances. On the other hand, initiatives such as Tamix Multimedios and Radio Cantautor reflected on and sought independence from this structure of data and surveillance capitalism by harnessing affordances for "our own" contents. Media outlets which set up multiple small islands of autonomy in the middle of capitalist information technology networks contributed to decolonializing the internet. On the ground in Los Angeles, such media facilities often formed part of the Oaxacan fiesta economy. Shop owners, self-employed migrants, videographers, and artists engaged in the production of the supplies necessary for organizing meetings, celebrations, and other events. Although this economic niche is embedded in the capitalist market, the Indigenous peoples involved carve out room for ideas and practices based on communality. The trophy sponsors mentioned earlier are an example of the Oaxacan businesspeople in Los Angeles helping to establish this space and time on which self-determined mediamakers set their spotlight.

Finally, in these media spaces and temporalities, political ideas about the transformation described above were conceptualized as Comunalidad, Oaxacalifornia, and "our own" American Dream and circulated. Usually, they were expressed in impromptu speeches (like the one delivered in Tamazulapam), in short messages, and above all audiovisually by depicting how communal practices and Indigenous knowledges were in fact lived in different places. Making widespread practices visible and audible motivated a transnational audience to participate in migrant association meetings and their debates, food preparations, basketball tournaments, and community celebrations. This example too points in the direction of the diverse effects that media practices have on Indigenous lifeworlds (cf. Postill 2021). The media coverage from the multisited heart of Comunalidad attests to its ubiquity: from kermesses in the asphalt jungle of Los Angeles to the privacy of the everyday thoughts of a mother/comunera conveyed to a networked publics.

Building a future for Indigenous knowledges and lifeways meant decolonizing and redefining the present. Rooted in the past and anchored in the present they were also propelled into the future via the media practices described in this book. Self-determined media related current experience selectively to the past and conveyed an immediate future. The past was broached in a spectrum of issues concerning how to recuperate communal lifeways and "our own" knowledge, which was never conceived as static. This was demonstrated in the media activities themselves, which easily combined a range of communicative devices from body techniques like dancing and playing music to craft technologies such as carving masks and tailoring costumes and the most recent cybertechnology. They are separated only by hegemonic narratives that rely on dual categories such as traditional/modern, rural/urban, and artisanal/high-tech to subordinate Indigeneity by allocating it solely to the past—connoted with the terms traditional, rural, and artisanal. Mediamakers and users also counteracted this conceptual divide, which is at the core of racialized discrimination, when they networked and circulated images and sound that show the diverse living conditions that Indigenous people inhabit during their lifetime. This includes commuting for education and work and the deliberate linking of hometowns and new places of residence—both by interaction on the ground and by cyberspace sociality. In addition, their media practices documented reform movements that involved the transborder extension of sacred dance performances, death rituals, ethnic sports tournaments, and coming-of-age celebrations. Carrying them out on the ground and transmitting them depended not only on close cooperation between hometowns and satellite communities but also on a generational contract between mediamakers such as mothers/comuneras and the second generation with their cultural production, knowledge, and political initiatives. Text, image, and sound combined in futurograms connected the second generation's dance performances to their parents' aspirations for communal life. They were archived on social media, converting private memories to public aspirations. Engagement in performing, publishing, and archiving these cultural expressions on social media decolonized the imbalances often found in established archives where Indigenous knowledges are frequently marginalized or even omitted.

As mentioned in the introduction, decolonizing the internet calls for numerous measures that are by no means the exclusive duty of Indigenous collectivities but are the responsibility of society in general, as well as state entities and the international global community. The Zapotec and Ayuujk approaches contributed to the audiovisual decolonizing of the transnational setting on the ground and in cyberspace, which was crucial to building a future for Indigenous knowledge and lifeways beyond the villages of origin. This broader decolonizing enterprise was grounded in the diversity of perspectives depending on gender, education, occupation, age, legal status, and migrant generation, and how actors actually "make" communal lifeways. Self-determined media activities contributed decisively to digital formats of cross-border sociality premised on communal values that resonated beyond the transnationalized Sierra Norte communities. Relying on self-determined media in the Trump era, these communities had expanded as a form of social protection. At the same time the community life and better future to which they aspired were often conveyed in digital artifacts focusing on the hometown and its "village brand"—designed from several vantage points. The hometown was the anchor that grounded a diverse group of people in community meetings and other events transmitted via live hookups to raise funds for needs in the hometown and in Los Angeles. This translated into a vital experience of cross-border community despite the adverse circumstances of illegalization and immobilization. Self-determined media conveyed this tangible future as the Zapotec and Ayuujk version of the American Dream: the digital media initiatives made clear that it was the everyday engagement in communal lifeways in combination with pleasure that brought visions to life—and not alienated hard work in capitalist businesses. For decades, communality had been the winning formula that contributed to a sustainable social and economic life and well-being. Consequently, self-determined media communicated how some of these dreams had already come true with regard to transforming rural and urban settings and their societies, while enhancing the visibility and recognition of the people involved. In general, mediamakers and users invested their creativity in their immediate surroundings, then exported Indigenous sociality to urban, capitalist settings. Places like Los Angeles would be forever changed because of the transmission of communal practices such as gozona, tequio, and guelaguetza. These media strategies were grains of sand wielding significant power.

# ACKNOWLEDGMENTS

Cheers! With her arm stretched out slightly above our heads, Pam would take a cell phone snap of both of us toasting with mezcal just after I arrived in Los Angeles from Berlin. This photo would then cascade in real time through the interconnected Facebook pages that showcase Zapotec migrant communities as well as their hometowns—and announce my arrival. For those many moments in which my interlocutors generously enabled me to "be there" and guided me on this multi-sited journey, I express my profound gratitude. This applies to the protagonists who appear in the following pages, but whose real names in some instances I have omitted.

As for those who supported this ethnographic endeavor, sharing views from various places and vantage points in the hometowns and satellite communities of Yalálag and Tamazulapam, I owe special thanks to the Sierra Zapotec and Ayuujk people in general. I would like to acknowledge the valuable support I received from the usos y costumbres governments and migrant committees as I conducted this research from 2016 to 2021. My heartfelt gratitude goes to my hosts and friends in different places, to Pam; Isabel Ramírez; Angela Revilla and her husband David and their daughter Julia; Eliseo Martínez and his wife Guille; Leónides Calderón and his fiancée Olga; Fernando Aguilar and Herlinda Martínez, Elizabeth Eslava, Eduardo Molina and Edwin Molina, Juan Pablo González and Isabel Fernández de Alba, Freya Rojo, Juana and Teresa Vásquez. I would also like to honor the memory of Camilo Vásquez, a gifted Yalaltec musician who sadly passed away in July 2020.

I owe an extraordinary debt to the mediamakers who allowed me to accompany them, trusted me, and generously shared their wisdom with me in Tamazulapam, Yalálag, and Los Angeles: Eliel Cruz, Genaro Rojas, Hermenegildo Rojas, Rosita Román, Noé Aguilar, Adrián Beltrán, Arturo Vargas, Silvano Maldonado, Amado Aquino, Francisco Limeta, Juana Vásquez, Natalia López, Leti, Verónica Nicolás, Maricela Morales, Lisvelia Hilario, Edmundo Ambrosio, Antonio Cruz, Cecilia Mestas, and Jesús Ramón García. For their assistance in queries concerning the Zapotec and Ayuujk languages special thanks go to Juana Vázquez, Manolo Ortiz Chino, Pedro Ruiz Vásquez, and Yenny Aracely Pérez. I also express my gratitude to several dance experts and teachers, although I name only three: Malaquías Allende, Sebastián Chimil and Luis Rey Delgado.

In Los Angeles, Gaspar Rivera-Salgado, Odilia Romero, Isaí Pazos, and Dalila Castillo generously made time for multiple conversations and helped get this research off the ground, by showing their interest in it and providing profound insights on community life. Along this path I became acquainted with Xochitl Chávez, Rafael Vásquez, and Seth Holmes, to whom I also owe gratitude. Adriana

Cruz-Manjarrez was of crucial help in introducing me to the Yalaltec community in Los Angeles.

I have many more scholarly debts across the disciplines, and in these specific years I benefited from meetings on-site in Oaxaca City, Mexico City, Lima, and Berlin and in cyberspace with Salomón Nahmad Sittón, Oscar Ramos Mancilla, Antonio Zirión, Alejandra Leal, Nitzan Shoshan, Gisela Cánepa, María Eugenia Ulfe, and Freya Schiwy. I especially want to thank both anonymous reviewers who thoughtfully engaged with my original manuscript and offered both encouragement as well as suggestions as to how it could be improved. Any errors or shortcomings remain my own. Nevertheless, I hope that I have rendered as truly as possible the transborder media agency of the Sierra Zapotec and Ayuujk people and the ways they have met the challenges of difficult times.

My ethnographic research was supported by the Institute for Latin American Studies (LAI) of the Freie Universität Berlin, where I am based as a founding member of "Temporalities of Future in Latin America: Dynamics of Aspiration and Anticipation." I thank my wonderful colleagues at this International Research Training Group, which is funded by the German Research Foundation (DFG); they contributed to the development and refinement of concepts on the temporality of communities in flux in times of crises.

I would not have been able to convey my ideas in English as well as in German without the expertise of Sunniva Greve, who translated most of my writing. The revision of the final manuscript benefited considerably from Barbara Belejack's dedication, patience, and knowledge of the Mexican-U.S. context. Many thanks also go to Laura Malagón, Mario Martínez, and Mariana Almaraz who carefully transcribed the interviews revised the bibliography and prepared the index.

At Rutgers University Press, I received wholehearted support from editor Nicole Solano, for which I am truly grateful.

Finally, I would like to thank all those who in different places—from Amorbach in Franconia through the Mexican Sierra Norte up to Koreatown in Los Angeles—were willing to help me piece this story together. They regularly shared time and enthusiasm, commented on incipient ideas, advised me how to deal with obstacles, and suggested how to convey a vision in spoken language, in text, photography, and film. My hope is that this interlocking of understandings even from afar will allow for building elements of a common, more equal, and sustainable future—now, within our lifetimes.

# NOTES

## CHAPTER 1 INTRODUCTION

1. Zapotecs and Ayuujk ja'ay are the widely used names for ethnolinguistic groups whose members resort to different terms of self-reference depending on the scale of their sense of belonging. Zapotecs was originally coined as an exonym by the Nahuatl-speaking Aztecs (and means "inhabitants of the sapote place"); it has currently been resignified in the context of political struggle as a term that refers to any collectivity speaking a Zapotec language variant, which encompasses some 500,000 speakers. Ayuujk ja'ay ("people of the flowery language") is the term of self-reference of the ethnolinguistic group called Mixe (stemming from Nahuatl too; probably derived from the Ayuujk word for young man, mïx) by its exonym with around 190,000 speakers.

2. Pam is a pseudonym. In general, when only a first name appears in the text, it is a pseudonym used to protect the identity of the person in question for different reasons, among them their migration status in the United States.

3. The "interior arrests" or "administrative arrests" were implemented by the Trump administration with an executive order signed on January 25, 2017; on February 21, 2017, due to the memorandum issued by the Homeland Security secretary, the order went into effect in California. During the latter part of his presidential term, Barack Obama (2009–2017) had prioritized the arrests of unauthorized migrants who had committed serious criminal offences, while the Trump administration also arrested and deported migrants who lacked criminal records or had committed only minor offenses (Gramlich 2020; FitzGerald, López, and McClean 2019, 47). Nevertheless, Los Angeles County continued to offer refuge to unauthorized migrants as a "sanctuary city" and provide them assistance, a policy dating back to the 1980s. The city of Los Angeles limited its cooperation with Immigration and Customs Enforcement during the Trump administration.

4. This form of municipal governance, called *usos y costumbres* (literally: traditions and customs), was officially recognized by the state of Oaxaca in 1995. It grants the right to self-governance according to local principles, therefore offering an alternative to the national Mexican system of political parties. At the heart of this form of governance, now designated as the "internal normative system" (*sistema normativo interno*), municipalities run their own elections; a General Assembly decides all issues by consensus. Three-quarters of the municipalities in the state of Oaxaca (418 of 570) have chosen this system of governance.

5. With regard to the Southern California lifestyle, see Brunn et al. (2020, 65). Concerning the history of Indigenous Oaxacan migrants in Los Angeles, see Alarcón, Escala, and Odgers (2016), Quinones (2013), Aquino Moreschi (2012), and Malpica Melero (2005).

6. The disadvantages in these three sectors are reflected in the low indicators of Indigenous villages regarding infrastructure in education and telecommunications and control of the exploitation of natural resources. During the Peña Nieto administration, protests against the major education reform led to the deaths of seven civilians on June 19, 2016, in Nochixtlán after federal police fired into a crowd.

7. The numbers offered here are very rough estimates with regard to migrants of both ethnolinguistic groups living in the United States. The number of members of all Zapotec groups in Oaxaca (Sierra Norte, Sierra Sur, Valles Centrales, and Istmo) is between 405,583 and 474,298 based on official statistics from 2019 (see García Vargas 2018, 14 and http://sic.gob.mx/ficha .php?table=grupo_etnico&table_id=26); the number of Zapotecs living in the Sierra Norte

might be 20 percent of this group, or approximately 100,000. The Ayuujk ja'ay total 132,759 persons (García Vargas 2018, 14) or up to more than 190,000 based on official statistics from 2015 (Instituto Federal de Telecomunicaciones 2019, 120). According to Escala and Rivera-Salgado (2018, 39), there are 350,000 Indigenous Oaxacans established in California.

8. My ethnographic research in Tamazulapam, Yalálag, and Los Angeles took place during regular annual stays in the years from 2012 to 2021. I steadily developed a collaborative approach influenced by the communal discourses and practices of my interlocutors and discussed drafts of these chapters and video recordings with those involved and organized book presentations in the respective communities, making free copies available. In the period up to 2019, I conducted a total of 123 recorded interviews in Tamazulapam, 42 in Yalálag, and 41 in Los Angeles.

9. Current icons of Zapotec and Ayuujk culture such as the sacred la Danza de los Negritos and the music of brass bands were introduced by Spaniards and European missionaries during the colonial period for the purpose of evangelization. The autochthonous inhabitants adapted foreign dances and music to their own cosmology and the veneration of natural forces and combined them with existing artistic traditions. Due to the imbalance of power, the colonized used imported cultural elements for strategies of hybridization or masking local practices, while appearing to comply with colonial impositions. See Cruz-Manjarrez (2013, chap. 7) and Dorantes (2015).

10. Standardized, universal time concepts such as Judeo-Christian time and clock-calendar-time have been employed as crucial strategies of power and domination, as Johannes Fabian (1983, 2) examined in detail. James Clifford (1994, 311) reminds us that diasporas live in a temporal and spatial tension with their host society.

11. The minimum wage in Mexico in 2018 was 89 pesos, the equivalent of $4.50. A farmhand in California earned from $11 to $12 an hour, but undocumented workers were paid only around $7 an hour.

12. The notion of media is extended beyond telecommunication and mass media and understood in a broader sense to include a wide variety of communicative devices that transmit coded messages, from the human body and its gestures up to the latest mass media such as the internet (Kummels 2012, 14; Peterson 2003, 3–8).

13. For a discussion on "media sovereignty" based on how Native American scholars have developed this concept and political demand, see Ginsburg (2016). In contrast, claims made by Indigenous media in Mexico are more commonly couched in terms of requesting "media autonomy."

14. In Mexico self-determined, autonomous media are coerced into a marginalized and informal communication sector. As a result of the Federal Legislation of Telecommunication introduced in 2006, mega media conglomerates such as Televisa and TV Azteca control 80 to 90 percent of the market. Since the passing of the Reform of the Secondary Legislation of Telecommunication in July 2014, community-run media organizations have lower-cost access to transmission airspace. Nevertheless, they often avoid legalization since it implies the obligation to transmit governmental election advertising. In contrast, in the United States the media market is not centrally regulated by the federal government (Mercado 2015, 181). Numerous migrant media outlets operate legally without any particular commitment to the government.

15. Media appropriation processes cannot be understood solely via media-centric notions such as "mediation" (Bolter and Grusin 2000). Scholars of Indigenous media have coined the culturally specific dimension of media appropriation as "indigenization" (Appadurai 1996, 32; Schiwy 2009, 12–13). I mainly use the research term "mediatization" to capture the way "contemporary culture and society are permeated by the media, to the extent that the media may no longer be conceived as being separate from cultural and social institutions" (Hjarvard 2013, 2).

16. Moreover, a majority population in the state of Oaxaca identifies as mestizo, a category that is also diverse and draws on distinct histories of migration from Europe and the Middle East,

among other regions. The Afro-Mexican population lives mainly in the Costa Chica region. In addition, Indigenous Tsotsil and Zoque from Chiapas have immigrated to and settled in Oaxaca.

17.  The great number of municipalities in the Oaxacan Sierra Norte region is based on a history that can be traced back to the multitude of *altepetl* (city-states; a Nahuatl term) it harbored in the precolonial period. On the other hand, the Spanish colonial administration later fragmented these basic territorial-political units according to its politics of divide and rule and for the end of economic exploitation (Hernández-Díaz and Juan Martínez 2007, 31–39).

18.  As to village-specific characteristics of the self-determined video production, see chapter 2. The inhabitants' sense of belonging centers on the *pueblo*, which the state recognizes as an administrative unit or municipality. In Ayuujk the term for village is *kajp* and in Bene xhon *yell*. The village or municipality is governed internally according to its own norms and without intervention from the political party system in Mexico. In general, every community member is required to serve recurrently as a village official after a certain period of years and to finance this one-year duty out of his or her own pocket.

19.  A considerable proportion of the Ayuujk population and those descended from ethnically mixed marriages live in Yalálag as a result of internal migration. Particularly during the 1940s, Yalaltecs in search of land for cultivation migrated to Nigromante, Veracruz, where they established their first satellite community; in the meantime, Ayuujk ja'ay from neighboring villages worked for pay in Yalálag. Many eventually settled there and today account for around 20 percent of this village's population (Cruz-Manjarrez 2013, 196).

20.  For Yalálag, see the interviews with Malaquías Allende, Yalálag, September 14, 2017, and Conrado Alberto Montellano, Los Angeles, April 8, 2018; see also Gutiérrez Nájera (2007, 60–66). For Tamazulapam, see Kuroda (1984, 19).

21.  In the years between 2017 and 2019, the state of Oaxaca derived more than 10 percent of its GDP from migrant remittances; the sums amounted to $1.46 billion in 2017, $1.73 billion in 2018, and $1.80 billion in 2019. Oaxaca was in fifth place, among the highest remittance receivers, following the Estado de México, Guanajuato, Michoacán, and Jalisco. See https://www.oaxaca .gob.mx/ioam/confirma-ioam-aumento-del-21-3-en-captacion-de-remesas-para-oaxaca/.

22.  With regard to migration to the United States during this period, with considerable numbers of Indigenous people first leaving their hometowns in the Valles Centrales and later departing from the Sierra Norte, see Caballero and Ríos Morales (2003), López and Runsten (2004), Malpica Melero (2005), and Krannich (2017, 116–124); specifically concerning Yalálag, refer to Gutiérrez Nájera (2007), Aquino Moreschi (2012), and Cruz-Manjarrez (2013); concerning Tamazulapam, consult Kummels (2017a), León Himmelstine (2017), and Jiménez Díaz (2020).

23.  People from the Sierra Norte use the term *pueblitos* (tiny villages) in Spanish to refer to the numerous villages of Sector Zoogocho and Sector Villa Alta-Cajonos that—not least due to international migration—often have fewer than a thousand inhabitants.

24.  Concerning the Zapotec crew working at Hamburger Hamlet, consult Quinones (2013, 2015).

25.  The Immigration Reform and Control Act (IRCA) is called "amnesty" for short. While penalizing employers of unauthorized workers, the act also provided the latter with an avenue to legalize their residence status in the United States if they complied with certain requirements.

26.  In addition, a considerable proportion of migrants from Tamazulapam live in the state of Wisconsin, particularly Milwaukee, as well as in the Central Mexican industrial zone of the Bajío. The specific Tamazulapam migration pattern is one of considerable dispersion throughout Mexico and various parts of the United States due to the economic strategy of opening taco restaurants in towns that have not yet been tapped economically by fellow countrymen and -women. For a detailed account of Tamazulapam's migration pattern since the 1990s, see Jiménez Díaz (2020, chap. 3).

**27.** Yalálag and Tamazulapam are in no way the only mass media pioneers of the Sierra Norte. Beginning in the late 1980s, other villages too had embarked on a wide variety of media initiatives. For a comprehensive outline, see Smith (2005) and consult chapter 2.

**28.** There are only rough estimates of the number of Oaxacan migrants currently living in California; estimates are at 200,000 to 300,000 persons originating mainly from Indigenous villages (Equipo de Cronistas Oaxacalifornianos 2013, 24; Krannich 2017, 123). According to Escala and Rivera-Salgado (2018, 39), there are 350,000 Indigenous Oaxacans established in California; around 180,000 have settled in the southern portion of the state.

**29.** Hometown associations are societies that organize in the diaspora based on their relation to the Mexican village of origin. They have official recognition, for example of their nonprofit status according to registration within the United States (Bada 2014, 5). One of their "classic" activities is to raise funds for infrastructural measures and other needs of the hometown. They also collect to support diaspora members experiencing hardship. The funds are gathered out of many, small contributions. Depending on the governance of the hometown and their necessities in the United States, migrants there have developed different kinds of informal associations. Societies affiliated with Yalálag refer to themselves as *comisiones de los barrios* and not as "hometown associations." I agree with Cruz-Manjarrez (2013, 92), who specifies that the U.S. *barrio* committees "maintain strong social and economic relationships with their corresponding *barrio* committees in Yalálag, but not with other transnational migrant associations and organizations."

**30.** Mexican immigration in the Los Angeles metropolitan area includes a broad spectrum of Mexican sending states, particularly Zacatecas, Michoacán, Guanajuato, Nayarit, and Durango (Alarcón, Escala, and Odgers 2016, 46).

**31.** The degree of depopulation and population imbalances resulting from emigration and displacement from the Sierra Norte has been registered selectively and only for certain periods by scholarship. Worthen (2012) deals in-depth with Yatzachi El Bajo becoming a "ghost town."

**32.** State Indigeneity defines these ethnic groups in accordance with the constitution of Oaxaca, article 16, which recognizes the basically "multiethnic, multilingual and pluricultural composition" of the state and the "legal personality of its sixteen Indigenous peoples (*pueblos indígenas*). It privileges the peoples that settled in the state in precolonial times.

**33.** The concept of ascribing identity to an Indigenous tribe or nation in what is now the United States by referring to "blood," that is, to fractions of family ancestry, was imposed by European settlers in the eighteenth century. On this basis, the U.S. Indian Reorganization Act of 1934 developed blood quantum as a legal criterion for Native American identity. A certain percentage of Indigenous ancestry was a requirement for being legally classified as Indigenous, ancestry being reckoned in halves, quarters, and smaller fractions by the ascription of a person's ancestors to a "race." This established certain rights like living on a reservation and land rights, as well as obligations such as paying particular taxes. Many tribes adopted the blood quantum regulation, but some did not or adopted it only in combination with other criteria.

**34.** Tamix Multimedios, May 23, 2021. According to a message this same user posted two days later, it had been twenty-three years since she last experienced the village's patron saint celebration on site.

**35.** The videographer Leonardo Ávalos Bis from Yalálag explained the genre of *video de comunidad* (in Zapotec *xhen ke yell*) to me as follows: It corresponds to what village customers conceive as a representation of reality. Villagers "want to see what is real" ("lo que quiere ver es lo real"). To meet these expectations, village videographers record events in real time for as long as possible and avoid over-editing or manipulating images through animation. Interview with Leonardo Ávalos Bis, Yalálag, April 29, 2016. Early video production in Yalálag has been studied by Estrada Ramos (2001) and Gutiérrez Nájera (2007); for Tamazulapam, see Wortham (2013) and Kummels (2017a). Much of the credit for advancing the topic of early transnational video production goes to the Purhépecha filmmaker Dante Cerano, who studied media use in his hometown Cheranástico and its U.S. satellites (Cerano 2009; see also Kummels 2011 and 2017a, 21).

36. Interview with Francisco "Pancho" Limeta, Yalálag, May 25, 2016; see also Estrada Ramos (2001, 43).

37. Concerning the use of digital video made by Oaxacan Indigenous migrants in Los Angeles for transnational communication and mobilization, see Costanza-Chock (2014, 93) and Kummels (2016b). For accounts of the political media activities of ORO and FIOB, see Corkovic (2017) and Mercado (2019). Stephen (2013), Schiwy (2018), and Schiwy et al. (2017) provide examples of how media were employed in transnational outreach during the Oaxacan social movement in 2006.

38. The cyberactivists who use social media to promote Indigenous languages in Mexico form a significant cluster. The Ayuujk language is the main concern of Colegio Mixe, ColMix (https://de-de.facebook.com/pg/colmixe/reviews/), and the cause of Sierra Zapotec language is an issue raised by Dill Yel Nbán (https://en-gb.facebook.com/yelnban/). See the online lecture given by Genner Llanes Ortiz on "Digital Abiayala: Indigenous Heritage and Media in Latin America" (Ibero-Amerikanisches Institut, Berlin, October 27, 2020).

39. The concept of reconfiguration derives from Norbert Elias's (1997) notion of figuration as processes that emerge from the personal interdependencies of people with their affective, social, economic, spatial, and symbolic dimensions.

40. The one outstanding exception is the so-called internet guerrilla of the neo-Zapatista EZLN (Ejército Zapatista de Liberación Nacional). In 1994 the digital political activities of these insurgents in Chiapas, Mexico, were the focal point of much scholarly attention. The prose, figures of speech, and media format of the communiqués disseminated by Subcomandante Marcos via email contradicted the stereotype that equates Indigenous peoples with backwardness and Western society with modernity and technology (Cleaver 1995).

41. Based in Menlo Park in Silicon Valley, California, Facebook (CEO Mark Zuckerberg) also owns Instagram and WhatsApp. Since 2006, the video-sharing site YouTube has been a subsidiary of Google LLC. The microblogging platform Twitter is yet another central, online social network based in Silicon Valley since 2007. By connecting users, content, data, and advertising, all these companies have amassed both enormous wealth and power worldwide.

42. That corporations designed social media for the purpose of stimulating and marketing the sociality of users must be taken into account. Mediamakers, therefore, are forced to adapt—at least to a certain degree—to the tools predefined by the architecture of such platforms, their so-called affordances, to make people experience sociality. For example, Facebook encourages people to identify themselves via a profile page, on which the administrator integrates an image related to the person or enterprise. By limiting posts to 280 characters at a time, Twitter invites users to abbreviate and express ideas directly, often resulting in fast, hefty exchanges of words along threads. Social networking also relies on the economy of likes, in which liking itself is a short form of communication that can legitimate a community (Winocur 2019, 12). Finally, the tight entanglement of the offline and online dimensions of sociality deserves mention. Many researchers rightly point out that media actors frequently do not distinguish between both spheres of sociality. The cell phone is now often conceived of as an extension of the human body (Miller et al. 2021). But in the present case studies, we must take into account that actors sometimes separate offline and online as a strategy of concealing offline activities (see chapter 3).

43. In the United States there is a long-standing tradition of using racial and ethnic categories for collecting demographic data. Among its origins were concepts of race that the government employed to determine immigration quotas. On the other hand, panethnic terms such as "Hispanic" and "Latino" have in part been adopted and redefined by the populations categorized as such. Since the new millennium in particular, "Latino/a" and "Latinx" have been used as terms

of self-identification and empowerment by those claiming a specific history and cultural heritage in the United States (see the special issue of *Latino Studies* 15, no. 2, July 2017; Milian 2020).

44. The Global South is not a geographic term but instead refers to decolonial thinking and practices constructed "outside and in the borders and fissures of the North Atlantic Western world" (Mignolo and Walsh 2018, 2).

45. The meme takes its theme from the news event in March 2019 when Mexican president López Obrador demanded apologies from the Vatican and the Spanish Crown for human rights abuses committed during the Conquista.

46. Jaime Martínez Luna is a founder of the Organization in Defense of the Natural Resources and Social Development of the Sierra Juárez (Odrenasij), and Floriberto Díaz established the Committee of Defense and Development of Mixe Natural and Human Resources (Codremi). Comunalidad was first disseminated in written form in a hectographed document by these pioneer organizations representing the Zapotec and Ayuujk ethnic groups. Their members identified as "autochthonous peoples" (*pueblos autóctonos*) and claimed "communitarian self-determination" (*autodeterminación comunitaria*). A manifesto mentions Comunalidad in the demand of an independent education system "commensurate with our concepts of time and space" (see Mejía Piñeros and Sarmiento Silva 1987, 270). These ethnic organizations opposed the so-called national development, a euphemistic term of the Mexican government, which promoted the exploitation of forest and mining resources of the Sierra Norte by private enterprise.

47. See Aquino Moreschi (2012, 54) and interviews with Genaro Rojas, Tamazulapam, April 4, 2013, and Juana Vásquez, Yalálag, April 29, 2016.

48. Back then few Mexican anthropologists recognized Comunalidad as a theoretical approach that formed part of Mexican anthropology as a discipline.

49. At the Second International Congress of Comunalidad it was publicly announced that the Autonomous University Benito Juárez of Oaxaca (UABJO) would cooperate with Tlahuitoltepec with regard to academic training on Comunalidad. In November 2020, the Autonomous Communal University (UACO) was launched in Oaxaca under the intellectual leadership of Jaime Martínez Luna. See also Nava Morales (2020).

50. Recording of the Second International Congress of Comunalidad, Tlahuitoltepec, March 5, 2018.

51. Radio Jënpoj is currently accessible by web radio in the United States; see http://jenpojradio .info/inicio/.

52. Ojo de Agua Comunicación was and continues to be a pivotal alternative media organization with headquarters in Oaxaca City since 1998. It offered support to people from Indigenous villages who were developing media outlets such as communitarian radio stations and provided them with training. At the same time, Ojo de Agua Comunicación functioned as a film production company that accepted assignments in addition to designing its own projects. At the Fourth Encounter of Communitarian, Communication Ojo de Agua Comunicación relied on funding from the Angelica Foundation (United States) and Kultura Comunicación Desarrollo ONGD (Basque Country).

53. Interview with Genaro Rojas, Tamazulapam, September 9, 2019. In the meantime, the Rojas brothers have further elaborated the *exta'n* concept defining it as "symbolism, media and meeting spaces where memory that reinforces the cosmovision of the Ayuujk or Mixe people is shared" (Rojas et al. 2021). They stress that everyone may contribute to this community-building memory from a different perspective.

54. Odilia Romero, who comes from Zoogocho in the Sierra Norte and migrated with her family to Los Angeles at the age of eleven, has led a long career as an activist in FIOB. She has also been involved as an interpreter of Bene xhon (Sierra Zapotec language) in Los Angeles. During her leadership at FIOB between 2017 and 2020, she continued to work closely with the Los Angeles police to defend Indigenous rights at court proceedings and offered training to interpreters of Oaxacan Indigenous languages (see Blackwell 2009; Newdick and Romero 2017).

55. Odilia here refers to the concept of Guelaguetza, defined as forms of collaboration that imply reciprocity (see below and for a historical perspective Flores-Marcial 2015).

56. Interview with Odilia Romero, Los Angeles, March 21, 2016.

57. Interview with Gaspar Rivera-Salgado, Los Angeles, April 4, 2016.

58. The Guelaguetza Festival in Oaxaca can be traced back to the Homenaje Racial (Racial Homage) hosted by the Oaxacan state government in 1932 (Lizama Quijano 2006, 107–122). The mass event was later renamed Guelaguetza.

59. The Los Angeles Guelaguetza is essentially supported by the dance groups of migrant associations from Oaxaca and folklórico troupes (see Chávez 2013; Escala and Rivera-Salgado 2018).

60. Interview with Dalila Castillo and Isaí Pazos, Los Angeles, August 12, 2017.

61. The migrant associations that cooperate with ORO and host the Los Angeles Guelaguetza Festival are from villages with historic migration that began early in the twentieth century, such as San Pablo Macuiltianguis, whereas Ayuujk communities have remained peripheral (see the ORO website: http://www.guelaguetzaoro.com/, "Community & Groups Affiliated"). With regard to the boom of second-generation Oaxacan bandas, see Chávez (2017, 2020).

62. Telemundo 52 is a Spanish-language television channel that was launched by NBCUniversal in 1984 and has its headquarters in Los Angeles.

63. For a critical analysis of the disparity between the aspirations of the American Dream, defined as immigrants' possibility to advance economically regardless of class, gender, race, or ethnicity, see Valdez (2011); with regard to Zapotec and Tojolabal migrants pursuing the American Dream, see Aquino Moreschi (2012).

64. Young people who entered the United States before the age of sixteen without authorization may be eligible for recognition according to the Deferred Action for Childhood Arrivals (DACA) program implemented by the Obama administration in 2012. They are popularly known as Dreamers, a term referring to the DREAM Act (Development, Relief, and Education for Alien Minors Act), first introduced in 2001 but never passed. Under certain conditions DACA authorizes these migrant youth to pursue higher education and work legally. The Trump administration tried to end DACA, a move that was blocked by the courts.

65. See https://trademark.trademarkia.com/festival-guelaguetza-86184016.html.

66. Interview with Isaí Pazos, Los Angeles, March 9, 2016.


CHAPTER 2    HISTORIES OF MEDIATIC SELF-DETERMINATION

1. The number of patron saint festivals celebrated according to the Catholic calendar is extensive since each municipality honors at least one patron saint and within each municipality every *rancho* or *agencia* (settlement) venerates its own saint. In the case of Tamazulapam el Espíritu Santo (the Holy Spirit), Santa Rosa de Lima, and the patron saints of nine settlements are commemorated; Yalálag observes five saint days: San Antonio, San Juan, Santiago, Santa Rosa, and Santa Catarina. In the Sierra Norte I participated in the fiestas celebrated in Tamazulapam and its agencias, Tlahuitoltepec, Zacatepec, Alotepec, Huayapam, Chuxnabán (agencia of Quetzaltepec), Yalálag, and Xochixtepec. In Los Angeles I was present at the *kermesses* of the migrant associations of Yalálag (organized separately by four barrios), Roayaga, Solaga, Yojovi, and Yaganiza. In some communities one or two video enterprises operate on-site; in most cases they are family businesses. Specific outlets serve multiple villages within a larger region such as Video Cajonos, which covers most of the Sierra Juárez (see my film *Ayuujk Cameras*).

2. Currently these video enterprises offer their clients a variety of local and at the same time transnational genres such as patron saint fiesta videos, family rite-of-passage videos (*eventos sociales*), officeholder videos, and documentaries about political disputes (Kummels 2017a, 34–35). The range of genres varies depending on the village, the format offered by the videographer, and the time period. For Yalálag, see Estrada Ramos (2001) and Gutiérrez Nájera (2007); for Los Angeles, see Costanza-Chock (2014); for Tamazulapam and Los Angeles, consult Kummels (2017a).

3.  La Danza de la Malinche, for example, is performed in different versions in Yalálag and Tamazulapam and depicts the colonial Spanish invasion ("Conquista") with historical figures such as Moctezuma and Malinche (Malintzin). The perspectives of these dances and their embodied messages differ from hegemonic historiography, which formerly emphasized the agency and power of the colonizers.

4.  Salvador is a pseudonym.

5.  For a critical analysis of this version of media history that homogenizes the local and predominantly autonomous media initiatives of Indigenous communities and accredits the emergence of Video Indígena foremost to the *indigenismo* policies of the Mexican government, see Kummels (2017a, 4–5, 198–208) and Schiwy and Wammack (2017).

6.  Identification with the categories Indigenous, White, and so on always implies a conscious positioning of oneself and the making of a political statement. The misnomer *indio* or *india* (literally inhabitant of India) was imposed by the Spanish colonial empire on the autochthonous population to subordinate them to tribute payments. When Mexico gained its independence, "Indigenous" was eliminated as a legal category but was reproduced in other ways to marginalize this sector of the national population considered culturally and racially different. Since 1992, article 2 of the Mexican constitution has defined the nation as pluricultural and recognizes its Indigenous peoples (*pueblos indígenas*) as its foundation, because they already inhabited its territory before Spanish colonization. Nevertheless, they are simultaneously viewed as the nation's "Others." Their languages and social life are stereotyped, as, for example, occurs in television programs promoting tourism by depicting Indigenous peoples as relics of a remote past. In contrast, since the 1970s Indigenous movements have appropriated the term "Indigenous" and redefined it as a positive self-reference. They also call themselves *pueblos originarios* to emphasize their current demands of autonomy, that is, rights to their ancestral land, its conservation and exploitation of natural resources, and the organization of community life according to their own principles. "White" is an allegedly neutral category for race/people that is still recorded in official questionnaires in Mexico and the United States. People who identify as "White" in day-to-day life mostly claim a belonging to the dominant population group of Mexico (called "mestizo" in intellectual circles and scholarship), based on subjectively interpreted physical criteria of Whiteness; at the same time, they distance themselves from groups that they exclude and subordinate as "ethnic minorities." As to situate myself, I never identified as "White" since I was raised with the awareness of my culturally, ethnically, and socially diverse background and have cultivated the complexity of my roots (influenced by my Cuban mother, German father, Chinese grandfather, "mulatto" maternal grandmother, and paternal German grandmother from Middle Franconia). Besides, I have experienced school, training, and work in several countries of Europe and the Americas, in non-Indigenous and Indigenous lifeworlds. For the purposes of this study, I am a German woman with a Cuban/Latina mother who was born in Los Angeles; therefore, I am considered a partly non-White migrant who obtained U.S. citizenship by birthplace.

7.  Interview with Francisco "Pancho" Limeta, Yalálag, May 25, 2016. Pancho dedicates himself mainly to videography on weekends, while he butchers pigs during weekdays and earns a living selling meat, sausage, and pork rinds.

8.  Communal labor mandated by the village's General Assembly often consists of contributions to the construction or maintenance of buildings, roads, and other infrastructure. Until the 1980s, in Yalálag this form of service obligation was restricted to men, with some exceptions for single women and widows as heads of households. Whoever complies with this form of public work is recognized as a full-fledged member/citizen of the village.

9.  Interview with Juana Vásquez, Yalálag, April 29, 2016.

10.  Interview with Israel Monterrubio and Bernarda Salvador, May 24, 2016.

11.  Interview with Francisco "Pancho" Limeta, Yalálag, May 25, 2016.

12.  Interview with Juana Vásquez, Yalálag, April 29, 2016.

13. Most villages invest considerable efforts in lining up the largest and most musically adept municipal brass band possible. The band promotes internal cohesion and represents the community's strength to others. Participation as a musician (until the 1990s limited to men) is recognized as a form of village service. Members of influential families formerly constituted the majority in these bands and sometimes used their position to control village governance.

14. Lourdes Gutiérrez Nájera (2007, 161–166) describes how videos showing conflict and violent confrontation in Yalálag between 1989 and 1998 were consumed and commented on by Yalaltec migrants living in Los Angeles in 1999.

15. Interview with Francisco "Pancho" Limeta, Yalálag, May 25, 2016. The following excerpts also derive from this interview. Patron saint fiestas have been recorded since 1987, the celebration for San Antonio since 1988 (see Estrada Ramos 2001, 112).

16. San Antonio became important as the patron saint of cattle in the 1940s. He was then added to the traditional group of four saints that represent barrios (San Juan, Santiago, Santa Rosa de Lima, and Santa Catarina Mártir) as a saint that serves the whole community (De la Fuente [1949] 1977, 261–264, 284). Subsequently San Antonio became the icon of the transnational Yalaltec community (Cruz-Manjarrez 2013, 79–82).

17. Informal conversations with Jaime Morales and others, Yalálag, April 2017.

18. Interview with Leonardo Ávalos Bis, Yalálag, April 29, 2016.

19. The Yalaltec brass band Uken ke Uken included musical training and membership for girls in 2003. Email from Juana Vásquez, February 24, 2022.

20. Pancho Limeta resides in the neighborhood of Santa Catarina, Víctor Monterrubio of San Juan and Héctor Bis and Leonardo Ávalos Bis of Santiago. Videographers give preference to commissions from their neighborhood.

21. These videographers had immigrated to California at the end of the 1980s.

22. Interview with Arturo Vargas, Los Angeles, April 1, 2016; the following excerpts also derive from this interview.

23. *Pozontle* is a fresh drink made of chocolate and the wild plant *cocolmeca*. *Tlayudas* consist of large tortillas on which crushed beans are spread and topped with Oaxacan cheese and a dry meat called *tasajo*. *Mermelas* are small tortillas adorned with different ingredients. *Quesadillas* consist of Oaxacan cheese folded in fried tortillas.

24. Interview with Juana Vásquez, Yalálag, April 29, 2016.

25. At these early workshops, which were organized by state National Indigenist Institute (INI) and later by the independent media center Ojo de Agua Communicación in the 1990s, the expectation was that Indigenous trainees would develop their own original documentary style. Paradoxically, at these workshops films made by non-Indigenous anthropologists showing Indigenous peoples were screened as models for filmmaking (Kummels 2017a, 205–208).

26. Informal conversation with Antonio Hilario, Xochixtepec, September 30, 2017.

27. Informal conversation with Ignacio Hernández, Xochixtepec, September 30, 2017. The price to smuggle a person across the border at the end of the 1970s was $600. Concerning the banda of Xochixtepec, see also https://boomingbandas.com/en-espanol/.

28. Informal conversation with Melissa Pablo-Hernández, Xochixtepec, September 30, 2017.

29. Informal interview with Emanuel Pérez Morales, Xochixtepec, October 2, 2017.

30. See, for example, https://id-id.facebook.com/pg/benexhonvideos/videos/?ref=page_internal.

31. Interview with Edmundo Ambrosio, Lachiroag, August 19, 2015.

32. Interview with Erik and Fernanda, Tamazulapam, January 4, 2019.

33. Interview with Antonio Cruz of Video Richi, Güilá, March 10, 2018.

34. Interview with Juana Vásquez, Yalálag, April 29, 2016.

**35.** Interviews with Hermenegildo Rojas, Tamazulapam, September 4, 2013, and Arturo Vargas, Los Angeles, April 1, 2016.

**36.** According to the U.S. Motion Picture Association, between February and October 2004 alone 12.9 million pirated VHS cassettes, 6.1 million (music) CDs, and 4.4 million DVDs were sold at the informal market of Tepito in Mexico City. See also Cross (2011).

**37.** Interview with Salvador, Los Angeles, July 28, 2017.

**38.** A number of media anthropologists, political scientists, and communication scholars have examined—particularly since the so-called Twitter Revolution of the Arab Spring—the specific characteristics of communities that essentially network via social media and online platforms. In such cases they become a community in the process of online networking (for examples from Latin America, see Treré 2019). In contrast, preexisting communities that merely expand their social life via online activities have different features. A team of researchers conducted a comparative investigation of small preexisting communities (with several thousands of inhabitants) in Trinidad, Italy, and China and discovered that to a significant extent users reproduce online the social control and norms of the offline community (McDonald, Nicolescu, and Sinanan 2017, 89).

**39.** See https://www.facebook.com/artvo/. The slogan of this streaming outlet is "Connected with Our People." Its website proclaims, "Our streaming covers every aspect of the patron saint fairs of the Sierra Mixe."

**40.** To date, the majority of Yalálag's General Assembly has rejected investment in the acquisition of an antenna and services of a private enterprise because of concerns about expense, among other reasons. As an alternative, users resort to local private suppliers who offer internet services. Through an informal arrangement, they also use the internet at the local clinic. Connectivity in Yalálag was bound to increase starting in September 2022. The state program "Internet for Everyone" ("Internet para todos"), which the López Obrador administration had announced in 2019, had recently installed an antenna covering the village.

**41.** See https://de-de.facebook.com/KanzioLizeFilms/.

**42.** Interview with Eliel Cruz, Tamazulapam, September 13, 2019.

**43.** During the Santa Rosa festivities in 2021, I was often able to accompany Eliel at his transmissions and exchange views with him about his media work.

**44.** See Kummels (2017a, 228). Compare with the Tamix Multimedios website covering the Santa Rosa fiesta, https://www.facebook.com/Tamixmultimedios/.

## CHAPTER 3    ZAPOTEC DANCE EPISTEMOLOGIES ONLINE

**1.** This chapter evolved from Kummels (2021 and the preceding conference in 2017). I conducted this part of the research as head of a subproject at the Collaborative Research Center titled "Affective Societies. Dynamics of Social Coexistence in Mobile World," supported by the German Research Foundation (DFG).

**2.** The Acervo de Cine y Video Alfonso Muñoz mainly stores ethnographic documentaries produced by non-Indigenous Mexican anthropologists from the late 1950s to the early 1990s. Sierra Zapotec dances are dealt with in two documentaries: *Danza de Conquista* by Fernando Cámara Sánchez (1978) and *De bandas, vida y otros sones* by Sonia Fritz (1985). A number of important community archives exist in the state of Oaxaca that may also house additional films concerning Sierra Zapotec dances. For example, the independent media organization Ojo de Agua Comunicación maintains a large video repository that has been digitalized. Nevertheless, its descriptive metadata are still incomplete.

**3.** Interview with Pam, Los Angeles, July 31, 2017.

**4.** *Polaca* is a game of chance that uses boards with emblematic figures of Mexican flora, fauna, and culture. Players who draw cards need to match them with the same figures on their boards and usually make bets. Children use corn kernels and beans as the game's currency.

5. These are the expressions often used by my interlocutors.

6. The term "heart," or *lhall* in Zapotec, refers to what Zapotec people consider the source of affects. Interlocutors would refer, for example, to a heart that "shrinks" and provokes sadness, or one that "opens itself" and generates joy (notes from a conversation with Juana Vásquez, Yalálag, April 15, 2017). Following Brian Massumi (2002, 27), I differentiate affects from emotions and attribute to the first a more dynamic quality. While emotions correspond to culturally shaped conceptualizations, affects refer to the impact and agitation that "affected" persons experience during relational interaction, relations concerning those between persons as well as those between a person and an entity or an object. Affects are often experienced as the intensity of what is perceived as a new difference in contrast to what had existed before (see also SFB 1171 Affective Societies 2016, 3–5).

7. Interview with Cecilia Mestas, Yalálag, July 26, 2016.

8. La Danza de los Negritos is, for example, claimed by the neighborhood of Santa Rosa; La Danza de los Cuerudos and La Danza de los Negritos Colmilludos are deemed to be property of the neighborhood of Santiago; La Danza de San José is claimed by the neighborhood of Santa Catalina; and Los Huenches is considered property of the neighborhood of San Juan.

9. Interview with Malaquías Allende, Yalálag, September 13, 2017. As a resident of the Santiago barrio in Yalálag, Malaquías began to document dance history, precisely to substantiate the neighborhood's claim on dances such as La Danza de los Cuerudos.

10. Interview with Salvador, Los Angeles, April 8, 2018.

11. Interview with Sebastián, February 26, 2017.

12. Interviews with Román Delgado, Yalálag, October 4, 2017; Francisco "Antelmo" Aquino, Yalálag, September 4, 2017; Víctor Hugo Díaz, Los Ángeles, April 10, 2018; and Malaquías Allende, Yalálag, September 14, 2017.

13. Interview with Román Delgado, Yalálag, October 4, 2017.

14. The second performance of La Danza de la Negritas in Yalálag was published on YouTube. See https://www.youtube.com/watch?v=9yGAUDfXMV0.

15. Interview with Marta and José, Los Angeles, February 27, 2017.

16. Interview with Sebastián, Los Angeles, February 26, 2017.

17. On YouTube one can view recordings of dances performed by a group of second-generation descendants from San Bartolomé Zoogocho in that same Mexican village. They include young women born in Los Angeles, but whose parents come from the communities of Zoochina, Yatzachi el Alto, Zoogocho, and Xochixtepec. These villages are near Yalálag in the Oaxacan Sierra Norte and make up the so-called Sector Zoogocho. The female group of the Zoogocho community in Los Angeles was the first to coin the term La Danza de las Negritas. See https://www.youtube.com/watch?v=SGq_FMWDW8g; https://www.youtube.com/watch?v=IM44XolWe58; https://www.youtube.com/watch?v=c7FqTwZi2lM. See also Nicolas (2021).

18. Interview with Lisvelia Hilario, Los Angeles, January 8, 2017. The quotes in this section are from this same source, unless otherwise indicated.

19. Informal conversation with Kanzio Lize, Yalálag, July 26, 2016.

## CHAPTER 4   THE FIESTA CYCLE AND TRANSNATIONAL DEATH

1. The internet radio pages are https://www.facebook.com/radiocantautoroaxaca/, https://www.facebook.com/Radio-Gobixha, https://www.facebook.com/radioestrelladeoaxaca/, https://sq-al.facebook.com/pages/category/Radio-Station/Super-Antequera-Radio-HD-181669498903045/ and https://www.facebook.com/pages/category/Fan-Page/La-Voz-de-yalalag-1027-Los-Angeles-Ca-1178930105612165/.

2. With regard to the distinction between a migrant committee and a formal hometown association, see chapter 1, note 29. I estimate that there are around twenty migrant associations affiliated with Yalálag and Sector Zoogocho in Los Angeles.

3. The president of the barrio committee of Santiago had provided his private home for the event. The migrant associations from Yalálag and further villages of the Zapotec Sierra region solemnize each of the nine days before a *kermés* (a period called *novenario*) with a rosary for the respective patron saint.

4. Enfoque Latino broadcasts from Studio City, a district in North Los Angeles. The activist Ruben Tapia launched the radio station in 1986 to support refugees from El Salvador and Guatemala who had come to Los Angeles in large numbers fleeing from civil wars and persecution in their home countries. From January 2017 on the radio station began to broadcast via its Facebook page as well; see https://www.facebook.com/EnfoqueLatinoKPFK90.7FM/. Reporter Cristina Ramírez from Enfoque Latino specifically engaged with migrant associations from Yalálag and disseminated their activities via her Facebook page "Crónicas de OaxaCalifornia."

5. Cuban American sociologist Rubén G. Rumbaut coined the term "one-and-a-half" or "1.5" generation to distinguish Latin American immigrants who passed their childhood and part of their adolescence in their country of origin before migrating to the United States. Rumbaut distinguishes life stages in order to analyze their influence on integration in the target county.

6. In the course of the 1990s a great number of migration policies were implemented on a national level as well as by the U.S. states bordering Mexico to block illegal entries of Mexican migrants. They impeded the pattern of a circular migration common up to then and instead paradoxically enhanced mass immigration and long-term residence (Trevizo and Lopez 2018, 24–30). In the past years it has become increasingly difficult and expensive to cross the border back into the United States without documents. According to my interlocutors, coyotes charged up to $10,000 to smuggle persons to the United States in the period between 2016 and 2021.

7. I visited several wakes in Yalálag and Los Angeles, including one in Los Angeles commemorating Enriqueta, at the beginning of April 2016, and another commemorating Jairo Diego Aquino on March 27, 2018. Both of them passed away in Yalálag. Ten interviews specifically on the topic of parallel wakes in Los Angeles were conducted. Depending on their life stage, migrants from Yalálag identified with distinct primary places of belonging; in the course of life, they changed their opinion with regard to the community that they believed would remember them most after death. In some cases, persons at retirement returned to their hometown Yalálag after having spent many years in Los Angeles, in agreement with their children in the United States. They took advantage of their retirement stage to engage in the hometown's governance. Returnees are required to serve as officials in Yalálag. Pensioners who had opted to reintegrate to the hometown envisaged their burial there.

8. In Yalálag the home wake is only one element of an elaborate funerary process for a deceased person. It includes nine days of daily rosaries and on the ninth day the Lifting of the Cross (*Levantada de Cruz*), with which the public mourning rituals conclude. In Los Angeles these traditional rituals are condensed on one day.

9. Already in the 1930s anthropologist Julio de la Fuente ([1949] 1977, 205) mentions that when an unchristened child died in Yalálag "a wake is considered a 'good one' when there was much dancing, rejoicing and a lot of liquor and food were offered."

10. Because volunteering in Los Angeles is not recognized as serving in an office in Yalálag, migrants cannot ascend rapidly in the political governance when returning to their hometown. When they assume service there, they are first elected to a low-ranking office.

11. Los Angeles committees normally coordinate their work tightly with the committee of the same name in Yalálag. The collaboration concerns the handing over of the donations from the United States and the supervision of construction work in the hometown financed with these funds.

12. The migrant associations in general tend to develop sports facilities and a communal kitchen or a dining room in the compound surrounding the chapel of the patron saint of a

neighborhood. That is, they provide for infrastructure to host numerous guests at patron saint celebrations.

13. In 2018 the costs for a grave at the Holy Cross Park Cemetery amounted between $7,000 and $15,000.

14. Fueled by remittances and the investments of hometown associations in their native villages, in 2002 the Mexican government began to support their projects by cofinancing them through the Three-for-One program. When formally recognized hometown associations finance a project in Mexico, their investment is matched and tripled with federal, regional, and local subsidies. Experts have since either highly praised or heavily criticized the program. From a critical perspective, Sarah Lynn Lopez (2015, 73) points out that the Mexican government's Three-for-One program is a means of reducing its own contribution to rural development, instead tasking migration with the role of driving development. In 2004, the attempt to implement a Three-for-One program in Yalálag sparked ongoing tensions between migrant associations in Los Angeles and the hometown governance in Yalálag. A Yalaltec businessman managing the program from Los Angeles was accused of embezzlement and using inferior materials for building a wall on the compound at the Church of San Antonio, which collapsed (see Cruz-Manjarrez 2013, 92).

15. In Yalálag only a very rudimentary equipped state clinic exists. Patients are forced (among others for childbirth) to travel two hours to Villa Alta or three hours to Oaxaca City. Emergencies are at risk of receiving medical support much too late.

16. *Dazangurhe llin dekze gak chenhakrhe gakhren ben yell, kerhe nhazen iz dazan da yalljze, ba brhekzerhen rhao bxhenha*; transcription and translation by Pedro Ruiz Vásquez.

17. I estimate the number of migrant associations from Sierra Norte in Los Angeles is greater than the number of the sixty-eight municipalities they originate from. The associations from Yalálag and the villages of Sector Zoogocho foster particularly tight relationships. There are six associations affiliated with Yalálag in Los Angeles, and further villages, such as San Pablo Yaganiza, are represented by separate associations for Catholics and Evangelicals.

18. See https://www.lataco.com/an-ode-to-oaxacan-l-a-friday-nights-at-ponchos-tlayudas/.

19. Interview with Adrián Beltrán, Los Angeles, March 27, 2018.

20. "The Voice of Our Villages" ("La Voz de Nuestros Pueblos") is the leading motto of Radio Cantautor.

21. The climax of the love song of a man for a woman is a Yalaltecan-style marriage proposal ("Tell me how many pairs of turkeys do you want") and an offer that reveals adaptation to the Los Angeles labor market: "Ask for anything that you want señorita. And I'll get even two jobs."

22. Interview with Leti, Los Angeles, April 2, 2019. The following excerpts also derive from this interview.

23. Interview with Verónica, Los Angeles, March 31, 2018. The following excerpts also derive from this interview.

24. Interview with Maricela, Los Angeles, April 12, 2018.

## CHAPTER 5      AYUUJK BASKETBALL TOURNAMENT BROADCASTS

1. In parallel with López Obrador's visit to the Copa Benito Juárez tournament, a regional convention of village officials took place in Guelatao, Oaxaca, in support of a constitutional reform recognizing Indigenous peoples as legal entities. The latter was the purpose of the presidential political tour to Oaxaca in March 2019. See https://www.gob.mx/inpi/articulos/pueblos-indigenas-conmemoran-el-ccxiii-aniversario-del-natalicio-del-licenciado-benito-juarez-garcia-en-guelatao-de-juarez-oaxaca?tab=.

2. For a more detailed version, see Kummels (2017a, 151–156) and Kummels (2018).

3. Interview with Leandro Hernández, Zacatepec, October 16, 2019. Leandro was well acquainted with Luis Rodríguez as a youth since Rodríguez was his godfather. The Ministry of

Education SEP promoted basketball shortly after the Mexican Revolution as part of its rural education program aimed at the assimilation of Indigenous peoples throughout Mexico. In the case of the Distrito Mixe, however, this program was not as successful in popularizing basketball as the Ayuujk strongman Rodríguez's policy on sports.

4. At flash championships the duration of a match is adapted to the number of teams participating in the competition and the total time available to compete.

5. The Comité de Defensa y Desarrollo de los Recursos Naturales y Humanos Mixe (Codremi), founded in the late 1970s, was one of the first ethnically based Ayuujk organizations.

6. Informal conversation, Tamazulapam, September 9, 2019.

7. Interview with Constantino Vásquez, Tamazulapam, September 17, 2019. At the re-initiation of the basketball tournament, one of the first to act as a sponsor was a village woman. See the Tamix Multimedios film of the Copa Mixe in 2005, https://fb.watch/7DPWGGRdQ2/.

8. Interview with Joaquín Ortiz Aguirre, Tamazulapam, August 23, 2016. In 2016 there was growing talk of the *nación Ayuujk* in connection with the broad resistance of Indigenous teachers organized in the union Sección 22 to the educational reform implemented by the Peña Nieto government.

9. Most inhabitants of Tamazulapam profess *costumbres* or "our own religion"; that is, they worship the forces of wind, lightning, and water at natural sacred sites. Ritual offerings of a complex composition are determined by consulting a diviner. The diviners figure out the exact numbers and precise mixture of the elements to be offered. These include poultry of a certain color, size, and age (fowl blood is a central element of the sacrifices), and symbolic food such as *tamales* and maize dough figures. The offerings are gathered according to numbers related to the Mesoamerican calendar. This has been combined with the veneration of Catholic saints introduced by European missionaries. The offering of *päknë* is also performed as a public act at the Guelaguetza Festival.

10. I acted as a trophy sponsor of the Copa Ayuujk tournaments in 2016 and 2019, which allowed for ethnographic insights from this perspective too, even though my sponsorship as a non-Ayuujk person was a special case.

11. Village governance issues official certification of the investment and exemption from service. The trophies are challenge cups; a team that wins it three times may keep the cup. A silver trophy may cost up to 52,000 pesos ($2,500).

12. Only some of the online viewers follow the playoffs live. Instead, most watch them shortly after. The administrator of the Facebook page gave me information on the total number of viewers.

13. The administrator of the Facebook page provided insight into the composition of its audience during this match: Oaxaca 46.7 percent, California 20.2 percent, Distrito Federal 5.82 percent, Guanajuato 3.07 percent, Wisconsin 2.38 percent, Querétaro 2.31 percent, State of Mexico 1.92 percent, Washington 1.73 percent, San Luis Potosí 1.66 percent, Georgia 1.24 percent. Interview with Eliel Cruz, Tamazulapam, September 13, 2019.

14. Broadcasting in 2019 still required paying for private internet services, whose costs due to the region's scarce supply of antennas and providers are substantial, around $100 for a daylong broadcast.

15. These are symbols of Ayuujk culture that also decorate the woven sashes of the typical women's attire of Tamazulapam.

16. In 2022, after reaching an agreement on the border demarcation between both neighboring villages, Ayutla basketball teams resumed participation in the Copa Ayuujk in Tamazulapam, highlighting the achievement of peace after years of intense conflict.

17. The Bajío, a transitional region between Northern Mexico and the Central Mexican Plateau, includes parts of the states of Aguascalientes, Jalisco, Guanajuato, Querétaro, San Luis Potosí, and Zacatecas.

**18.** *Costumbres*, sacrifices of fowl to Mother Earth and forces of nature, are mainly carried out at natural sites in the homeland. They are now practiced in the Bajío primarily within the taco restaurants in order to safeguard them.

**19.** Interview with Eliseo Martínez, Celaya, March 8, 2019.

**20.** Interview with Leónides Calderón, Querétaro, March 5, 2019.

**21.** See "Un fracaso, el operativo, Golpe de Timón! Guanajuato no deja de sangrar . . . ," *Proceso*, March 17, 2019, 23–25.

**22.** *Fútbol 7* is a version of soccer with only seven players and modified rules.

**23.** The basketball teams came from the states of Guanajuato, Guadalajara, San Luis Potosí, Pachuca, Morelia, Aguascalientes, Ciudad de México, and Querétaro. The fútbol 7 teams also included the state of Veracruz.

**24.** This way of collecting prize money from the teams and distributing it between the three first-place teams is called *el botín*, the booty.

**25.** The administrator of the page provided insight into the composition of the audience at the final game: Oaxaca 24.4 percent, California 18.9 percent, Guanajuato 9.15 percent, Distrito Federal 8.8 percent, Querétaro 5.34 percent, Washington 4.57 percent, Tennessee 4.33 percent, Durango 3.84 percent, Wisconsin 3.83 percent, and Aguascalientes 3.76 percent.

**26.** See https://www.elsoldelbajio.com.mx/deportes/realizan-torneo-mixe-bajio-2019-sexta-edicion-basquetbol-futbol-unidad-deportiva-celaya-equipos-campeones-edicion-3188262.html.

**27.** Interview with Rolando, Los Angeles, March 28, 2019.

**28.** See https://elnuevosol.net/2018/06/radio-nepantla-cesar-bravo/.

**29.** *Baby fút* is a fast version of soccer played with five players on a fifteen- by twenty-five-meter field.

## CHAPTER 6    TURNING FIFTEEN TRANSNATIONALLY

**1.** Interview with Sandra, Los Angeles, August 1, 2019.

**2.** According to estimates by the videographer, costs for a quinceañera celebration range from $12,000 to $30,000; interview with Salvador, Los Angeles, August 8, 2018. In the case of Francis's party, the costs amounted to $28,000 according to her mother; interview with Eustolia, Los Angeles, March 29, 2019.

**3.** Salvador gained expertise in filmmaking with the help of an experienced friend. He owns equipment worth around $10,000. His professionalism relies on detailed knowledge of the manual settings required to produce certain images and moods, like white balance to record clear images.

**4.** Salvador showed me his filled-up order book. Because of the demand he now employs two or three assistants on weekends or an additional videographer when two events are booked for the same time.

**5.** Thanks to the generosity of Salvador and his wife Yolanda, I would occasionally spend several hours at their home, where I was a casual witness to conversations with the hosts of an upcoming quinceañera about the commissioning of a video. This particular conversation took place in Los Angeles on August 4, 2017.

**6.** Popular features of a quinceañera video throughout the United States and Mexico are the presentation of her attendants during the morning; life of the quinceañera in souvenir photos; excursion with her chamberlains; mass at church; photo session with the chamberlains at a park; luxury vehicle (like a Hummer limousine) for her court along these routes; dinner buffet; entrance and dance performance, including waltz with family members, *padrinos*, and *madrinas*; toast; short speeches; handing over the last doll to the quinceañera; her coronation; as well as the cotillions with her court.

7. Interview with Salvador, Los Angeles, July 28, 2017.

8. I later found out that this property belonged to a distant cousin of Eustolia who had lent it to her for the five-day celebration.

9. I estimate that half of the community group has papers, while the other half is undocumented.

10. Interview with Francis, Los Angeles, March 29, 2019. The following quotes also derive from this interview.

11. Interview with Matilde, Los Angeles, March 29, 2019. The following quotes also derive from this interview.

12. An entry as a tourist is possible but often time-consuming and expensive. Mexicans applying for a visa have to seek out the embassy in Mexico City or another city and undergo an interview. They must prove their regular earnings and comply with further requisites to acquire a visa.

13. The three DVDs were arranged according to the following chapters: DVD 1: Intro, Francis—My Story, Excursion with the chamberlains to Santa Monica, My clothing in the morning, Santo Tomás Church, Photos and video in the park, Our reception, Chocolate fountain, "Las Mañanitas"; DVD 2: Presentation (Last doll), Coronation, Toast, Main waltz, *Sones* and *jarabes*, Surprise dance; DVD 3: Dance in Yalalatec costume, "El Ratón."

14. Aldo Cruz migrated 15 years ago from Oaxaca to Los Angeles. Since then, he has been active in forming the umbrella group Organización Regional de Oaxaca (ORO) and participating in the multi-ethnic cultural life of Los Angeles. I became acquainted with him at large events in the city like Oaxacan Heritage Month and the Guelaguetza Festival.

15. Interview with Francisco, Los Angeles, March 29, 2019.

16. Interview with Eustolia, Los Angeles, March 29, 2019. Matilde mentioned in a positive vein that because she had grown up with her aunt, she was able to learn Zapotec when she was a child.

17. Informal conversations with guests at the quinceañera, Los Angeles, April 14, 2018.

18. Their adult daughters were the ones who drew my attention to this behavior. Informal interview with Erika, Los Angeles, April 8, 2018.

19. In the municipality of Yalálag, concerns about the cost of an antenna and services from a private company (among other reasons) have led the majority to reject the investment. Private suppliers offer internet services, and clinic facilities are available for informal use.

20. In 2012, Deferred Action for Childhood Arrivals (DACA) was implemented by President Barack Obama as a policy that grants unauthorized immigrants brought to the United States as children renewable, two-year permits that protect them from deportation and allow them to work legally.

21. Besides engaging in cultural events, this umbrella organization of numerous Indigenous migrant communities in Los Angeles also promotes Three-for-One projects. The Three-for-One projects of the Mexican government are matching funds programs for investments that formal hometown associations from the United States undertake in Mexico. In 2001 Gerardo Vásquez from Yalálag founded the umbrella organization FOCOICA in Los Angeles. One of their Three-for-One projects triggered a controversy in Yalálag (see chapter 4 and Cruz-Manjarrez 2013, 92).

22. Zine is a collective term for low-circulation publications produced with accessible means like a photocopier. These author editions are in general subcultural forms of art that propose an alternative to or extension of conventional publications. Their precursors were the fanzines produced for the fan groups of subcultural bands.

23. See chapter 2 concerning this incident at a *kermés* celebrated in honor of Santa Rosa de Lima.

24. See https://www.cbc.ca/news/indigenous/indigenous-nativetwitter-influencers-1.4824534.

25. The university had announced plans to commercialize this "miracle corn plant," which a UC Davis professor "discovered" in 1992 in the Ayuujk village of Totontepec with the help of Indigenous aides (Pskowski 2019).

26. In January 2015, Oaxacan artist Susana Harp discovered that the exclusive Dallas-based department store Neiman Marcus was selling Tlahuitoltepec blouses (see https://ar-ar .facebook.com/SusanaHarp/posts/sobre-el-plagio-del-huipil-de-tlahuitoltepec-oaxaca -debido-a-esta-tercera-ola-qu/10153113783271481/). The Ayuujk village used its community radio Jënpoj and other resources to widely disseminate its protest of the infraction of their cultural rights by French designer Isabel Marant and its demands for a legal framework to protect Mexican textile art. In January 2022, the Mexican government passed legislation to protect autochthonous designs, but Yalaltec political scientist Ariadna Itzel Solís Bautista has criticized its shortcomings. See https://www.elmanana.com/combate-a-la-apropiacion-cultural-la-nueva-ley-muy -mercantil-/5493815.

## CHAPTER 7   EPILOGUE

1. Newspaper headlines expressed similar complaints about other Sierra Norte and Valles Centrales villages, for example: "Alotepec Celebrating Its Fiesta Despite Covid" or "People Insist on Infection with Covid: Patron Saint Fiesta to Take Place in Suchilquitongo." See https://www.rioaxaca.com/2020/04/05/autoridades-de-tamazulapam-desacatan-cuarentena-y -realizan-baile-popular/, https://www.eluniversal.com.mx/estados/alotepec-celebra-fiesta-pese -covid, and https://www.nssoaxaca.com/2020/07/25/insiste-gente-en-contagiarse-de-covid -realizan-fiesta-patronal-en-suchilquitongo/, published by the newspapers *Rioaxaca*, *El Universal*, and *NSS Oaxaca*.

# REFERENCES

Abidin, Crystal. 2016. "'Aren't These Just Young, Rich Women Doing Vain Things Online?' Influencer Selfies as Subversive Frivolity." *Social Media + Society* 2 (2): 1–17. https://doi.org/10.1177/2056305116641342.

Abrego, Leisy, and Genevieve Negrón-Gonzales, eds. 2020. *We Are Not Dreamers: Undocumented Scholars Theorize Undocumented Life in the United States*. Durham, NC: Duke University Press.

Acevedo Conde, María Luisa. 2012. *Sierra Norte*. Serie: Imágenes de una identidad. Oaxaca City: CIESAS.

Aguilar Gil, Yásnaya. 2020. *Ää: manifiestos sobre la diversidad lingüística*. Mexico City: Almadía/Bookmate.

Alamillo, José M. 2020. *Deportes: The Making of a Sporting Mexican Diaspora*. New Brunswick, NJ: Rutgers University Press.

Alarcón, Rafael, Luis Escala, and Olga Odgers. 2016. *Making Los Angeles Home. The Integration of Mexican Immigrants in the United States*. Berkeley: University of California Press.

Alberto, Lourdes. 2017. "Coming Out as Indian: On Being an Indigenous Latina in the US." *Latino Studies* 15 (2): 247–253.

Alinejad, Donya. 2017. *The Internet and Formations of Iranian American–ness. Next Generation Diaspora*. Cham: Palgrave Macmillan.

Anderson, Benedict. 1991. *Imagined Communities. Reflections on the Origin and Spread of Nationalism*. New York: Verso.

Andrews, Abigail Leslie. 2018. *Undocumented Politics: Place, Gender, and the Pathways of Mexican Migrants*. Berkeley: University of California Press.

Appadurai, Arjun. 1995. "Playing with Modernity: The Decolonization of Indian Cricket." In *Consuming Modernity: Public Culture in a South Asian World*, edited by Carol Breckenridge, 23–48. Minneapolis: University of Minnesota Press.

———. 1996. *Modernity at Large: Cultural Dimensions of Globalization*. Minneapolis: University of Minnesota Press.

———. 2003. "Archive and Aspiration." In *Information Is Alive: Art and Theory on Archiving and Retrieving Data*, edited by Joke Brouwer and Arjen Mulder, 14–25. Rotterdam: V2_Publishing and NAI.

Aquino Moreschi, Alejandra. 2012. *De las luchas indias al sueño americano. Experiencias migratorias de jóvenes zapotecos y tojolabales en Estados Unidos*. Mexico City: CIESAS and UAM-X.

———. 2013. "La comunalidad como epistemología del Sur: Aportes y retos." *Cuadernos del Sur* 34: 7–19.

Aufderheide, Patricia. 2007. *Documentary Film: A Very Short Introduction*. Oxford: Oxford University Press.

Bada, Xóchitl. 2014. *Mexican Hometown Associations in Chicagoacán: From Local to Transnational Civic Engagement*. New Brunswick, NJ: Rutgers University Press.

Baldassar, Loretta, and Raelene Wilding. 2020. "Migration, Aging, and Digital Kinning: The Role of Distant Care Support Networks in Experiences of Aging Well." *Gerontologist* 60 (2): 313–321.

Barabas, Alicia, and Miguel Bartolomé. 1984. *El Rey Cong-Hoy: Tradición mesiánica y privación social entre los Mixes de Oaxaca*. Oaxaca City: INAH.

Basch, Linda, Nina Glick Schiller, and Cristina Szanton-Blanc. 1994. *Nations Unbound: Transnational Projects, Postcolonial Predicaments and Deterritorialized Nation-States*. London: Routledge.

Basu, Paul, and Ferdinand De Jong. 2016. "Utopian Archives, Decolonial Affordances: Introduction to Special Issue." *Social Anthropology* 24 (1): 5–19.

Baym, Nancy K., and danah boyd. 2012. "Socially Mediated Publicness: An Introduction." *Journal of Broadcasting & Electronic Media* 56 (3): 320–329.

Beltrán, Cristina. 2015. "Undocumented, Unafraid, and Unapologetic: DREAM Activists, Immigrant Politics, and the Queering of Democracy." In *From Voice to Influence: Understanding Citizenship in a Digital Age*, edited by Danielle Allen and Jennifer S. Light, 80–104. Chicago: University of Chicago Press.

Berg, Ulla, and Ana Ramos Zayas. 2015. "Racializing Affect: A Theoretical Position." *Current Anthropology* 56 (5): 654–677.

Besnier, Niko, Susan Brownell, and Thomas F. Carter. 2018. *The Anthropology of Sport: Bodies, Borders, Biopolitics*. Berkeley: University of California Press.

Bird, Steven. 2020. "Decolonising Speech and Language Technology." In *Proceedings of the 28th International Conference on Computational Linguistics*, 3504–3519. Barcelona.

Blackwell, Maylei. 2009. "Mujer rebelde: testimonio de Odilia Romero Hernández." *Desacatos* 31: 147–156.

———. 2017. "Geographies of Indigeneity: Indigenous Migrant Women's Organizing and Translocal Space of Politics." *Latino Studies* 15 (2): 156–181.

———. 2018. "Indigeneity." In *Keywords in Latino/a Studies*, edited by Deborah R. Vargas, Nancy Raquel Mirabal, and Lawrence La Fountain-Stokes, 100–105. New York: New York University Press.

Bloom, Peter Lawrence. 2015. "La Telefonía Celular Comunitaria como alternativa ante el sistema hegemónico de telecomunicaciones en México. Un estudio de caso de las nuevas iniciativas en la Sierra Juárez, Oaxaca." Master's thesis, Universidad Autónoma Metropolitana–Xochimilco.

Boehm, Deborah A. 2013. *Intimate Migrations: Gender, Family, and Illegality among Transnational Mexicans*. New York: New York University Press.

Bolter, Jay David, and Richard Grusin. 2000. *Remediation: Understanding New Media*. Cambridge, MA: MIT Press.

Bonini, Tiziano. 2014. "The New Role of Radio and Its Public in the Age of Social Network Sites." *First Monday* 19 (6). https://doi.org/10.5210/fm.v19i6.4311.

Bourdieu, Pierre, and Marie-Claire Bourdieu. (1965) 2004. "The Peasant and Photography." *Ethnography*, 5 (4): 601–616.

boyd, danah. 2010. "Social Network Sites as Networked Publics: Affordances, Dynamics, and Implications." In *Networked Self: Identity, Community, and Culture on Social Network Sites*, edited by Zizi Papacharissi, 39–58. London: Routledge.

Bravo, Vanessa. 2017. "Coping with Dying and Deaths at Home: How Undocumented Migrants in the United States Experience the Process of Transnational Grieving." *Mortality* 22 (1): 33–44.

Bravo Muñoz, Loreto Alejandra. 2017. "Soñando nuevas infraestructuras. Telefonía Celular Autónoma, la hija prodigio de la radio comunitaria en México." In *Radio, redes e Internet para la transformación social*, edited by Vicente Barragán and Iván Terceros, 99–112. Quito: CEISPAL.

———. 2020. "Practitioner Perspective. Autonomous Infrastructures: Community Cell Phone Networks in Oaxaca, Mexico." In *Digital Activism, Community Media, and Sustainable Communication in Latin America*, edited by Cheryl Martens, Cristina Venegas, and Etsa Franklin Salvio Sharupi Tapuy, 163–173. Cham: Palgrave Macmillan.

Brown, Anna, Gustavo López, and Mark Hugo Lopez. 2016. "Digital Divide Narrows for Latinos as More Spanish Speakers and Immigrants Go Online." Pew Research Center, July 27, 2016. https://www.pewresearch.org/hispanic/2016/07/20/digital-divide-narrows-for-latinos-as-more-spanish-speakers-and-immigrants-go-online/.

Brunn, Stanley D., Donald J. Zeigler, Maureen Hays-Mitchell, and Jessica K. Graybill, eds. 2020. *Cities of the World: Regional Patterns and Urban Environments*. Lanham, MD: Rowman & Littlefield.

Bryceson, Deborah Fahy. 2019. "Transnational Families Negotiating Migration and Care Life Cycles across Nation-State Borders." *Journal of Ethnic and Migration Studies* 45 (16). doi.org /10.1080/1369183X.2018.1547017.

Budka, Philipp. 2019. "Indigenous Media Technologies in 'the Digital Age': Cultural Articulation, Digital Practices, and Sociocultural Concepts." In *Ethnic Media in the Digital Age*, edited by Sherry S. Yu and Matthew D. Matsaganis, 162–172. London: Routledge.

Caballero, Juan Julián, and Manuel Ríos Morales. 2003. "Impacto de la migración trasnacional entre los *Ñuu Savi* (mixtecos) y los *Béné Xhon* (zapotecos de la Sierra Norte) de Oaxaca." In *La Ruta Mixteca*, edited by Silvia Escárcega and Stefano Varese, 137–202. Mexico City: UNAM.

Çağlar, Ayse. 2018. "Chronotopes of Migration Scholarship: Challenges of Contemporaneity and Historical Conjuncture." In *Migration, Temporality and Capitalism*, edited by Pauline Gardiner Barber and Winnie Lem, 21–42. Cham: Palgrave Macmillan.

Cantú, Norma Elia. 2002. "Chicana Life-Rituals." In *Chicana Tradition: Continuity and Change*, edited by Norma Elia Cantú and Olga Nájera Ramírez, 15–34. Urbana: University of Illinois Press.

Castellanos, M. Bianet. 2015. "Idealizing Maya Culture: The Politics of Race, Indigeneity, and Immigration among Maya Restaurant Owners in Southern California." *Diálogo* 18 (2): 67–78.

———. 2017. "Rewriting the Mexican Immigrant Narrative: Situating Indigeneity in Maya Women's Stories." *Latino Studies* 15 (2): 219–241.

Castells, Manuel. 1996. *The Rise of the Network Society*. Vol. 1, *The Information Age: Economy, Society and Culture*. Malden, MA: Blackwell.

Castells i Talens, Antoni. 2011. "¿Ni indígena ni comunitaria? La radio indigenista en tiempos neoindigenistas." *Comunicación y Sociedad* 15 : 123–142.

Cave, Martin, Rubén Guerrero, and Elisa Mariscal. 2018. "Bridging Mexico's Digital Divide: An Inside-Out/Outside-In View of Competition and Regulation." https://ceeg.mx/publicaciones /ESTUDIO_2_2018-Bridging_Mexicos_digital_divide_Final_2018_12_20.pdf.

Cerano, Dante. 2009. "Purhépechas vistos a través del video. Comunicación y nostalgia en ambos lados de la frontera." Master's thesis, El Colegio de Michoacán.

Chávez, Xochitl. 2013. "Migrating Performative Traditions: The Guelaguetza Festival in Oaxacalifornia." PhD diss., University of California, Santa Cruz.

———. 2017. "Booming Bandas of Los Angeles: Gender and the Practice of Transnational Zapotec Philharmonic Brass Bands." In *The Tide Was Always High: The Music of Latin America in Los Angeles*, edited by Josh Kun, 260–266. Berkeley: University of California Press.

———. 2020. "La creación de Oaxacalifornia mediante tradiciones culturales entre jóvenes oaxaqueños de Los Ángeles, California." *Desacatos* 62: 172–181.

Cleaver, Harry. 1995. "The Zapatistas and the Electronic Fabric of Struggle." https://la.utexas .edu/users/hcleaver/zaps.html.

Clifford, James. 1994. "Diasporas." *Cultural Anthropology* 9 (3): 302–338.

Comaroff, John, and Jean Comaroff. 2009. *Ethnicity Inc*. Chicago: University of Chicago Press.

Cook, Scott. 2014. *Land, Livelihood, and Civility in Southern Mexico. Oaxaca Valley Communities in History*. Austin: University of Texas Press.

Cordero Avendaño de Durand, Carmen. 2009. *Supervivencia de un derecho consuetudinario en el Valle de Tlacolula*. Mexico City: Porrúa.

Corkovic, Laura M. 2017. *Indigenes Erbe im Internet: Zur Identitätspolitik der Chicano–Fotografie im digitalen Zeitalter*. Bielefeld: Transcript.

Costanza-Chock, Sasha. 2014. *Out of the Shadows, into the Streets! Transmedia Organizing and the Immigrant Rights Movement.* Cambridge, MA: MIT Press.

Couldry, Nick. 2004. "Theorising Media Practice." *Social Semiotics* 14 (2): 115–132.

Couldry, Nick, and Ulises Mejias. 2019. *The Costs of Connection: How Data Is Colonizing Human Life and Appropriating It for Capitalism.* Stanford, CA: Stanford University Press.

Cremoux Wanderstok, Daniela. 1997. "Video Indígena, dos casos en la Sierra Mixe." BA thesis, Universidad Intercontinental.

Cross, John C. 2011. "Chapter 6: Mexico." In *Media Piracy in Emerging Economies*, edited by Joe Karaganis, 305–325. New York: SSRC.

Cruz, Emiliana, and Tajëëw Robles. 2019. "Using Technology to Revitalize Endangered Languages." In *Indigenous Interfaces: Spaces, Technology, and Social Networks in Mexico and Central America*, edited by Jennifer Gómez Menjívar and Gloria Elizabeth Chacón, 79–96. Tucson: University of Arizona Press.

Cruz-Manjarrez, Adriana. 2012. "Engendering Indigenous Mexican Migration into the United States: A Case of Study of the Yalálag Zapotec Women." *Diversities* 14 (2): 87–101.

———. 2013. *Zapotecs on the Move: Cultural, Social, and Political Processes in Transnational Perspective.* New Brunswick, NJ: Rutgers University Press.

———. 2014. "Transnacionalismo y género en una comunidad oaxaqueña." *Amérique Latine. Histoire et Mémoire. Les Cahiers ALHIM* 27. http://alhim.revues.org/4975.

Cwerner, Saulo B. 2001. "The Times of Migration." *Journal of Ethnic and Migration Studies* 27 (1): 7–36.

Darieva, Typilma, Nina Glick Schiller, and Sandra Gruner-Domic. 2016. *Cosmopolitan Sociability: Locating Transnational Religious and Diasporic Networks.* London: Routledge.

Davalos, Karen Mary. 1996. "La Quinceañera: Making Gender and Ethnic Identities." *Frontiers* 16 (2–3): 101–127.

De Genova, Nicholas. 2005. *Working the Boundaries: Race, Space and "Illegality" in Mexican Chicago.* Durham, NC: Duke University Press.

De la Cadena, Marisol, and Orin Starn, eds. 2007. *Indigenous Experience Today.* Oxford: Berg.

De la Fuente, Julio. (1949) 1977. *Yalálag. Una villa serrana zapoteca.* Mexico City: INI.

De León-Pasquel, María de Lourdes. 2018. "Entre el mensaje romántico y el etnorock en YouTube: repertorios identitarios en los paisajes virtuales de jóvenes mayas tsotsiles." *LiminaR. Estudios Sociales y Humanísticos* 16 (1): 40–55.

Derrida, Jacques. 1995. "Archive Fever: A Freudian Impression." *Diacritics* 25 (2): 9–63.

Díaz, Floriberto. (1995) 2007. "El pasado que es presente." In *Floriberto Díaz. Escrito. Comunalidad, energía viva del pensamiento mixe. Ayuujktsënää'yen—ayuujkwënmää'ny—ayuujk mëk'äjtën*, edited by Sofía Robles Hernández and Rafael Cardoso Jiménez, 148–158. Mexico City: UNAM.

Dorantes, Felipe Flores. 2015. "Las bandas de viento: una rica y ancestral tradición de Oaxaca." In *Bandas de viento en México*, edited by Georgina Flores Mercado, 183–206. Mexico City: INAH, Colección Etnología y Antropología Social, Serie Testimonios.

Elias, Norbert. 1997. *Über den Prozeß der Zivilisation.* Vol. 1. Frankfurt am Main: Suhrkamp.

Equipo de Cronistas Oaxacalifornianos. 2013. *Voces de jóvenes indígenas oaxaqueños en el Valle Central: Forjando nuestro sentido de pertenencia en California* (Informe de investigación no. 1. Julio 2013). Santa Cruz: UC Center for Collaborative Research for an Equitable California.

Eriksen, Thomas Hylland. 2021. "Filling the Apps: The Smartphone, Time and the Refugee." In *Waiting and the Temporalities of Irregular Migration*, edited by Christine M. Jacobsen, Marry-Anne Karlson, and Shahram Khosravi, 57–72. New York: Routledge.

Ernst, Wolfgang. 2013. "Underway to the Dual System: Classical Archives and Digital Memory." In *Digital Memory and the Archive*, edited by Jussi Parikka, 81–94. Minneapolis: University of Minnesota Press.

Escala, Luis, and Gaspar Rivera-Salgado. 2018. "Festivals, Oaxacan Immigrant Communities and Cultural Spaces between Mexico and the United States: The Guelaguetzas in California." *Migraciones Internacionales* 9 (3): 37–63.

Estrada Ramos, Alicia. 2001. "La tecnología video y las practicas jurídicas de la comunalidad: El caso de Yalalag, Villa Hidalgo, Oaxaca." BA thesis, Universidad Nacional Autónoma de México.

Fabian, Johannes. 1983. *Time and the Other: How Anthropology Makes Its Object*. New York: Columbia University Press.

Featherstone, Mike. 2010. "Archiving Cultures." *British Journal of Sociology* 51 (1): 161–184.

Félix, Adrian. 2018. *Specters of Belonging: The Political Life Cycle of Mexican Migrants*. Oxford: Oxford University Press.

Fernández L'Hoeste, Héctor, Robert Irwin McKee, and Juan Poblete, eds. 2015. *Sports and Nationalism in Latin/o America*. New York: Palgrave Macmillan.

Figueroa, Mercedes. 2016. "Gazing at the Face of Absence: Signification and Re-signification of Family Photographs of Disappeared Students in Peru." In *Photography in Latin America: Images and Identities across Time and Space*, edited by Gisela Cánepa and Ingrid Kummels, 195–217. Bielefeld: Transcript.

FitzGerald, David Scott, Gustavo López, and Angela Y. McClean. 2019. *Mexican Immigrants Face Threats to Civil Rights and Increased Social Hostility*. San Diego: University of California, San Diego, Center for Comparative Immigration Studies.

Flores-Marcial, Xóchitl. 2015. "A History of Guelaguetza in Zapotec Communities of the Central Valleys of Oaxaca." PhD thesis, University of California, Los Angeles.

Foucault, Michel. 1969. *L'archéologie du savoir*. Paris: Gallimard.

Fox, Jonathan, and Gaspar Rivera-Salgado, eds. 2004. *Indigenous Mexican Migrants in the United States*. La Jolla: University of California, San Diego, Center for Comparative Immigration Studies.

Fuchs, Christian. 2018. *Digital Demagogue: Authoritarian Capitalism in the Age of Trump and Twitter*. London: Pluto Press.

García Vargas, Lenin A. 2018. "Radiografía demográfica de la población indígena en Oaxaca." Población Indígena. Oaxaca Población Siglo XXI, *Nueva Época* no. 41: 7–20. Oaxaca City: Dirección General de Población de Oaxaca.

Garcini, Luz M., Thania Galvan, Ryan Brown, Michelle Chen, Elizabeth A. Klonoff, Khadija Ziauddin, and Christopher P. Fagundes. 2020. "Miles over Mind: Transnational Death and Its Association with Psychological Distress among Undocumented Mexican Immigrants." *Death Studies* 44 (6): 357–365.

Garde-Hansen, Joanne. 2009. "My Memories? Personal Digital Archive Fever and Facebook." In *Save as . . . Digital Memories*, edited by Joanne Garde-Hansen, Andrew Hoskins, and Anna Reading, 135–150. New York: Palgrave Macmillan.

Geismar, Haidy. 2017. "Instant Archives?" In *The Routledge Companion to Digital Ethnography*, edited by Larissa Hjorth, Heather Horst, Anne Galloway, and Genevieve Bell, 331–343. New York: Routledge.

Gill, Harjant. 2019. "Multimodality and the Future of Anthropological Research and Scholarship." https://theartsjournal.net/2019/03/28/multimodality-anthropology/.

Ginsburg, Faye. 2016. "Indigenous Media from U-Matic to YouTube. Media Sovereignty in the Digital Age." *Social Anthropology* 6 (3): 581–599.

Goffman, Erving. 1959. *The Presentation of Self in Everyday Life*. New York: Doubleday.

Gómez Cruz, Edgar. 2012. *De la cultura Kodak a la imagen en red. Una etnografía sobre fotografía digital*. Barcelona: Editorial UOC.

Gómez Menjívar, Jennifer, and Gloria Elizabeth Chacón, eds. 2019a. *Indigenous Interfaces. Spaces, Technology, and Social Networks in Mexico and Central America*. Tucson: University of Arizona Press.

————. 2019b. "Introduction: No Static: Re-Indigenizing Technology." In *Indigenous Interfaces: Spaces, Technology, and Social Networks in Mexico and Central America*, edited by Jennifer Gómez Menjívar and Gloria Elizabeth Chacón, 3–30. Tucson: University of Arizona Press.

Gómez Navarro, Dulce Angélica, and Marlen Martínez Domínguez. 2020. "Brechas digitales indígenas en tiempos de Covid-19." https://ichan.ciesas.edu.mx/brechas-digitales-indigenas-en-tiempos-de-covid-19-2/.

González, Robert J. 2020. *Connected: How a Mexican Village Built Its Own Cell Phone Network*. Berkeley: University of California Press.

————. 2021. "Virtual Village. Zapotec Migrants in the Digital Era." In *Handbook of Culture and Migration*, edited by Jeffrey Cohen and Ibrahim Sirkeci, 372–385. Northampton: Edward Elgar.

González-Martin, Rachel V. 2016. "Digitizing Cultural Economies: 'Personalization' and U.S. Quinceañera Practice Online." *Ethnology and Folkloristics* 15 (1): 57–77.

Goulbourne, Harry, Tracey Reynolds, John Solomos, and Elisabetta Zontini. 2011. *Transnational Families: Ethnicities, Identities and Social Capital*. London: Routledge.

Gramlich, John. 2020. "How Border Apprehensions, ICE Arrests and Deportations Have Changed under Trump." Washington, DC: Pew Research Center. https://www.pewresearch.org/fact-tank/2020/03/02/how-border-apprehensions-ice-arrests-and-deportations-have-changed-under-trump/.

Griffiths, Melanie, Ali Rogers, and Bridget Anderson. 2013. "Migration, Time and Temporalities: Review and Prospect." Centre on Migration, Policy and Society (COMPAS) Research Resources Paper.

Gruzinski, Serge. 2001. *Images at War: Mexico from Columbus to Blade Runner (1492–2019)*. Durham, NC: Duke University Press.

Gutiérrez Nájera, Lourdes. 2007. "Yalálag Is No Longer Just Yalálag. Circulating Conflict and Contesting Community in a Zapotec Transnational Circuit." PhD diss., University of Michigan.

————. 2012. "Reconstructing Zapotec Transnational Identities and Localities in a Virtual Environment." *Cahiers Dialog*, no. 2: 9–14.

Gutiérrez Nájera, Lourdes, and Ana D. Alonso Ortiz. 2019. "Expressing Communality: Zapotec Death and Mourning across Transnational Frontier." In *Transnational Death*, edited by Samira Saramo, Eerika Koskinen-Koivisto, and Hanna Snellman, 85–99. Helsinki: Finnish Literature Society.

Guttman, Allen. 2004. *Sports: The First Five Millenia*. Amherst: University of Massachusetts Press.

Hall, Stuart. 2001. "Constituting an Archive." *Third Text* 15 (54): 89–92.

Härkönen, Heidi. 2011. "Girls' 15-Year Birthday Celebration as Cuban Women's Space Outside of the Revolutionary State." *Journal of the Association of Social Anthropologists* 1 (4): 1–41.

Harvey, David. 1989. *The Condition of Postmodernity: An Enquiry into the Origins of Cultural Change*. Cambridge, MA: Blackwell.

Haynes, Nell. 2016. *Social Media in Northern Chile*. London: UCL Press.

Hepp, Andreas. 2015. *Transcultural Communication*. Chichester: Wiley Blackwell.

Hernández Castillo, Rosalva Aída, and Andrew Canessa, eds. 2012. *Género, Complemetariedades y Exclusiones en Mesoamérica y los Andes*. Copenhagen: IWGIA.

Hernández-Díaz, Jorge, and Víctor Leonel Juan Martínez. 2007. *Dilemas de la institución municipal. Una incursión en la experencia oaxaqueña*. Mexico City: Porrúa.

Hill, Juniper, and Caroline Bithell. 2014. "An Introduction to Music Revival as Concept, Cultural Process, and Medium of Change." In *The Oxford Handbook of Music Revival*, edited by Caroline Bithell and Juniper Hill, 1–43. New York: Oxford University Press.

Hine, Christine. 2000. *Virtual Ethnography*. London: Sage.

Hjarvard, Stig. 2013. *The Mediatization of Culture and Society*. London: Routledge.

Hjorth, Laurissa. 2007. "Snapshots of Almost Contact: The Rise of Camera Phone Practices and a Case Study in Seoul, Korea." *Continuum: Journal of Media & Cultural Studies* 21 (2): 227–238.

Hochschild, Arlie. 2000. "Global Care Chains and Emotional Surplus Value." In *On the Edge: Living with Global Capitalism*, edited by Will Hutton and Anthony Giddens, 130–146. London: Jonathan Cape.

———. 2016. *Strangers in Their Own Land: Anger and Mourning on the American Right.* New York: New Press.

Hof, Karina. 2006. "Something You Can Actually Pick Up: Scrapbooking as a Form and Forum of Cultural Citizenship." *European Journal of Cultural Studies* 9 (3): 363–384.

Huizinga, Johan. (1938) 1980. *Homo Ludens: A Study of the Play-Element in Culture.* London: Routledge & Kegan Paul.

Iber, Jorge, Samuel Regalado, José Alamillo, and Arnoldo De León. 2011. *Latinos in U.S Sport: A History of Isolation, Cultural Identity, and Acceptance.* Champaign, IL: Human Kinetics.

Instituto Federal de Telecomunicaciones. 2019. "Diagnóstico de Cobertura del Servicio Móvil en Pueblos Indígenas 2018." Mexico City. https://usuarios.ift.org.mx/indigenas2019/.

Jiménez, Carlos. 2020. "Radio Indígena and Indigenous Mexican Farmworkers in Oxnard, California." In *Digital Activism, Community Media, and Sustainable Communication in Latin America*, edited by Cheryl Martens, Cristina Venegas, and Etsa Franklin Salvio Sharupi Tapuy, 27–52. Cham: Palgrave Macmillan.

Jiménez Díaz, Telmo. 2020. "Redes migratorias, migración de retorno e inserción laboral: El caso de los mixes de Tamazulapam, Oaxaca." PhD thesis, Universidad Nacional Autónoma de México.

Jonsson, Hjorleiffur. 2003. "Mien through Sports and Culture: Mobilizing Minority Identity in Thailand." *Ethnos* 68 (3): 317–340.

Karim, Karim H. 2015/2016. "Virtual Diasporas and Their Communication Networks: Exploring the Broader Context of Transnational Narrowcasting." Nautilus Institute. http://oldsite.nautilus.org/gps/virtual-diasporas/paper/Karim.html.

Kaun, Anne. 2016. "Archiving Protest Digitally: The Temporal Regime of Immediation." *International Journal of Communication* 10: 5395–5408.

Kaun, Anne, and Fredrik Stiernstedt. 2014. "Facebook Time: Technological and Institutional Affordances for Media Memories." *New Media and Society* 16 (7): 1154–1168.

Kearney, Michael. 1995. "The Effects of Transnational Culture, Economy, and Migration on Mixtec Identity in Oaxacalifornia." In *The Bubbling Cauldron: Race, Ethnicity, and the Urban Crisis*, edited by Michael Peter Smith and Joe R. Feagin, 226–243. Minneapolis: University of Minnesota Press.

Kearney, Michael, and Federico Besserer. 2004. "Oaxacan Municipal Governance in Transnational Context." In *Indigenous Mexican Migrants in the United States*, edited by Jonathan Fox and Gaspar Rivera-Salgado, 449–468. La Jolla: University of California, San Diego, Center for Comparative Immigration Studies.

Krannich, Sascha. 2017. *The Reconquest of Paradise? How Indigenous Migrants Construct Community in the United States and Mexico.* Münster: LIT Verlag.

Kummels, Ingrid. 2007a. "*Adiós soccer, here comes fútbol!*: La transnacionalización de comunidades deportivas mexicanas en los Estados Unidos." *Iberoamericana* 7 (27): 101–116.

———. 2007b. *Land, Nahrung und Peyote: Soziale Identität von Rarámuri und Mestizen nahe der Grenze USA-Mexiko.* Berlin: Reimer.

———. 2011. "*Cine Indígena*: Video, Migration and the Dynamics of Belonging between Mexico and the USA." In *Ethnicity, Citizenship and Belonging: Practice, Theory and Spatial Dimensions*, edited by Sarah Albiez, Nelly Castro, Lara Jüssen, and Eva Youkhana, 259–281. Frankfurt am Main: Vervuert.

———. 2012. "Introducción: Espacios mediáticos: cultura y representación en México." In *Espacios mediáticos: cultura y representación en México*, edited by Ingrid Kummels, 9–39. Berlin: Tranvía.

———. 2015. "Negotiating Land Tenure in Transborder Media Spaces: Ayuujk People's Videomaking between Mexico and the USA." Paper for the EASA Media Anthropology Network E-Seminar, October 2015. http://www.media-anthropology.net/index.php/e-seminars.

———. 2016a. *La producción afectiva de comunidad: Los medios audiovisuales en el contexto transnacional México-EE.UU.* Berlin: Tranvía.

———. 2016b. "Búsquedas más allá del 'original': reflexiones sobre la comunidad que creamos a partir del cine. Entrevista con la cineasta Yolanda Cruz." In *La producción afectiva de comunidad: Los medios audiovisuales en el contexto transnacional México-EE.UU*, edited by Ingrid Kummels, 357–379. Berlin: Tranvía.

———. 2017a. *Transborder Media Spaces. Ayuujk Videomaking between Mexico and the US*. New York: Berghahn.

———. 2017b. "Fiesta Videos: 'Home' and Productive Nostalgia between Oaxaca and California." *Sociologus* 67 (2): 131–149.

———. 2018. "Das Basketballturnier Copa Mixe/Ayuujk: Die sportive Ethnopolitik einer transnationalen indigenen Gemeinde." In *Ballspiele. Transkulturalität und Gender. Ethnologische und altamerikanistische Perspektiven*, Berliner Blätter 76, edited by Julia Haß and Stephanie Schütze, 36–56. Berlin: Panama Verlag.

———. 2020. "An Ayuujk 'Media War' over Water and Land: Mediatized Senses of Belonging between Mexico and the U.S." In *Theorising Media and Conflict*, edited by Philipp Budka and Birgit Bräuchler, 196–214. New York: Berghahn.

———. 2021. "Archivar aspiraciones entre México y EE.UU.: *Influencers* étnicos y el archivo dancístico zapoteco online." In *Antropología y archivos en la era digital: usos emergentes de lo audiovisual*, vol. 2, edited by Ingrid Kummels and Gisela Cánepa, 175–205. Lima: IDE/PUCP.

Kummels, Ingrid, and Gisela Cánepa. 2016. "Introduction: Photography in Latin America. Images and Identities across Time and Space" In *Photography in Latin America: Images and Identities across Time and Space*, edited by Gisela Cánepa and Ingrid Kummels, 7–31. Bielefeld: Transcript.

———. 2021. Los archivos y su transformación digital: una introducción. In: *Antropología y archivos en la era digital: usos emergentes de lo audiovisual*, Vol. 2, edited by Ingrid Kummels and Gisela Cánepa, 7–39. Lima: IDE/PUCP.

Kuroda, Etsuko. 1984. *Under Mount Zempoatepetl. Highland Mixe Society and Ritual*. Osaka: National Museum of Ethnology.

Lange, Patricia G. 2014. "Commenting on YouTube Rants: Perceptions of Inappropriateness or Civic Engagement?" *Journal of Pragmatics* 73: 53–65.

———. 2019. *Thanks for Watching: An Anthropological Study of Video Sharing on YouTube*. Louisville: University Press of Colorado.

Lefebvre, Henry. (1974) 2009. *The Production of Space*. Malden, MA: Blackwell.

León Himmelstine, Carmen. 2017. "The Linkages between Social Protection and Migration: A Case Study of Oportunidades and Migration in Oaxaca, Mexico." PhD thesis, University of Sussex.

Lizama Quijano, Jesús. 2006. *La Guelaguetza en Oaxaca: Fiesta, relaciones interétnicas y procesos de construcción simbólica en el contexto urbano*. Mexico City: CIESAS.

López, Felipe, and David Runsten. 2004. "Mixtecs and Zapotecs Working in California: Rural and Urban Experiences." In *Indigenous Mexican Migrants in the United States*, edited by Jonathan Fox and Gaspar Rivera-Salgado, 249–278. Berkeley: University of California Press.

Lopez, Sarah Lynn. 2015. *The Remittance Landscape: Spaces of Migration in Rural Mexico and Urban USA*. Chicago: University of Chicago Press.

Lugones, María. 2010. "Toward a Decolonial Feminism." *Hypathia* 25 (4): 742–759.

Madianou, Mirca. 2016. "Ambient Co-presence: Transnational Family Practices in Polymedia Environment." *Global Networks* 16 (2): 183–201.

Madianou, Mirca, and Daniel Miller. 2012. *Migration and New Media: Transnational Families and Polymedia*. London: Routledge.

Maldonado, Sandra. 2019. *No'l Yara'rj*. Los Angeles: Zine.

Malpica Melero, Daniel. 2005. "Indigenous Mexican Migrants in a Modern Metropolis. The Reconstruction of Zapotec Communities in Los Angeles." In *Latino Los Angeles: Transformations, Communities, and Activism*, edited by Enrique Ochoa and Gilda L. Ochoa, 111–136. Tucson: University of Arizona Press.

Martens, Cheryl, Etsa Franklin Salvio, Sharupi Tapuy, and Cristina Venegas. 2020. "Transforming Digital Media and Technology in Latin America." In *Digital Activism, Community Media, and Sustainable Communication in Latin America*, edited by Cheryl Martens et al., 1–24. Cham: Palgrave Macmillan.

Martín-Barbero, Jesús. 1987. *De los medios a las mediaciones*. Mexico City: Universidad Autónoma Metropolitana.

Martínez Luna, Jaime. 2010. *De eso que llaman comunalidad*. Oaxaca City: CNCA.

Massey, Doreen. 1994. *Space, Place, and Gender*. Minneapolis: University of Minnesota Press.

Massumi, Brian. 2002. *Parables for the Virtual: Movement, Affect, Sensation*. Durham, NC: Duke University Press.

Mbembe, Achille. 2002. "The Power of the Archive and Its Limits." In *Refiguring the Archive*, edited by Carolyn Hamilton, Harris Verne, Jane Taylor, Michele Pickover, Graeme Reid, and Razia Saleh, 19–26. Dordrecht: Kluwer.

McDonald, Tom, Razvan Nicolescu, and Jolynna Sinanan. 2017. "Small Places Turned Inside-Out: Social Networking in Small Communities." In *The Routledge Companion to Digital Ethnography*, edited by Larissa Hjorth, Heather Horst, Anne Galloway, and Genevieve Bell, 89–101. London: Routledge.

Mejía Piñeros, María Consuelo, and Sergio Sarmiento Silva. 1987. *La lucha indígena: un reto a la ortodoxia*. Mexico City: Siglo XXI.

Meneses, Guillermo Alonso, and Luis Escala. 2015. *Offside / Fuera de lugar. Fútbol y migraciones en el mundo contemporáneo*. Tijuana: El Colegio de la Frontera Norte.

Mercado, Antonieta. 2015. "*El Tequio*: Social Capital, Civic Advocacy Journalism and the Construction of a Transnational Public Sphere by Mexican Indigenous Migrants in the US." *Journalism* 16 (2): 238–256.

———. 2019. "Decolonizing National Public Spheres: Indigenous Migrants as Transnational Counterpublics." In *The Handbook of Diaspora, Media and Cultures*, edited by Jessica Retis and Roza Tsagarousianou, 269–282. Hoboken, NJ: Wiley Blackwell.

Mignolo, Walter. 2000. *Local Histories / Global Designs: Coloniality, Subaltern Knowledges and Border Thinking*. Princeton, NJ: Princeton University Press.

Mignolo, Walter, and Catherine Walsh. 2018. *On Decoloniality: Concepts, Analytics, Praxis*. Durham, NC: Duke University Press.

Milian, Claudia. 2020. *LatinX*. Minneapolis: University of Minnesota Press.

Miller, Daniel, et al. 2016. *How the World Changed Social Media*. London: UCL Press.

———. 2021. *The Global Smartphone: Beyond a Youth Technology*. London: UCL Press.

Mollerup, Nina Grønlykke. 2017. "'Being There,' Phone in the Hand: Thick Presence and Anthropological Fieldwork with Media." Paper for the EASA Media Anthropology Network E-Seminar, February 2017. http://www.media-anthropology.net/index.php/e-seminars.

Nava Morales, Elena. 2011. *Prácticas culturales en movimiento. Internet en Santa María Tlahuitoltepec, Oaxaca*. Saarbrücken: Editorial Académica Española.

———. 2019. "Para que las lenguas indígenas también puedan tener presencia: indigenizando el ciberespacio." *Canadian Journal of Latin American and Caribbean Studies* 45 (1): 122–142.

———. 2020. "Ecos de la *Comunalidad* en Oaxaca a inicios del siglo XXI." *IdeAs Idées d'Amériques* 16: 1–18. http://journals.openedition.org/ideas/9121.

Nedelcu, Mihaela. 2019. "Digital Diasporas." In *Routledge Handbook of Diaspora Studies*, edited by Robin Cohen, and Carolin Fischer, 241–250. London: Taylor & Francis.

Newdick, Vivian, and Odilia Romero. 2017. "Interpretation Is an Act of Resistance: Indigenous Organizations Respond to 'Zero Tolerance' and 'Family Separation.'" *Forum* 50 (1): 30–34.

Nicolas, Brenda. 2021. "'Soy de Zoochina': Transborder *Comunalidad* Practices among Adult Children of Indigenous Migrants." *Latino Studies* 19 (1): 47–69.

Papacharissi, Zizi. 2015. *Affective Publics. Sentiment, Technology, and Politics.* Oxford: Oxford University Press.

Peña, Leopoldo. 2017. "Danza de los superhéroes: Zapotec Immigrant Tradition in Transnational Transfer." *Boom California*, July 17. https://boomcalifornia.com/2017/07/17/danza-de-los-superheroes-zapotec-immigrant-tradition-in-transnational-transfer/.

Peterson, Mark Allen. 2003. *Anthropology and Mass Communication: Media and Myth in the New Millennium.* New York: Berghahn.

Ponzanesi, Sandra. 2019. "Migration and Mobility in a Digital Age: (Re)Mapping Connectivity and Belonging." *Television & New Media* 20 (6): 547–557.

Postill, John. 2021. "The Effects of Media Practices." Paper for the EASA Media Anthropology Network E-Seminar, February 2021. https://www.easaonline.org/downloads/networks/media/66p.pdf.

Pskowski, Martha. 2019. "Indigenous Maize: Who Owns the Rights to Mexico's 'Wonder' Plant?" *YaleEnvironment 360*, July 16. https://e360.yale.edu/features/indigenous-maize-who-owns-the-rights-to-mexicos-wonder-plant.

Quijano, Aníbal. 2000. "Coloniality of Power, Eurocentrism, and Latin America." *Nepantla: Views from the South* 1 (3): 533–580.

Quinones, Sam. 2001. "Zeus and the Oaxacan Hoops." In *True Tales from Another Mexico: The Lynch Mob, the Popsicle Kings, Chalino and the Bronx*, edited by Sam Quinones, 117–135. Albuquerque: University of New Mexico Press.

———. 2013. "Hamburger Hamlet Still Serving Up His American Dream." *Los Angeles Times*, February 23. https://www.latimes.com/local/la-xpm-2013-feb-23-la-me-oaxaca-kitchen-20130224-story.html.

———. 2015. "How Three Pioneering Immigrants Forever Changed the Course—and the Culture—of L.A." *Los Angeles Magazine*, December 4. https://www.lamag.com/longform/how-three-pioneering-immigrants-forever-changed-the-course-and-the-culture-of-l-a/.

Quinones, Sam, and Alan Mittelstaedt. 2000. "A League of Their Own." *LA Weekly*, February 2. https://www.laweekly.com/a-league-of-their-own/.

Ramírez Ríos, Bernardo. 2019. *Transnational Sport in the American West.* Lanham, MD: Rowman & Littlefield.

Ramos Mancilla, Óscar. 2016. "Internet y pueblos indígenas de la Sierra Norte de Puebla, México." PhD thesis, Universitat de Barcelona.

———. 2018. "Acceso a internet desigual y heterogéneo en los pueblos indígenas de la Sierra Norte de Puebla (México)." *Revista Española de Antropología Americana* 48: 9–27.

———. 2020. "El agregado digital en las juventudes indígenas: entre desigualdades y representaciones locales." *Perspectivas em Ciência da Informação* 25 (1): 263–281.

Rappaport, Joanne. 2005. *Intercultural Utopias: Public Intellectuals, Cultural Experimentation, and Ethnic Pluralism in Colombia.* Durham, NC: Duke University Press.

Reyes Gómez, Juan Carlos. 2017. *Tiempo, cosmos y religión del pueblo Ayuujk (México).* Leiden: Leiden University Press.

Risam, Roopika. 2018. "Decolonizing the Digital Humanities in Theory and Practice." *Faculty Publications* 7 (January 5). https://digitalcommons.salemstate.edu/english_facpub/7.

Robson, James Patrick, Dan Klooster, Holly Worthen, and Jorge Hernández-Díaz. 2017. "Migration and Agrarian Transformation in Indigenous Mexico." *Journal of Agrarian Change* 18 (2): 1–25.

Rodriguez, Evelyn Ibatan. 2013. *Celebrating Debutantes and Quinceañeras: Coming of Age in American Ethnic Communities.* Philadelphia: Temple University Press.

Rojas García, Marciano. 1975. *Antecedentes históricos del Campeonato Regional Deportivo y Cultural Mixe.* Tamazulapam del Espíritu Santo: Ms.

Romero, Mary. 2012. *The Maid's Daughter: Living Inside and Outside the American Dream.* New York: New York University Press.

Rosa, Hartmut. 2015. *Social Acceleration: A New Theory of Modernity.* New York: Columbia University Press.

Rose, Gillian. 2010. *Doing Family Photography: The Domestic, the Public and the Politics of Sentiment.* Surrey: Ashgate.

Ruiz Medrano, Ethelia. 2011. *Mexico's Indigenous Communities: Their Lands and Histories, 1500–2010.* Boulder: University Press of Colorado.

Salazar, Juan Francisco, and Amalia Córdova. 2020. "Indigenous Media Cultures in Abya Yala." In *Media Cultures in Latin America: Key Concepts and New Debates*, edited by Anna Cristina Pertierra and Juan Francisco Salazar, 128–146. London: Routledge.

Santos, Boaventura de Sousa. 2009. *Una epistemología del Sur. La reinvención del conocimiento y la emancipación social.* Mexico: CLACSO and Siglo XXI.

———. 2018. *The End of the Cognitive Empire: The Coming of Age of Epistemologies of the South.* Durham, NC: Duke University Press.

Savage, Rebecca. 2012. "Towards the Ethnography of Filmic Places: Video-Based Research and Found Footage Filmmaking in the Anthropological Investigation of Mexican Migrant Event Video." PhD thesis, University of Westminster.

Scherer, Jay, and David Rowe. 2014. *Sport, Public Broadcasting, and Cultural Citizenship: Signal Lost?* London: Routledge.

Schiwy, Freya. 2009. *Indianizing Film: Decolonization, the Andes, and the Question of Technology.* New Brunswick, NJ: Rutgers University Press.

———. 2018. "Decolonization and Collaborative Media: A Latin American Perspective." In *Oxford Research Encyclopedia of Critical Communication Studies.* Oxford: Oxford University Press. https://doi.org/10.1093/acrefore/9780190228613.013.641.

———. 2019. *The Open Invitation: Activist Video, Mexico, and the Politics of Affect.* Pittsburgh: University of Pittsburgh Press.

Schiwy, Freya, Amalia Córdova, David Wood, and Horacio Legrás. 2017. "New Frameworks. Collaborative and Indigenous Media Activism." In *Routledge Companion to Latin American Cinemas*, edited by Marvin D'Lugo, Ana López, and Laura Podalsky, 204–222. New York: Routledge.

Schiwy, Freya, and Byrt Wammack. 2017. "Adjusting the Lens: An Introduction." In *Adjusting the Lens: Community and Collaborative Video in Mexico*, edited by Freya Schiwy and Byrt Wammack, 3–38. Pittsburgh: University of Pittsburgh Press.

SFB 1171 Affective Societies. 2016. "A Glossary. Register of Central Working Concepts: Affective Societies." Working Paper 1. Berlin: Freie Universität Berlin.

Smith, Benjamin. 2008. "Inventing Tradition at Gunpoint: Culture, Caciquismo and State Formation in the Región Mixe, Oaxaca (1930–1959)." *Bulletin of Latin American Research* 27 (2): 215–234.

Smith, Laurel C. 2005. "Mediating Indigenous Identity: Video, Advocacy, and Knowledge in Oaxaca, Mexico." PhD diss., University of Kentucky.

Soch, Konstanze. 2018. *Eine große Freude? Der innerdeutsche Paketverkehr im Kalten Krieg (1949–1989)*. Frankfurt am Main: Campus.

Solis Bautista, Ariadna Itzel. 2021. "¿Miradas desde adentro? Dinámicas de representación de mujeres yalaltecas en la actualidad." *Revista Digital Universitaria* 22 (3). http://doi.org/10.22201/cuaieed.16076079e.2021.22.3.3.

Speed, Shannon. 2017. "Structures of Settler Capitalism in Abya Yala." *American Quarterly* 69 (4): 783–790.

Stephen, Lynn. 2013. *We Are the Face of Oaxaca: Testimony and Social Movements*. Durham, NC: Duke University Press.

Strunk, Christopher. 2015. "Practicing Citizenship: Bolivian Migrant Identities and Spaces of Belonging in Washington DC." *Journal of Intercultural Studies* 36 (5): 620–639.

Taylor, Diana. 2003. *The Archive and the Repertoire: Performing Cultural Memory in the Americas*. Durham, NC: Duke University Press.

Treré, Emiliano. 2019. *Hybrid Media Activism: Ecologies, Imaginaries, Algorithms*. London: Routledge.

Trevizo, Dolores, and Mary Lopez. 2018. *Neighborhood Poverty and Segregation in the (Re-)Production of Disadvantage: Mexican Immigrant Entrepreneurs in Los Angeles*. London: Palgrave.

Valdez, Zulema. 2011. *The New Entrepreneurship: How Race, Class, and Gender Shape American Enterprise*. Stanford, CA: Stanford University Press.

Van Dijck, José, Thomas Poell, and Martijn De Waal. 2018. *The Platform Society: Public Values in a Connective World*. Oxford: Oxford University Press.

Vang, Chia Youyee. 2016. "Hmong Youth, American Football, and the Cultural Politics of Ethnic Sports Tournaments." In *Asian American Sporting Cultures*, edited by Stanley Thangaray et al., 199–220. New York: New York University Press.

Vásquez, Rafael. 2019. "Zapotec Identity as a Matter of Schooling." *Association of Mexican American Educators Journal* 13 (2): 66–90.

Vásquez García, Carolina. 2018. *Ser mujeres y hombres en la filosofía Ayuujk. Ja yää'tyëjk ja të'ëxyëjk ja jyujky'äjtïn, ja tsyënää'yïn, tyanää'yïn, yä'et näxwiiny*. Oaxaca City: Colectivo Editorial Casa de las Preguntas.

Velasco Ortiz, Laura. 2008. *Migración, fronteras e identidades transnacionales*. Mexico: El Colegio de la Frontera Norte/Porrúa.

Vertovec, Steven. 2004. "Cheap Calls: The Social Glue of Migrant Transnationalism." *Global Networks* 4 (2): 219–224.

Virilio, Paul. 2006. *Speed and Politics*. Los Angeles: Semiotext(e).

Vokes, Richard. 2016. "Before the Call: Mobile Phones, Exchange Relations, and Social Change in South-western Uganda." *Ethnos* 8 (2): 1–16.

Vokes, Richard, and Katrien Pype. 2016. "Chronotopes of Media in Sub-Saharan Africa." *Ethnos* 8 (2): 207–217.

White, Kyle Powys. 2017. "Indigeneity and US Settler Colonialism." In *The Oxford Handbook of Philosophy and Race*, edited by Naomi Zack, 91–101. New York: Oxford University Press.

Williams, Raymond. 1977. *Marxism and Literature*. New York: Oxford University Press.

Wilson, Kenneth L., and Alejandro Portes. 1980. "Immigrant Enclaves: An Analysis of the Labor Market Experiences of Cubans in Miami." *American Journal of Sociology* 86 (2): 295–319.

Winocur, Rosalía. 2019. "La tribu de los memes. Un territorio virtual de inclusión–exclusión entre los adolescentes." *Comunicación y Sociedad* 1–22. https://doi.org/10.32870/cys.v2019i0.7327.

Wolfe, Patrick. 1999. *Settler Colonialism and the Transformation of Anthropology*. London: Cassell.

Wortham, Erica Cusi. 2013. *Indigenous Media in Mexico: Culture, Community, and the State*. Durham, NC: Duke University Press.

Worthen, Holly. 2012. "The Presence of Absence: Indigenous Migration, a Ghost Town, and the Remaking of Gendered Communal Systems in Oaxaca, Mexico." PhD diss., University of North Carolina at Chapel Hill.

———. 2015. "Indigenous Women's Political Participation: Gendered Labor and Collective Rights Paradigms in Mexico." *Gender & Society* 29 (6): 914–936.

Zuboff, Shoshana. 2019. *The Age of Surveillance Capitalism: The Fight for a Human Future at a New Frontier of Power.* New York: Public Affairs.


## FILMOGRAPHY

Cámara Sánchez, Fernando. 1978. *Danza de Conquista.*

Fritz, Sonia. 1985. *De bandas, vida y otros sones.*

Kummels, Ingrid. 2018. *Ayuujk Cameras.* https://vimeo.com/293855233.

———. 2021. *The Very First Fiesta Video.* https://vimeo.com/638306466.

Limeta, Pancho. 2016. *La Danza de los Negritos ejecutada por señoritas radicadas en Los Ángeles, California.*

Rojas, Hermenegildo, Genaro Rojas, Carlos Martínez, and Eliel Cruz. 2021. *Exta'n Pyëjk Mujk Tajk. Memoria Audiovisual Tamix.*

Tamix Multimedios. 2020. 2005. *Segunda etapa de la "COPA REGIONAL MIXE" con el primer partido femenil, TOTONTEPEC VS CUATRO PALOS.* https://fb.watch/7DPWGGRdQ2/.

TV Tamix. 1994. *Fiesta animada / Animated Feast.*

# INDEX

# ABOUT THE AUTHOR

INGRID KUMMELS is an anthropologist based at the Institute for Latin American Studies of the Freie Universität Berlin. She is head of the binational collaborative project Shared Soundscapes: Music Revivals and Identity Politics in Peru. Her long-term ethnographic research specializes on Mexico, Cuba, Peru, and the United States and focuses on transborder community building and crafting cultural knowledge from the perspective of media anthropology.

## AVAILABLE TITLES IN THE LATINIDAD: TRANSNATIONAL CULTURES IN THE UNITED STATES SERIES

Luis F. B. Plascencia, *Disenchanting Citizenship: Mexican Migrants and the Boundaries of Belonging*

Catherine S. Ramírez, Sylvanna M. Falcón, Juan Poblete, Steven C. McKay, and Felicity Amaya Schaeffer, eds., *Precarity and Belonging: Labor, Migration, and Noncitizenship*

Israel Reyes, *Embodied Economies: Diaspora and Transcultural Capital in Latinx Caribbean Fiction and Theater*

Cecilia M. Rivas, *Salvadoran Imaginaries: Mediated Identities and Cultures of Consumption*

Jayson Gonzales Sae-Saue, *Southwest Asia: The Transpacific Geographies of Chicana/o Literature*

Mario Jimenez Sifuentez, *Of Forest and Fields: Mexican Labor in the Pacific Northwest*

Maya Socolovsky, *Troubling Nationhood in U.S. Latina Literature: Explorations of Place and Belonging*

Susan Thananopavarn, *LatinAsian Cartographies*

Melissa Villa-Nicholas, *Latinas on the Line: Invisible Information Workers in Telecommunications*